What people are saying...

"Allison's book should never leave your sight. It contains a clear path for living your dream and getting more out of life. Here is your chance to stop dreaming about it once and for all and start making something great happen in your life and work. It is your desktop and bedside table companion for life!"

MARK LeBLANC, author of *Growing Your Business!*, president of Small Business Success, past president, National Speakers Association

"Allison Maslan bares her soul in this authentic book about living passionately and fully from the inside out. In Blast Off! *she skillfully weaves the power of divine energy and the soul's purpose with nuts and bolts strategy and raw determination. The result is mesmerizing. After reading this book, you will not only know for certain that you can achieve your heart's desire, you will be equipped with the tools make it happen. She is brilliant at teaching others to tap into the deepest part of themselves and then helping them create their individual formula for success. I highly recommend this book."*

ERNEST D. CHU, author of *Soul Currency,* spiritual community leader and counselor

"Allison Maslan is amazing. My dreams have come true after working closely with her program. Blast Off! *is completely unique and led me to my road of success. Years of dreaming are now manifesting as a speaker and writer due solely to her program. Thank you, Allison!"*

JEANNE STRYKER, M.D.

"Allison Maslan has given us a book that not only inspires us but also shows us the path for our newfound passion to follow. This is a rare self-help tutorial with a road map. Ms. Maslan has ingeniously shed the light on 'how to do it' after she has delivered the 'what to do.' The ingredients for success are motivation, inspiration, and passion. This is the book that makes it clear how to put them to use."

JOE HARPER, president of Del Mar Thoroughbred Club and Racetrack

*"*Blast Off! *is an entertaining guidebook that reveals how to make your dreams become a reality—complete with your own personal flight plan, prelaunch check list, and enough fuel to reach the stratosphere in personal achievement. Allison shows that harnessing your passion and fulfilling your soul's goals 'ain't rocket science!' She's helped countless others before, and now* Blast Off! *can prepare you to lift off on your own mission of sky-high success."*

C. RUSSELL BRUMFIELD, bestselling author of *Whiff!*

"How sweet is this! A beautifully crafted book, jam-packed full of bright wisdom, heartwarming stories, and brilliant ideas. Let it be your personal coach and you cannot go wrong. It will guide, advise, encourage, and even cheer you on at each and every step of your way, as you craft a vision, breathe life into your dreams, and make them come true."

MIRANDA CASTRO, FSHOM, CCH, homeopath and author, *The Complete Homeopathy Handbook; Homeopathy for Pregnancy, Birth, and Your Baby's First Years;* and *A Homeopathic Guide to Stress*

"This is a wonderful book of great assistance to anyone seeking the next step in life's journey. It is a user manual to manifesting one's dreams. Often in my practice, my patients who get well will ask, 'Now what?' Allison's book provides the answer."

TODD ROWE M.D., M.D. (H), CCH, DHT, president of The American Medical College of Homeopathy and author, *Homeopathic Methodology* and *The Homeopathic Journey*

"In Blast Off! *Allison Maslan provides us with the keys to manifesting what in the yogic tradition are called the Four Fruits of Life—dharma (the true path), artha (prosperity), kama (love), and moksha (freedom). Allison shares generously from her life experiences and humorously recounts how from them she learned to discover her true calling, find the man of her dreams, build a successful business, face her fears, and have a lot of fun along the way. Allison's gift is to present universal and eternal principles in a way that is easy to understand and apply.*"

TIM MILLER, owner/director, Ashtanga Yoga Center (Encinitas, California) The first American certified to teach by Pattabhi Jois at the Ashtanga Yoga Research Institute in Mysore, India

"In Blast Off! *Allison shares the story of her personal journey from despair to triumph. It's an insightful and engaging book, filled with specific actions you can take right now. It will inspire you to transform your own life from so-so to supersonic, just like Allison did. What a great read!*"

SARAH Z. SLEEPER, award-winning journalist and past vice-president of The National Writers Union

"Allison Maslan's powerful book, Blast Off! *gives the most direct path in inventing the career and personal life of your dreams. Her easy-to-follow flight plan is a profound mix of inspiration, passion, and success in the real world.*"

DIGBY DIEHL, *New York Times* and *London Times* bestselling author of over 30 books, including *Million Dollar Mermaid,* and *Remembering Grace,* literary correspondent for ABC-TV's "Good Morning America," and founding editor of *The Los Angeles Times Book Review*

BLAST Off!

The Surefire
Success Plan to
Launch Your Dreams
into Reality

Allison Maslan, HHP, CCH

New York

Blast Off!
The Surefire Success Plan to Launch Your Dreams into Reality
Allison Maslan, HHP, CCH

ISBN 978-1-60037-679-5 (paperback)
Library of Congress 2009932357

Published by:
MORGAN · JAMES
THE ENTREPRENEURIAL PUBLISHER™
www.morganjamespublishing.com

Morgan James Publishing
1225 Franklin Ave. Ste 325
Garden City, NY 11530-1693
Toll Free 800-485-4943
www.MorganJamesPublishing.com

Blast Off! Life Coaching™, *Blastation*™, *Interactive Life Coaching Software*™, *Mile Steps Spreadsheet*™, *Weekly Flight Assessment Log*™, *Big Picture Vision Board*™ and *Mini Feat Calendar*™ are trademarks of Allison Maslan.

*Mini Feats*ˢᴹ, *Weekly Flight Assessments*ˢᴹ, *Mile Steps*ˢᴹ, *Rocket Words*ˢᴹ, *Blast Off! Group Facilitation Certificate*ˢᴹ, *Big Picture Vision*ˢᴹ, *Sun-Up Scripts*ˢᴹ and *Wow Frequency*ˢᴹ are service marks of Allison Maslan.

Blast Off! A Surefire Success Plan to Launch Your Dreams Into Reality™ is a trademark of Allison Maslan and printed in this material as *Blast Off! Program.*

Edited by Sarah Z. Sleeper and Robin Quinn
Book cover and interior designed by Peri Poloni-Gabriel, Knockout Design
Cover photo and author photo by Leslie Bohm
Illustrations by Mia Fortescue

To Mike and Gabriella Bella
and in memory of Wilbur...
and to every believer, seeker,
survivor, visionary, idealist
and pioneer who is
impassioned to live the life
of their dreams.

Dreams are gifts of the soul.
We need to make every effort
to cherish them, to live them.
Otherwise they only surface in our sleep.
A soulful life is an awakening
and actualizing of our
deepest dreams within.

~Allison Maslan

How This Book Is Different

There are many books available that share and teach principles that will help you to reach your dreams and attain success. Often the reader completes one of these books feeling inspired and motivated, but then becomes perplexed about what steps to actually take to reach their goals, and how to apply them to their own life on a daily basis.

What sets *Blast Off!* apart from these books is that I won't just share my philosophy on how to attract your desires. I will also teach you step-by-step how to get there from start to finish. This book will provide you with proven tools that you can use every day for the rest of your passionate life.

You're not just reading a book that's offering great insight; you're holding in your hands a complete program that will launch you to the life of your dreams. This book's *Blast Off! Program* is simple, workable and very valuable.

BLASTATION
Interactive Life Coaching Software

Blastation is a completely unique interactive life-coaching software program that can be utilized to work the *Blast Off! Program*. I developed *Blastation* when I was unable to find adequate goal-setting software to use with my *Blast Off! Life Coaching* clients. It's a lively software that helps keep you organized, optimistic and inspired so you can stay on track to make your dream life a reality.

Blastation is like no other goal-setting/life-planning software. It's Web-based like Yahoo or Google, so it is at your disposal anywhere that you can get Internet access. This is a one-of-a-kind software that enables you to clarify and attain your large and small life dreams and visions in an exciting and stimulating way. Then *Blastation* helps you break these goals down into easy-to-follow incremental steps, called *Mini Feats*, that make your bigger projects much easier to achieve. These steps are then posted on your personalized online *Blastation Calendar* to keep your personal and professional life organized. You don't have to worry about using too many programs at once, because *Blastation* can send e-mails and host your online address book. Allow *Blastation* to be the catalyst to help you envision your dreams, then strategize to make them come true!

> "Blastation is your virtual space to dream, design, envision and implement the life you've always wanted."
> ~Allison Maslan

As you work with the *Blast Off! Program* offered in this book, it's perfectly fine to work strictly with the book and a journal or *The Blast Off! Workbook* for the exercises. However, I recommend that you also consider accessing the tools contained in the *Blastation* program for added reinforcement. Visit the website, www.InteractiveLifeCoach.com for more information.

Table of Contents

Foreword

As a little boy, I had no idea what I wanted to do when I grew up. No dreams of being a doctor, lawyer, policeman—*no particular desire to do anything*. My uncertainty about a career direction becomes totally obvious if you look at the list of jobs I later racked up between the ages of twenty and forty: welding shop clerk, advertising agency junior account executive, assistant marketing manager of a retail sporting goods chain, pizza delivery driver (not as bad as you'd think), TV studio production assistant (worse than you'd think), frozen yogurt franchisee, real estate agent, cookware store assistant manager, biotech company director of operations, television travel show host, and biotech facilities consultant. And the list doesn't even include the three hours I spent as a telemarketer—I couldn't even make it to lunchtime.

With all these job changes, it came as no surprise to anyone that I was once again trying my hand at something new—this time, hosting a cooking show. Was I a great cook? *No.* In fact, I'd not really done much cooking at all. Did I have years of television experience? *No.* Was I related to a well-placed television executive who could land me a job? *No.* Honestly, I didn't have much.

But what I did have would ultimately become much more powerful than anything else I could put on a resume. First, I was really ready to make a career change. I needed to change so badly that I would have done almost anything. Turns out desire is a ridiculously strong motivator. And second, I had Allison Maslan. Allison had coached me a couple years before about making changes in my work life, but I wasn't ready back then. It's the old, "you-can-lead-a-horse-to-water" concept with me as the horse. Now, *finally,* I was ready to drink.

Starting any business is difficult and certainly full of its own challenges, but my brand new TV career brought one additional challenge that I hadn't anticipated. This challenge was that pretty much everyone I knew thought that I was making a mistake—and a big one at that. I had expected a certain amount of skepticism—I mean I was trying to go from the biotech industry to becoming the host of a TV cooking show! And then there was that pesky little thing about having virtually no experience. For friends and family to question me would have been okay—but everyone thought I was insane. And if they didn't say this directly to me, they said it to someone I knew. The whole, "You're-a-fool" thing came to a head the day my two oldest brothers called to ask, "What will happen when it *doesn't* work?" Not "if," but "when!" *What?* Where was the support? Where were the cautious yet brotherly love, advice and counsel? After this phone conversation with my brothers, I pulled over to the side of the road and called Allison. I've never been in AA, but I imagined that this was what calling your sponsor would be like. I really wanted—no, make that *really needed*—to talk to her.

From the beginning, Allison's coaching was always about *me finding me*. And somehow she recognized a more creative Sam inside. Through her questions and our conversations, Allison started nudging me towards something that she knew I needed and would be good at. And an interesting thing happened. You know how there are bazillions of car ads every day on TV and you barely notice them? But the day you wake up and say, "Today I need to buy a car," that's when you start noticing? Well, finally one day I woke up and knew that it was time to make a change. And this was when everything that Allison had coached me about finally started to take root.

But on that day of my brothers' phone call, while I sat in my car at the side of the road, Allison's advice took on a whole new form. Her gentle probing and casual conversation, as in our past coaching sessions, was now gone, and like a coach preparing an athlete for a huge race, Allison took charge. Her advice was simple, straightforward and, well, kind of tough. She said, "They're feeding you negative energy. Just stop talking about it, Sam. Your career changes are triggering their own fears. They can't be supportive of you taking a risk; it's too scary for them. Tune them out. Get back in touch with your inner focus and just do it."

Right from the start, Allison told me to keep my new passion to myself. She said, "People will tell you that you're not being realistic. They'll say you're a dreamer. There will always be people who will think you'll fail and they'll tell you that. And then there are those who act somewhat supportive, but also ask the questions that will make you question everything you're working toward." In my case, that second kind of feedback went something like this, "That's so great that you're going into television. How exciting! But isn't it really complicated? And doesn't everyone want to be in TV? And how do you even know where to start?" Five minutes with someone like that and you'll question everything you're doing. You'll start thinking: "They're right. It *is* complicated, everyone *does* want to be in this business, and I *don't* know where to start."

"But it's not about them," Allison counseled, "it's about you." She paused, then added, "Quit talking about it and quit asking people what they think, because it doesn't matter. None of that will help you, but more likely it will throw you off track. Just put your head down and keep moving forward toward your dream. Do your work, exactly as you know it needs to be done, and you'll find success."

So I did. I just shut up and did my thing. I created a demo tape and sent it out. I became my own cheerleader, because I knew no one would do it as well as me. When I found rejection—I moved around it. I made positive steps towards what I wanted every day. And I ended up on TV. And then on more TV. And then I won a bunch of Emmys. And then ended up with a national TV show. And then the first book deal came through. And so on. All this because I found myself and what I was meant to do. I'm now happy in a way I couldn't have imagined.

What's special about Allison is that she saw something in me right from the very beginning. In fact, with her keen awareness, she was able to see what I couldn't. This reminds me of a study I read about that involved two groups of people. Group A considered themselves lucky, and Group B didn't. The study organizers had both groups walk a specific route, where $5 bills had been hidden in exactly the same places for each group. The "lucky" group found more of the $5 bills than the unlucky group. But not because they were lucky—they simply were more "aware" of their surroundings.

In this book, Allison details her own journey, and then clearly explains what it takes for you to find your life of passion and success. Reading it will be like sitting and talking with her. Like me, you'll need to ask yourself if you're really ready for a change. Because if you're not, you won't find the answers here or anywhere else. At the same time, different readers will be looking for different kinds of changes. For me, it was a search for happiness in a career.

Some of us find our way the minute we start looking for a change, and some of us need a little help getting our direction. I needed help, but *however* you succeed doesn't really matter—just as long as you get there. Allison's *Blast Off! to Success Program*, if you're truly ready, will help you get there.

SAM ZIEN
The Cooking Guy
Author, *Just a Bunch of Recipes*
Host/Producer, *Just Cook This!*
Discovery Health Channel
www.thecookingguy.com

Preface

I love my life! I married my soulmate two years ago and just sent my daughter off to college. I run two thriving businesses and am in the process of building another. My husband and I travel the world and spend a great deal of time laughing to the point of crying. We share a beautiful oceanview home where we love to entertain close family and friends.

STOP! Before you groan in disgust and slam this book shut, know that it was not always this way and that my personal roadmap has been one filled with tragedy, tears, frustration, loneliness, poverty, over-whelm, confusion and exhaustion. Luckily, along the way, I acquired three qualities that pushed me through the darkest times: *determination, passion and hope...* always hope.

So let's begin with my story of *then...*

> "If we did all the things we are capable of doing, we would literally astound ourselves."
>
> ~*Thomas Edison, Businessman and inventor with more than a thousand patents in his name (1847-1931)*

Young and Determined

The drive has been there since I can remember. At age five, I wanted a Crissy doll that my mother said I could not spend my savings on. Because "no" didn't seem like a viable option to me, I took my piggy bank and slipped out of our house. I then walked two miles over the hill, which seemed like a mountain, to the neighborhood TG&Y dimestore. I bought the Crissy doll and proceeded to walk home with a sensation of elation and accomplishment like I had never experienced before. This smugness was quickly deflated when my mother came squealing across the road in her 1968 blue Buick and threw me into the back seat. Although I knew I was in big trouble, it did not dampen my sense of determination that I continued to maintain, and which became especially helpful in carrying me through the next several years.

As a child, I was often found dancing, and would spontaneously break out into cartwheels and somersaults down the hallways. I started gymnastics at age five and, as I grew older, I competed nationally for my team, The Tulsa OKs. My gymnastic coach built me a set of uneven parallel bars in my backyard and I spent hours upon hours doing flips from the high bar into the mud. That was my first experience of being truly in love with life.

As I grew older, our team practiced five hours a day. My coach, Mr. Childers, pushed us hard, and if we were heard uttering the two most vile words, "I can't," we had to do our entire floor routine with tumbling passes five times consecutively, without stopping. You do not have to experience this more than once to learn that "I can't" does not get you very far. Though this was a pretty dictatorial style of coaching, which would probably not be acceptable today, it taught me that if I worked through the pain and fear, triumph would eventually appear at the other end.

In addition to having determination, I inherited entrepreneurial skills from both sides of my family. My father, who I idolized, built the largest privately owned U.S. women's clothing chain of his day which he ran for thirty years. As a young girl, I used to accompany him as he traveled from store to store. I thought he had the easiest job in the world. All my dad did was say, "Hello!" to everyone and stop for ice cream in between locations. I told myself, "I can do this."

A Rude Awakening Brings Change

At age twenty, I was in for a rude awakening when my father, who was a pillar in the community and a powerful businessman, went bankrupt. The circumstances were shocking and while I felt very sad for him, I was also really worried about myself and my future. I had always counted on my dad for financial support. Up to that point, I didn't have a clue about the mighty dollar or what it took to make one. At the time, the bankruptcy seemed like a catastrophe. Looking back, it was the best thing that could have ever happened to me. Little did I know that it was time for me to jump into the Big World, whether I was ready or not.

I knew then that if I wanted to be able to live the lifestyle I was accustomed to, I would need to apply some of my determination into a fiscally rewarding activity. Okay, I needed a job. And I did manage to get hired numerous times. However, since I never succeeded in following orders, two weeks seemed to be the longest period that I was able to remain employed.

Passion is birthed when an unexpected twist or turn, an opportunity, or maybe even a tragedy falls into your path and sparks an inner fire. Whether the manifestation you eventually produce is a lovely romance, a creative endeavor, or your altruistic life work/purpose, passion is an energy that is influenced externally but created internally. Thank goodness it came to possess my being because this inner spark, which I call my *Secret Spark*, kept me feeling alive during the most challenging and deadening times of my life.

I started my first business venture, *Expressions by Allie,* when I was attending college. I was hired by fellow classmates to write personalized poetry for special occasions. I enjoyed learning about the people's lives and creating gifts that brought joy to both the giver and receiver. It ignited an entrepreneurial spark inside of me and I naively thought, "I can make a living at this." Reality set in when at $25 a poem, I had to furiously write and sell day and night to cover my rent and the costs of daily living. One week, after writing eight gift poems, I realized that I was still hundreds of dollars short of my expenses. I was sick with panic, and for the first time in my life, I became consumed with self-doubt. I questioned whether I had the capability to make it on my own. I questioned whether I would ever find my true calling.

> "Yesterday I dared to struggle. Today I dare to win."
>
> ~Bernadette Devlin McAliskey, Political activist in Northern Ireland

Even though fear was running amuck within me at age twenty-two, I did possess, on a deeper level, a belief that I could make it in the business world. As karma would have it, I met my first husband and started down a ten-year path of a marriage that was a barrage of loneliness, conflict and gut-building challenges. Looking back, it was also a tremendous time for personal growth. My strength was tested countless times and somehow my spirit prevailed. At age twenty-five, the silver lining was that I was blessed with a beautiful daughter, Gabriella.

Achieving a Success I Couldn't Love

We moved to San Diego, and since my husband was starting over in his career, financial survival became a big motivator for me. It was also the launching pad that forced me to face my fears of competency in the professional world. One day I walked into Merrill Lynch to offer the brokers my services for personalized poetry, and they invited me to their afternoon sales meeting to present my wares. I was shell-shocked with fear and I have no idea what I said, but I left that sales meeting with four orders for personalized greeting cards. You would have thought I had just won the lottery. I was beside myself with pride until my inner voice screamed, "You have absolutely no idea how to create or print greeting cards!" Well, my drive and passion kicked in and I did a pretty terrific job.

The snowball started rolling and before I knew it, I was hired by MCI to create greeting cards for their national branches. This led to clients such as Charlotte Russe clothing stores, Supercuts and Charter Hospital, asking me to develop brochures, buy radio and television time, and develop effective public relations campaigns. I launched *The Barali Group Advertising and Public Relations Agency,* accepting each business request as if I knew exactly what to do, and then I would work feverishly to figure out how to make it happen. Of course, I had absolutely no experience in marketing or advertising.

In the meantime, my marriage was suffering. And the lonelier I became in the relationship, the more I poured myself into my work. I remember nights when I didn't want to go home, but my responsibility as a mom kept me pursuing the promise of matrimony.

The Barali Group, named from a compilation of me, Allie, and my eventual partner, Barbara, became a huge success with a long list of national clients, many deadlines, and a schedule that didn't include rest stops. In the advertising world, you are only as good as your last campaign so there was always a new challenge. The money was also great, but somehow something very crucial felt missing in the equation. Through soul searching, I discovered that the missing piece was *meaning*—a deeper purpose in my work that really mattered to me. I lacked the kind of rewarding energy from my work that you can lose yourself in. I knew my meaning had to be out there, but I had no clue where to look, or how to find the courage to make any changes.

Hitting Bottom

Six years later, I was beyond burnout. This became blaringly obvious when I managed to run over myself with my car one day on the way to get my daughter Gabriella at daycare. Yes, you read correctly. This feat is clearly the biggest faux pas of my life thus far. Rushing out of my car in a panic, feeling the shame of being tardy to pick up my child, I failed to put my car fully into park. As it began rolling backward with me in its grips, halfway in and halfway out of the driver's seat, I thought my manic pace had finally done me in. Though the car did literally run over part of my body (my legs), the Universe spared my life and my extremities as it attempted to jolt me into some form of sanity.

At that point in my life, I had become so disconnected from myself that I had no idea who the hell I was or what the hell I was doing. My soul cried out, but the tears wouldn't come. I felt dead inside and there seemed to be absolutely no solution in sight. I felt trapped in my loveless marriage, stuck in a thriving business that I didn't enjoy and that was killing me, and guilt-ridden because I was failing as a parent.

That night, the tears finally came flooding through. I was sobbing and crying loudly to the heavens, to anyone who would listen. "Help me, please!" I pleaded. I was in a space of complete desperation and hanging on by a thread. Then the strangest thing occurred. I felt a loving hand on my forehead that offered the most calming, soothing and loving touch that I had ever experienced. Except that in my visual awareness, no one was there. At that moment, for reasons I couldn't explain, my crying ceased and I knew deep in my soul that everything was going to be all right.

> "How many cares one loses when one decides not to be something but to be someone."
>
> ~Coco Chanel,
> *Pioneering French*
> *fashion designer*
> *(1883-1971)*

I knew deep down that there had to be more to life. I suddenly had the awareness that if I continued operating blindly in this manner, I would not be long for this world. That very day, a business associate called and I shared my grief with her. She referred me to a special husband and wife team who practiced homeopathy, Rolfing and psychotherapy. I had no idea that this would be the beginning of an entirely new path. Never having experienced holistic healing before, I was a bit reluctant and pessimistic. In fact, when I approached their office door, I almost turned back. My thinking was, "I'll get over this. I can work through the rough spots on my own." Then I thought, "Obviously, what I'm doing is not working or I wouldn't be standing here with tire tracks on my legs." I really wanted to figure out how to get unstuck and find the meaning and fulfillment that was missing in my life.

An Awakening

I started to explore homeopathy and holistic medicine while still running The Barali Group. Quickly, I became fascinated with the concept of treating the whole person and healing the body and mind from the inside out. Through this work, I found a greater understanding of why I seemed to struggle so much in my life. I finally grasped why I worked myself to exhaustion and never felt like I was doing enough, and also why I chose such a challenging intimate relationship.

My father saw the world through his work. The only time I could connect with him was through conversations about my business and accomplishments. I was driving myself so hard in order to receive his approval and love.

I had married a businessman fifteen years older than myself who treated me like a child. On some level, the marriage let me play out a deep desire to work through my father-daughter dynamic. The Universe had given me just what I was looking for. But when I finally clued into the awareness of my true spirit and began maturing into "Allison," separate from my childhood deficits, I wanted to be respected as an adult.

My desire to have that father-daughter connection was colliding with my career-relationship crash and burn. That's why I never felt totally fulfilled by my marriage or in my work at the agency. The agency work didn't reflect my true career choice. It was work for approval's sake. And the difficult part was that I appeared successful outwardly, but remained an inner disaster. As the façade of Allie the Marketing Mogul started to appear more and more promising, I realized that just because I was good at running the agency, this didn't mean that I was supposed to spend my life doing it. That little girl swinging excitedly on the parallel bars still resided inside of me and she knew that she wanted more.

I took a month-long leave of absence from my business to heal. During that time, I attended a one-woman modern dance performance that triggered my memory of that passionate little girl flipping around in the backyard. I immediately started taking modern dance classes and became reconnected to the joyous feeling of moving my body through space. The dance and music awakened my soul and spirit, and I felt so alive for the first time in years. From this place of awareness, I knew that I must reach out and grasp hold of my precious life—or lose it forever.

Courageous Adjustments

After a year of studying homeopathy piecemeal, while working through all the puzzle pieces of my childhood and undergoing intensive marriage counseling, I had a brilliant new sense of courage that gave me the strength to walk away from the impossible limits and expectations I had placed upon myself. I took a graceful exit from The Barali Group, asked my husband for a divorce, and set out on my own as a single parent with absolutely no money and no idea what would happen next. Was I scared? *Terrified.* But I felt incredibly free for the first time in years.

I knew that I couldn't hide behind a rock or suppress what I had gained. I didn't want to live incongruently anymore.

In the meantime, I had become fascinated with homeopathic medicine and I decided to go back to school full-time with the determination to eventually start a practice. I buried myself in my studies, but it didn't seem like work because it fascinated me so much. My daughter and I laughed and danced together. My heart and soul were singing. Yet on the practical side, I was completely broke and couldn't make my house or car payments.

My ex-husband and family were critical of my new path. Neither was willing to help with my tuition. There were frequent arguments over quitting "this crazy hobby," as they saw it. My mother thought I had joined a religious cult. I had one friend tell me that I would never make a living practicing natural medicine and that I was throwing my life away. It's amazing, when you follow your dreams, how many people are quick to judge and criticize. I realized that my bravery was bringing up their fear of change. I learned to put my head down, move intently forward in my beliefs, and listen to no one who was negative or unsupportive. The more they said, "You can't," the more determined I became. I had gone through such a maze to find my true calling, nothing and no one would stop me now.

The reality of my finances was hard to ignore when I didn't have enough money to buy a cup of coffee. I almost applied for food stamps, but felt the welfare agency wouldn't take me seriously as I pulled up in my Lexus. My craving for a passionate life, along with my ingrained stubbornness, kept me hopeful and positive in my bleakest moments. I refused to forget that it could be much worse. I could still be lonely in my marriage. I could still be burned out and miserable in my career. I chose poverty instead because I knew my calling

> "I have learned that if one advances confidently in the direction of his dreams, and endeavors to live the life he has imagined, he will meet with a success unexpected in common hours."
>
> *~Henry David Thoreau,*
> *Author, transcendentalist,*
> *naturalist and philosopher*
> *(1817-1862)*

was to help people heal and find their way, and if I stayed on course, my financial circumstances would change. I maintained that ever-glimmering power of hope. I would not entertain failure as an option.

Learning to Blast Off!

And here's what happened. I earned the knowledge and personal satisfaction that comes with graduating as a Licensed Holistic Health Practitioner, but I couldn't get my diploma until I paid the $6,000 balance in tuition. I called my mom for a loan. I can't remember if I was more upset by the fact that she turned me down or by her statement that I was ruining my life with "this silly holistic stuff" and "needed to get my head on straight and find a job." Instead of allowing my anger to immobilize me, I took the only possible course of action that I could fathom. I directed that mad-adrenaline, my freeing sense of independence and flaming passion for life, into full-throttle emergency empowerment.

With my new high-octane energy, I started pounding the pavement to promote myself and my new private practice. I created some promotional flyers and went door-to-door introducing myself and my services to anyone who didn't run the other way. That very first day, four people set appointments and I booked two lectures at health food stores. Six months later, as I awaited back child-support payments, I was busy enough to pay off my debts and began making enough money to care for my daughter.

Fourteen years later, I have been blessed to have helped thousands of people transform their lives. I developed a school of homeopathy, built a scuba-diving business, became a real estate investor, and began coaching students, individuals, entrepreneurs and those in life transitions. Needless to say, my mom, whom I love dearly, is thankful that I didn't listen to her.

The Birth of Blast Off! Life Coaching

Over the years, as my homeopathy clients were feeling rejuvenated with a newfound sense of balance and health, an interesting thing started to happen. Many of them, who knew about my knack for entrepreneurship, asked me to coach them in their business or help them create an action plan for their goals. This natural evolution was the birth of my *Blast Off! Life Coaching Program* (info at www.MyBlastOff.com).

Through assisting, guiding and supporting so many individuals in actualizing their dreams, I came to understand why and how so many people become stuck by unconsciously placing limits and roadblocks upon themselves and their lives. Through my own personal journey and witnessing thousands of client transformations, I developed a compelling process to help get them unstuck so that they could realize their amazing potential. I grasped the ability to facilitate others to tap into their passions and universal inspiration and bring them into being with the power of *intention* combined with *clear action*. Their special gifts had always been right there within. They just needed a catalyst to stir their desire and ignite their inner fire. To witness my clients tear down their walls of fear and turn floating possibilities into concrete realities has been like watching rockets soar into the heavens. They access a powerful level of internal energy and the result is nothing less than 3-2-1… *Blast Off!*

Statements from some of my clients:

★ "I never thought I could be this happy!"

★ "I'm getting so much more accomplished in my day and I feel calmer than ever."

★ "The coaching has come back to me 100-fold. I am making so much more money and having a hell of a lot more fun."

★ "I feel in tune with my life… with myself. Finally!"

An Overview of Your Flight Plan

> "Somewhere there is a map of how it can be done."
>
> ~Ben Stein,
> Entertainment personality,
> political figure, attorney

You know you have the potential to attain more in your life. But you aren't sure exactly what steps to take to find your true calling. Help has arrived! In this book I provide the guidance and structure to make sure you stay true to your path, the courage to support you through the necessary changes, and the step-by-step strategies and solutions to bring your boldest visions into reality.

To create *Blast Off! A Surefire Success Plan to Launch Your Dreams into Reality* I drew upon my awareness of the varied roadblocks in human nature and my proven ability to move people beyond them. The powerful program in these pages can give you the inspiration to envision your biggest life dreams and desires, what I call your *Big Picture Vision*.

Over many years as a homeopathic physician and owner of *Blast Off! Life Coaching*, I have helped thousands of people bring their passions to life, just as I have forged my own rags-to-riches journey. I encourage you to think of this book as your personal life coach that will teach you how to access your Universal Inspiration and build your path of love, health, prosperity and adventure.

If you're truly ready to change or improve your life, I challenge you to take the initial step of beginning to explore this program today. *Blast Off!* is your clear and precise flight plan. It shows you how to connect with your hidden talents and dreams, and then it guides you step-by-step in bringing these dreams into reality.

Right now, you may be operating in high gear in one or two sectors of your life, while the other sectors lag behind. In this book I teach you how to drive your life into *Supersonic Gear,* where you will experience the most extreme, complete and strongest forward motion with the minimum effort.

Although it's fine to do the *Blast Off! Program* solo, sharing the book and program with a partner or a *Blast Off! Group* can be a powerful experience. Your partner or group can stimulate ideas, offer support, and help you stay accountable to your goals and commitments. Remember too that *Blastation,* my new interactive software, is also available to provide further support as you work the program (www.InteractiveLife-Coach.com).

My *Blast Off! Program* addresses the best of *wealth, career, business, love, personal fulfillment, adventure and health.* It will propel you forward and enable you to drive on all cylinders in every sector, instead of succeeding in only one or two. It will help you achieve abundance in all areas of your life.

> "They must often change, who would be constant in happiness or wisdom."
>
> *~Confucius,*
> *Chinese philosopher*
> *(551 BC-479 BC)*

Your Daily Launch Tools

There are some *Daily Launch Tools* that you'll use throughout the *Blast Off! Program.* They are referenced in each chapter and forms to help you do them are in the back of the book.

It is my hope that you'll continue to use these tools now and after you've completed the book. I've found that people are more successful in actualizing their dreams and goals when they operate within a certain routine or structure. This doesn't mean that your life must be predictable or stifling. Quite the opposite! The structure provided by the tools is a source of power and strength that you can draw from, and also a stable framework to ground you when fear or uncertainty arise. Think of them as your fear fighters. These

Daily Launch Tools will let you create a foundation so that you can attain and maintain your success.

1. **Sun-Up Scripts**—Your first tool is called the *Sun-Up Scripts*. This is a free-association writing exercise to assist you in releasing the negative thought process or any gunk in your brain that you may be starting your day with. It's also a modality to explore your hidden talents, inspiring thoughts, creative artistry and ingenious ideas.

   Rocket Words—You will use these along with your *Sun-Up Scripts*. They are your daily mantra, a phrase of strength for the day, which will assist you in flip-switching any negative attitudes or vibes into positive, energetic frequencies.

This is how the *Sun-Up Scripts* and *Rocket Words* work. Each morning use a journal or my *Blastation* software to create them. At the top of a blank page, write the first word or statement that comes to your mind. This is your *theme word or phrase*. Then write as much as you need to about that word or statement including whatever comes up spontaneously. You're not allowed to analyze or judge your thoughts, just spill out all the beauty or ugliness right onto the page or into the computer. Release every bit of pent-up energy or feelings from your brain, your heart, your gut and your spirit through your pen to the paper or through your fingers to the computer.

When you feel that you've fully addressed the word or phrase, after about a page or more of subconscious scribbling or typing, ask yourself if you feel complete. Have your feelings about this theme word or phrase changed at all? I liken this process to a good cry or scream. The *Sun-Up Scripts* are a vehicle for you to release an incredible amount of negative energy, or a catalyst to pump up your already positive mindset. This passionate writing may offer words or insight that you had not considered. Those words can offer effective solace and solutions to get you back on track or move you to the next level. You can start each *Sun-Up Script* with up to three theme words or phrases.

***Sun-Up Script* Example**
Theme Word: *Overwhelmed*

I have so much work to do this week! I am not sure how everything is going to get done. Why do I pile so much onto myself? Errrggghhh! I am so exhausted and I have no help. I just want to crawl back in bed. I have so much I want to do, but I have no time. When is it ever going to be my time? I am so sick of doing for everyone else and I have no energy left for me. So why do I keep saying "yes" when I really want to say "no"?! I am going to practice saying "no" every day this week and see how it feels. The thought of it seems so freeing. "No No No No No No No!!!" I feel soooo much better!

Then finish up the *Sun-Up Script* with your *Rocket Words* for the day, a summarizing sentence with a positive twist. If your theme words or phrases are already positive, your *Rocket Words* will provide added support to keep you in this positive flow.

For instance, in the case of the writer of the "Overwhelmed" *Sun-Up Script*, the *Rocket Words* for the day might be,

"I feel ready and able to take on whatever today brings."

> "We all have big changes in our lives which are more or less a second chance."
>
> ~*Harrison Ford,*
> *Movie actor known for his*
> Indiana Jones *and*
> Star Wars *film series*

Post your *Rocket Words* wherever you focus your attention—on your bathroom mirror, the fridge, on your computer desktop on *Blastation* software, etc. Every time you catch a glimpse of your *Rocket Words* for the day, they will remind you to stay tuned to this high frequency. And the more time you spend in this upbeat easy flow, he more likely your day will grace you with energy, productivity and fun.

2. Mini Feats—Another important tool is your *Mini Feats*. These are successive small accomplishments that add up to greater achievements. They involve courage, strength and commitment. They are action steps in small increments that require only five minutes to do.

Sometimes our goals can feel so huge and daunting. We often make lists with the best intentions of accomplishing everything on them. And then, because life takes over, we are not able to get the tasks done. We keep transferring those tasks to the next day or the next week. This only adds feelings of frustration and self-criticism to our already full plate.

Fractioning a project into five-minute increments makes it easy and fun. And surprisingly, you will finish the task and reach your goal much faster than you would expect. You can do just about anything for five minutes! And often, once you get started, you will be even more motivated to finish your task and may give it more time. But remember, you are only required to spend five minutes on each *Mini Feat*.

You may be thinking, "How much progress can be made in five minutes?" Well, if you do three valuable five-minute tasks each day, that will be twenty-one tasks completed by the week's end. The secret is to spend less time doubting, and more time doing. Write down your *Mini Feats* with the date and time you are committing to take action. For this effort, you might use the *Mini Feat Calendar* form provided in the back of this book, a day-planner, or the weekly or monthly calendar provided in the *Blastation* software.

Mini Feat Example

Let's use the example of procrastinating on paying your bills. You might set up your *Mini Feats* for the week like this:

Tuesday at 6:30 PM: *Put all bills together with the envelopes, stamps, checkbook and calculator.*

Wednesday at 8:00 PM: *Take bills out of the envelopes, and apply stamps and return address stickers on the return envelopes.*

Thursday at 7:00 PM: *Write checks and then stuff and seal envelopes.*

Friday at 8:00 AM: *Balance my check register and mail the bills.*

If cleaning your office is an overwhelming task, try this:

Monday at 10:00 AM: Clear off top of desk for five minutes.

Tuesday at Noon: Clear out the top right drawer.... and so on.

If finding a new career is your *Big Picture Vision* (your large goal for specific areas, explained in detail later in the book), your *Mini Feats* might be:

Monday at 7:00 AM: Spend five minutes doing Google searches on career ideas. (Save your findings to read through later.)

Tuesday at 10:00 PM: Research local business networking activities around town via the Internet or local newspapers.

Wednesday at 9:30 AM: Make call to sign up for networking meeting.

Thursday at 11:30 AM: Make call to arrange lunch meeting with recent acquaintance to find out more about their career and possible helpful connections.

By Thursday of the first week, you'll already be making terrific progress!

In the *Blast Off! Program* I ask that you perform a minimum of three *Mini Feats* per day. They can be from any area of your life that you are working on, or relate to any goals you've set. They need to be three activities that will assist you in working toward your objectives or your *Big Picture Vision*. So feeding the fish or watching your favorite reality TV show doesn't count.

You should thoughtfully write out your *Mini Feats* the night or the week before you plan to do them. Sunday is a good day to plan your week. This way, you'll hit the ground running on Monday morning. When you write your *Mini Feats*, you are also directing your intentions out into the Universe about what you want your days to entail. The energy will already be at work—even while you're sleeping—helping to create the dreams you plan to achieve.

3. Weekly Flight Assessments—Your next tool is the *Weekly Flight Assessment,* which helps you evaluate and track your weekly progress, gains and roadblocks. It's a quick way to assess your week, keep yourself on track, and see areas you may need to work on. Make a commitment to complete the *Weekly Flight Assessment* log every seven days, using a copy of the form in the back of this book.

Over the next several weeks, it will be fun to look back on your earlier flight assessments to see just how much progress you've made and how much closer you are to reaching your *Big Picture Vision.* For a further guarantee that you'll keep this promise to yourself, make it a habit to fax or e-mail your *Weekly Flight Assessment* to a supportive friend, co-worker or a member of your *Blast Off! Group.* This practice will help you to stay on track with your goals and be accountable to your commitments. It's kind of like weighing in at Weight Watchers. If you know that you're going to be accountable for your diet goals, you're more likely to skip the potatoes and choose extra broccoli instead.

> "Change always comes bearing gifts."
>
> ~Price Pritchett, Business advisor and author

How to Use the Blast Off! Program

The chapters of *Blast Off!* will give you insight, urge you to search inwardly, and help you to see your life and its possibilities through a completely new perspective. Each chapter's philosophy and prescriptions expound on one another, so it is most effective to start with Chapter One and move forward, completing a single chapter every one to two weeks.

However, if you see a chapter theme that you connect with strongly, such as career or relationship, you can fly directly there once you have completed the first three chapters. By then, you'll be eager to keep your forward momentum going. And the more consistent you are in keeping the pace moving, the sooner you'll soar to new dimensions in your *Blast Off! Program.*

Each chapter contains topic-specific *Launchtime Practices*. They are challenging yet insightful exercises designed to help you develop and actualize your success. You can do them on your own, or with a partner or a *Blast Off! Launching Group*. (See page 265 for details on How To Create Your Own *Blast Off! Launching Group*.) As well, my *Blastation Interactive Life Coaching Software*, available at www.InteractiveLifeCoach.com, can help you work through selected exercises from the chapter, in any order you choose.

I also suggest that you create a *Daily Launch Tools Checklist* to help you track your daily use of *Sun-Up Scripts*, *Mini Feats* and *Weekly Flight Assessments*. The checklist will help you acknowledge and revel in your amazing progress.

The Gears

I have defined three gears you can use as you cruise along your path of life—**Floating**, **Exploration** and **Supersonic**. Unfortunately, many people exist in the *Floating* stage. They are in neutral, floating in the margins of life while moving neither forward nor backward. Basically, they're stuck!

80 percent of the people I've coached come to me in the *Floating* stage, feeling that there has to be more to life but having no idea how to accelerate beyond the grip of gravity into the vast galaxy of opportunity. However, once you commit to making some kind of change, you'll naturally enter the *Exploration* stage—an investigative phase of your personal path and a period of decision making.

Finally, your star will ignite as you shift into the third stage, *Supersonic*, where you are finally in sync with your true nature, your innate potential, and the universal frequency and wisdom. In the *Supersonic* stage, where I believe you will be after reading this book, you'll begin actualizing your purpose as you reap the rewards of your intention and actions.

FLOATING— This is a state in which you are floating in a static mode where there's no electric charge or potential for any energy or movement. You have no power or frequency radiating from your core outwards toward the rest of your life. You're idling in mid-air or in a black hole, feeling stuck, trapped, frustrated and confused about what action or direction to take to propel yourself forward. In this stage you may be gripping the wheel with hopes of controlling your destination instead of flowing in the zone of your own intuition and inspiration.

EXPLORATION— This stage starts you down the path of discovery, in which you are cruising the skyways, plotting, directing, searching and researching your many fruitful options. Whether your exploration is in the realm of relationship, career, wealth, health, personal satisfaction, spiritual fulfillment or all the above, you are creating a roadmap to your *Blast Off!* You have momentum and are moving forward and you also stop, question, meditate and analyze as necessary. This is a time of trial and error, of u-turns, of rerouting, and of revisiting your map to confirm that you're on the right flight path. You're beginning to develop confidence in yourself and your vision. The all-knowing voice of your newfound faith and trust begins to emerge from your gut and says, "Yes, this is it! I have found my desired path and it feels right."

SUPERSONIC— This is the stage where you'll experience the most extreme, complete and strongest movement forward while putting out minimum effort. You are cruising on all cylinders with high-octane power and at supersonic speed. All your destinations are programmed into your personal GPS system and you fully believe in yourself and your path. You are in sync with the wind and in flow

> "Growth is the only evidence of life."
>
> ~John Henry Newman,
> Theologian and writer
> (1801-1890)

with the universal motion. You are flexible when the road splits and lights change. You have an agenda, yet at the same time you're letting go of the wheel to embrace each new adventurous turn of the open skies. You're soaring on the path of abundance, reaping the rewards of your embrace of determination, passion and hope.

Supersonic Story

Janice—Getting Unstuck and Finding Her Passion

Here's how one woman used my *Blast Off! Program* to achieve true happiness and success.

Janice came to me in search of a new career path. To most people Janice's life looked successful. She was a medical doctor employed at a hospital in Los Angeles. But, though she had worked for many years in her chosen field, her primary motivation was money. She saw her job as a means for survival and security. What she lacked was a passionate spark about her work. So, she felt unfulfilled, uninspired and stuck.

The first thing I suggested to Janice was that she meditate on and then make a list of all the things that inspired her or that she dreamt of doing in the past. After some thought, Janice wrote down dancing as the first item on her list. She explained that she used to love dancing, but with the demands of medical school and then her long hours at the hospital, it had been years since she had made time to dance. With this revelation, I had helped her see what she couldn't before—dancing was the best place for her to start to change her life. I felt sure that it would help her clear her head and spur her creative juices.

Just a few weeks after our first meeting, Janice signed up for classes at a dance studio near her home. Over the next few months Janice and I continued to work together, outlining new career options that interested her. We discussed interior design, event planning, music production, a board-and-care home for dogs, owning a restaurant or club and architecture. I asked Janice to research options for each of these areas, and then we began to brainstorm. It was through this ongoing creative process and also because of Janice's more open spirit—accessed through dancing—that she realized she was most attracted to music production.

"I love music. I went to a fine arts school where I played the piano and the flute," she said. As soon as she had recognized her passion and stated it aloud, it began to materialize. She found a music production program in Los Angeles that she could attend on the evenings and weekends when she wasn't working. I asked Janice to keep the momentum going by creating her *Big Picture Vision* of a career in music production. At this point she began to visualize what her life would be like in *Blast Off!* mode.

As part of her commitment to changing her life, I asked her to read her *Big Picture Vision* notes daily. This helped her stay connected to her intention and start manifesting her new personal life path. She became more and more excited about the possibilities as well as aware of some of the potential roadblocks. We identified an important concern, the need for her make a plan to manage what was sure to be a considerable drop in income when she first entered the music business. She knew it would probably take a few years before her music production business could replace her medical income. Together we realized the Janice's next step was to define a bridge that could help her transition from medicine to music.

Then, something amazing happened. The next time I saw Janice she was beaming from head to toe. She was two months into dance lessons and was feeling supercharged. And, she had connected with the owner of the dance studio, who happened to be a former medical student and entrepreneur himself. He shared his dream with her—he wanted to open a medical spa and needed a doctor to oversee it. Because she had done the work to ready her spirit for a new, exciting change in her life, she recognized the bridge she needed when the Universe stepped in to provide it. She would be the medical director of her friend's spa, a job that allowed her to make a decent income and have flexible hours, while she honed her craft in the world of music production. Wow!

> "As an irrigator guides water to his fields, as an archer aims an arrow, as a carpenter carves wood, the wise shape their lives."
>
> ~*Buddha,*
> *East Indian spiritual*
> *teacher and philosopher*
> *(563 BC-483 BC)*

Janice had opened up her world, mind and spirit through dance, an activity that brought passion back to her life. Through her daily *Blast Off!* work, she had discovered a whole new world of possibilities and connections. Janice got to experience what I call the *Secret Spark* for the first time in her life. With my guidance and the help of my *Blast Off! Program*, Janice had found her passion and was on her way to a new life.

We outlined the larger *Mile Steps* that needed to happen in order for her to reach her vision. From there, we broke them into daily *Mini Feats* so her progress would be attainable without feeling overwhelming. With my continued support she cleared all the psychological, legal and business hurdles to create a successful new career path. She attended conferences for medical spa technicians and spoke to business consultants for this particular field. The more information she gathered, the more motivated Janice became and the freer she began to feel.

In the end, she opted to open her own medical spa and also attend a music production education program. Right now she is blasting off to a whole new life adventure full of passion and meaning. **What a Supersonic Success Story!**

If Janice's story seems overwhelming or intimidating, take a deep breath. All that is required of you right now is to read one page at a time, to take one day at a time, to explore one galaxy at a time. Others have done it, and you can too. The tools I've included in this book will help you blast off with ease.

> "It takes a lot of courage to release the familiar and seemingly secure... But there is no real security in what is no longer meaningful. There is more security in the adventurous and exciting, for in movement, there is life, and in change, there is power."
>
> ~*Alan Cohen*
> *Author of* Dare to Be Yourself

Time to Blast Off!

The *Blast Off! Program* is comprehensive. Because of its wide-ranging positive impacts, it is important to complete the entire process so that you will reach your goals and ingrain your *Daily Launch Tools* as new healthy habits for your life. Just as exercise has a cumulative impact so does the *Blast Off! Program*.

If you're concerned about possibly being in conflict with some of the philosophies or spiritual principles in the book, know that I am not preaching *any* religious doctrines. In this book, the word "spiritual" is used to refer to personal growth. Personally, I visualize my life moving along a graceful, sometimes challenging, always changing path. At every corner, there are options, and from my choices, I learn and grow.

Through my own life process, I have been exposed to many ideas, methods, healing practices and principles. I have developed and incorporated my own systems that were inspired from my personal and professional trials, tribulations, achievements and joys.

The *Blast Off! Program* is a powerful combination of my own winning formulas and the most effective principles and practices that I have learned over the years.

It is an honor to share this book with you and it is my hope that you, too, will learn to revel in the life of your dreams in the near future, just as I do today.

CHAPTER 1

BLAST Off!
to a Life of Passion
and Meaning

* At this very moment, are you who you want to be?
* Is your daily life full of things you want to do?
* Are you attaining the goals and fulfillment that you want to have?

If you can answer "Yes" to each question, congratulations! You have either inherited or designed a life process that is working for you. In your case, the *Blast Off!* principles will only enhance your already satisfying journey.

On the other hand, if you've answered "No" to any or all of these queries, let me ask you one more very important question...

Do you want to be at the same place you are now,
with the same frustration, the same struggles,
and the same complaints, one year from now
or even ten years from now?

If the thought of being at this same juncture of your path, personally, professionally, emotionally and spiritually, ten years from now does not light a raging fire underneath your feet for moving toward transformation, then your fear of changing must be greater than your desire for it. If this is your story but you're still game, the *Blast Off! Program* can help you push past your fear and enter a more exciting state. And if your fire has been ignited, let's work together to infuse your life with the magic, joy, love and prosperity that you *so* deserve.

Fifteen years ago, I asked myself that same question, "How would I feel about being in the same place ten years from now?" Honestly, the thought of remaining stuck and frustrated with no movement forward on my life path made me nauseous. I had spent so much time fighting for what I wanted in relationships and in my career that I didn't know what else could be done. All I knew for sure was that the combination of a passion-less relationship *and* a career without meaning was absolutely killing me.

Your Personal Life Path

I'm pretty confident that you're yearning or reaching for your dreams and goals, or you wouldn't have picked up this book. As conscious human beings, we are most content when we're in motion. Well, here's some good news. Growing and expanding your mind, strengthening and nurturing your body, and creating a deeper connection with your spirit (or higher self) will give you a sense of wisdom, achievement, peace and understanding as you evolve on your Personal Life Path.

When I meditate, or close my eyes for a few moments of mental relaxation, I often visualize my Personal Life Path. My visual mindscape looks something like this:

The winding path of weathered cobblestones is set in firm sandy dirt. My path meanders through an endless field of changing landscapes. (A little "Wizard of Oz"-ish, I know. Just hang in there with me for a moment.) My skyscape is vast, and when I breathe in its blueness, I feel a sense of space and freedom in each and every cell of my body. There's an inviting breeze that blows in wisdom, inspiration and endless possibilities. The clouds can bring downpours of sadness, trauma and pain. Yet, on my Personal Life Path, the sun always comes up just around the bend. My path is rarely straight and the view alters quite frequently, keeping it new, interesting and full of adventure. Even when

I was stuck in many aspects of my life, I always visualized a curve in the path where the wind would shift, and hope was glowing in the trees.

I frequently meditate on this visual in order to assess where I am on my life path. This meditation helps me stay connected to my life purpose, make weighty decisions, and move through any little annoyance, frustration or stress that has arisen. By bringing my mind back to this visual of my life path, I quickly am reminded why I am here, what is important to me, and what my life is all about. In times of stress, this meditation reminds me that the rocky times will pass and there is always a new adventure or a smoother slope just around the bend.

> "All we need to know is waiting to be discovered."
> ~*Allison Maslan*

Blast Off! PRACTICE 1: Design Your Own Personal Life Path

In your journal or *The Blast Off! Workbook,* write a description of, or draw, your own life path. Be as detailed as possible. Your path can be as elaborate or as simple as you choose. No artistic skill is required. Keep your description or drawing within reach, and whether you feel stuck, get frustrated, or are cruising along in the Supersonic space, you can pull out your path artwork or description and ask yourself, "Where am I on my Personal Life Path?" ✪

Blast Off! PRACTICE 2: Where Are You Now?

Now I'm going to ask you to evaluate where you are on your Personal Life Path. When you think about this, you can include your career, relationships, financial state, health, personal fulfillment and spiritual life. Peruse this list of adjectives and ask yourself which one or two describes where you are on your path.

- ★ Stuck
- ★ Trapped
- ★ Drained
- ★ Frustrated
- ★ Indecisive
- ★ Unmotivated
- ★ Bored
- ★ Confused about what direction to take

- ★ Exploring new options
- ★ At a plateau, enjoyable but ready for more
- ★ So far so good, but time for the next level
- ★ Successful
- ★ Fulfilling
- ★ Inspiring and exciting
- ★ Supersonic Wow!

In one of your *Sun-Up Script* writing practices (this is a free-association writing exercise, which was described in the Introduction with the other Daily Launch Tools), jot down the theme word or words from above that best match your status on your Personal Life Path. Write this at the top of a page in your journal, or in The *Blastation* software. Then write a page or two about how this word (or words) describes your situation. At the end, write about how you would like to be different, and what you plan to do to make that change. If you don't know what to do to make the changes, not to worry. This book will be your guide through the changes that are needed. For now, you could just write about your excitement related to working with the *Blast Off! Program*. Next, write your *Rocket Words* (as described below) for the week, summarizing a positive feeling, truth or action related to changing.

For example:

If you chose the word "stuck," write a page or two about how, what and why this stuckness is present and what it represents in your life. Then at the end, write about the opposite of stuck, such as free, open, growing, and what that would feel like if it were really true. Then your Rocket Words from the Theme Word, stuck, could be: "I feel free, light and in motion in every choice and action in my life." ✪

From Stuck to Supersonic

Loren came to me feeling very stuck in her career. She had been a successful barber for twenty years. The salon where she'd been working all that time was closing down, and this was a catalyst for Loren to ask herself, "What is the next chapter of my life?" She felt stuck because her gut was saying, "Move on," but her head was wondering what else she could do.

In the relationship sector, Loren was also feeling stuck. She'd done an amazing job raising her kids as a single mom. She'd also been in a relationship with a man for the last few years. She enjoyed her boyfriend's company but felt there was no movement toward a deeper commitment or marriage. Any time that Loren brought up these concerns to her partner, he reacted with resistance, saying, "I'm happy with the way things are."

I worked with Loren to try to uncover what was really holding her back in both areas. Soon we determined that fear was the culprit—fear of loss of security concerning her career, and fear of losing her heartfelt connection in the relationship. Well, anytime you stay in a situation due to fear, rather than true choice, you are most likely making major sacrifices.

In working together further, I discovered that Loren really had a lot of life experience. I asked her to create a *Big Picture Vision*, a detailed description of what her dream career would look like. Through our coaching, she was able to flip her frustrations into passion and creativity. Loren broke through her boundaries and created an amazing vision of herself as an author, writing to her peers, the baby boomer generation, about what it takes to thrive emotionally during these years.

> "The willingness to create a new vision is a statement of your belief in your potential."
>
> ~David McNally, Motivational speaker, author and film producer

Through the *Blast Off! Life Coaching Program*, Loren realized she had been training for the past twenty years to be an author and teacher. As a barber, Loren had also played the role of confidant and therapist. She had offered her clients, who were already successful men, valuable insights from a woman's point of view. Loren had even helped save marriages. When we broke down her ideas and stories, Loren realized she had enough interesting content to be published into books. Her *Secret Spark* had been ignited!

With this newfound vision and passion for life, Loren was ready to address her relationship. In her *Big Picture Vision* for this area, she saw herself with a man like Robert, her boyfriend. But the new man had one more important characteristic; he was open-hearted and ready for marriage.

For the next several weeks, Loren read her vision statement and imagined this man in her life as if he had already arrived. And with her newfound confidence, she decided to tell Robert that their relationship was not enough for her anymore. Loren told him that if she stayed she would be denying herself what she truly desired—love and marriage with her soulmate.

> "You don't need to jump off a bridge to create positive change. Instead, create a bridge that unites you and the wisdom of your experience to the innocence of possibilities."
>
> ~Allison Maslan

Robert was floored. He felt the huge shift in Loren and knew she was moving on. He realized that if he didn't propose quickly to her, he would lose the best woman he had ever known. He also didn't feel pressure as he had in the past because there was no blame, guilt-evoking or ultimatums. Loren and Robert did get married.

I also helped Loren create a bridge with her barbering business to her new career as an author and speaker. She is working now only two days a week instead of five, but making more money because of her recent price increase. Loren now spends the rest of the week writing her book and spending time with her soulmate. Once she chose to walk through her fear, and release the beliefs that mired her in a state of stuckness, Loren cruised right into her new life of Supersonic Wow.

Blast Off! PRACTICE 3: Proclamation of the Day

Keep your *Rocket Words* (from Practice 2) in your wallet, on your computer screen, and/or on your bathroom mirror for a constant reminder of the expansive life you're beginning to create. Read this to yourself and out loud throughout the week. ✪

Owning Up and Letting Go

Let me clarify a point I made earlier in this chapter… it wasn't actually the relationship or my career that was killing me when I needed to change. It was the negative, tainted energy I owned around those two areas of my life, and the manner in which I chose to expend my energy toward them. The fact is that *I* was completely responsible for creating my own misery. *No one else. I* made the choice to be in that relationship. *I* chose the career. And *I* also chose to allow them both to affect me in a negative way. Hearing myself complain and wallow in my own anger, sadness and *stuckness* was draining and, in the end, only bred more anger, sadness and stuckness. The way I saw it, I had two choices:

1. Either I needed to accept my circumstances while making the best of them (which was not an option)…

2. Or I had to make a change (which is what my soul was crying out for me to do).

You may not want to hear this, but I assure you that you are responsible for the choices you have made in your life, and the circumstances that have resulted from those choices. *You are not a victim.* As a child, you may have been an unfortunate victim to traumatic, sad or frightening circumstances. As a child, you didn't have a choice. As an adult, thank goodness, you do. You are free to choose the right path for your life and it is never too late to start. Only when you fully accept this truth, take ownership of the repeated cycle of negative circumstances in your life, and learn to curb your habitual urge to repeat the insanity of such unhealthy choices will you begin to make powerful, positive changes one tiny step at a time.

Accepting responsibility may seem unfair or feel like a cop-out, as if you are letting someone or something off the hook for your pain. The truth is that taking ownership of your reality is so freeing and empowering because you get to shift your focus off of what is wrong in your life, and finally direct it toward the choices that are the best for you.

You are responsible for:

★ Not eating in a healthy way

★ Choosing to stay in an unhealthy relationship

★ Choosing to live without the love you desire

★ Choosing to stay in a stressful or unfulfilling job

★ Choosing to earn much less money than you deserve

★ Choosing friendships with pessimistic people

★ Choosing to get caught up in drama

★ Choosing to not gain the benefits of exercise

★ Choosing to not reach for your dreams

★ Choosing to stay miserable

This "aaahhaaaa" moment is not an exercise in self-punishment. This is an empowering wake-up call. *Because you are responsible for choosing and remaining in these circumstances, you can also choose to change them.* We make things much harder and much more complicated than they have to be. Whenever you are ready to choose joy, the Universe will hand it to you.

When my perspective shifted and I finally realized that I didn't have to fight for love, joy or acceptance by trying to control my situations, I put down my boxing gloves and began to trust in the process and the rhythm of the Universe. Yes, this felt scary because it was a whole new way of looking at the world. Old habits are limiting and, at the same time, familiarly comfortable.

What do I mean when I write that I didn't need to control every person, situation and aspect of my life? Well, I decided to let go of the past and encouraged myself to walk through the fear of the giant unknown. I finally cleared space in my life so only the most fortunate situations could appear. And all of a sudden, as if opportunity had been ready to pounce through my door for years, wonderful prospects started falling at my feet at an astounding pace. I began to attract the same frequency of positive energy that I was emitting. If I had known it was that easy, I would have stopped fighting for my joy long ago! I began making wonderful new friends, found bliss even in the little moments, and rediscovered a long-lost friend called laughter.

One day around this time, I was chatting away on the phone with my best friend and former college roommate, Susan. Suddenly we were laughing over something trivial that I cannot even remember. We laughed so hard that I started crying. My stomach was cramping and my body was convulsing with laughter to the point of suffocation, yet I felt such an explosion of happiness. There were so many tears of joy that I could not even see. *He He Ha Ha!!* Yeah, Allie was back.

Blast Off! PRACTICE 4: Let Go, Grow and Change

Resentment, anger and frustration keep us from moving forward in life. These feelings make sure that we stay connected to the past and to our negative situations and relationships. They can wreak havoc with your health and demeanor and at the same time block any potential for joy. If you want to move toward your potential for success, empowerment and love, you will need to begin to release this pain. In contrast, dwelling on the past will keep you stuck there, and I know you want to make a positive shift in your life. It's not a simple task to let go, especially when this person or situation creates a trigger or charge in your energy field.

Just remember that the anger or grief you generate and carry regarding someone else will only mirror the same frequency of energy back to you. So rather than hurting them, you are really hurting yourself. Come on already! Haven't you been through enough?

Take a moment to ask yourself the questions below. In your journal or *The Blast Off! Workbook*, write down the immediate thoughts that come to mind without censoring them. Be honest with yourself.

> "Resentment has been compared to holding onto a burning ember with the intention of throwing it at another, all the while burning yourself."
>
> ~Robin Casarjian, Author of Forgiveness: A Bold Choice for a Peaceful Heart

★ What resentments, anger and grief am I carrying around each day?

★ Who am I angry or resentful toward?

★ How can I take responsibility for this situation?

★ What have I learned from this situation that has been positive toward my growth?

★ Can I give myself permission to let go of these negative feelings?

★ How do I feel now that this energy-draining emotion is released? ✪

If you have gotten this far, you are definitely ready for change. You are working diligently to release the past and any negative blocks or energy that have held you back. You are letting go of any burdensome weight that could be slowing your progress. Once it is released, you'll feel like a hundred pounds of grief and stress have melted away. It's true; you'll actually feel physically lighter, freer and more present in the moment. And just think about how much more energy you'll have once you aren't working so hard to hold onto this negative load.

You may be thinking, how can I just let it go? In actuality, it is much easier to let something go than to hold onto it. Try lifting up something heavy. Feel the effort that it takes to keep the object suspended. How much energy does it take for you to grip the object? How many other body parts are involved? Your entire arm, your torso and your legs are probably all affected from this holding on—all in the effort to keep your equilibrium. Now, let it go. You can do it! Simply release your grip. (Please do not drop anything breakable and find a forgiving surface for the fall.)

> "Nothing great was ever achieved without enthusiasm."
>
> *~Ralph Waldo Emerson, Essayist, poet and 19th century leader of the Transcendental movement (1803-1881)*

Which movement took the least effort? Letting go is effortless. The illusion that letting go is hard is only the mental mania that we give it. Holding on is painful and often results in the exact thing we were trying to avoid—more pain! Well, here's an important truth: *When we allow the past to be in the past, we are making room for new positive energy and circumstances to appear.*

Now that you have let go of past resentments, your focus can shift to the present and the future. Congratulations... you are in motion again! Moving forward rather than hovering is energizing. The momentum feels productive which, in turn, gives you a sense of accomplishment. This is an uplifting place to be.

The Power of Your *Secret Spark*

It's time to connect with your passions in order to transform your life from where you are now to WOW! Once you finally connect with something that has meaning to you, and your internal passion regarding this is accessed and utilized, your once deadened perception and reality will be pumped with new and energized life blood. I call this your *Secret Spark*, a perfect mix of meaning and passion that enlivens your life purpose and gives you the drive and stick-to-it-ness to make things happen. When you discover your *Secret Spark*, your work will become stimulating and fun, and you'll be immersed in your satisfying activity and lose track of time. Yes, once you learn to access your *Secret Spark*, soul-enriching and mind-bending results will follow.

I liken the *Secret Spark* to your most addictive food craving. My all-time weakness is dark chocolate, and my closest friends know this about me. In fact, my second class of graduates from the school I founded, Homeopathic Academy of Southern California, gave me the biggest Hershey bar you have ever seen because I never teach a day without eating chocolate. In fact, my husband once hid some chocolate from me because he knew that if I found it, it would not last long. However, my sixth sense told me that chocolate was floating around somewhere. After ransacking my kitchen, I found it hidden on top of the shelf, wrapped with duct tape!

You know that feeling when you just have to have something. It's all you can think about. The good news is that if you develop a craving for a particular hobby or career (gambling, drinking, eating and sex do not apply!), your *Secret Spark*—that supercharged energy, drive and focus—will be activated. Warning: This healthy obsession may well take over your life for a period of time, and your friends and family may get very tired of hearing about it because this is your *Secret Spark*, not theirs.

Some people are blessed to find that special something that gives them the internal spark from a young age. Jake was just eleven years old when he walked into my office. He introduced himself and handed me his business card. "I have my own company. It is very successful," he informed me. Jake is the president of his own entertainment company through which he offers DJ services for parties and events. He saves his allowance money to invest back into the business. At the time of our first meeting, Jake had signed eight contracts for school dances and birthday parties. "At first I had a karaoke machine, just for fun. I just kept getting bigger speakers, and then I became a DJ! I feel good that I can do it. I want to keep the business my whole life and when I grow up, I can own a big business and have a bunch of DJs that work for me."

Needless to say, I was blown away by Jake's fascination, enthusiasm and intention. Jake is lucky enough to have found something that he is passionate about and he is good at. You don't meet too many eleven-year-old entrepreneurs. Most of us figure out what lights that *Secret Spark*, that electric adrenaline zing you receive when you tap into your bliss, through some personal life experiences or by being introduced or exposed to a certain activity later in our life.

Sherry's *Secret Spark*

When Sherry came to see me, she had been a realtor for several years. She was a hard worker, financially successful, and as Sherry so eloquently stated, "Bored to death!"

She told me: "Some people really love selling houses, but it does nothing for me but pay my bills. I am very good at pasting on a smile each morning and helping my clients buy and sell houses. I know I am good at this, but please help me. I am so uninspired! I wake up in the morning dreading my day, but I feel I have no choice. I need this job to survive."

The key word here is "uninspired." What Sherry had expressed to me was that she wanted to find that *Secret Spark* that would support her in feeling motivated, stimulated and excited about her career. The problem here is that Sherry and real estate simply were not a match. She just needed to transfer all the great qualities that made her successful in her current career, such as her gregarious nature and her ability to make the customer feel calm and confident in their transactions, into something that truly mattered to her.

I asked Sherry one powerful question, "If you could do anything you wanted for a hobby or career and you were not limited by time, financial obligations, or capability, what would you choose to do?"

Without hesitation, Sherry replied, "I've always loved fashion ever since I was a little girl dressing my Barbies. One of my favorite things in this world is to find creative and unique ways to coordinate my outfits. That is how I express myself." Sherry always dressed sharply, with the latest trends. "I study all the fashion magazines and then find a way to mirror them with items from my favorite treasure-filled second-hand stores. I can proudly replicate a thousand-dollar look with a hundred-dollar purchase."

> "Leap and the net will appear."
>
> ~Julia Cameron,
> Author of
> The Artist's Way

I then asked Sherry, "Tell me how you feel when you're shopping or coordinating these outfits?"

"Oh my gosh, I am in heaven!" Sherry exclaimed. "I spend hours hunting down a style or mixing and matching looks. I can completely immerse myself into the creative process. It's as if I am in another world and I completely lose track of time."

Flowing in the Zone

This in-sync flow of time and space that Sherry noted is her *Secret Spark*, a powerful yet energetic flow that occurs in your body and mind when you're completely synchronistic with your emotions, your mental focus and your actions. Runners experience this as an adrenaline high when their gait pattern is in rhythm with their breath, and they're running at a rapid pace with almost no effort at all. When you're madly in love with what you're doing, your *Secret Spark* will ignite, and you will experience life with joy in your heart. Even work will no longer feel like work. In fact, you would do it for free if you had to. *This is passion.*

When I asked Sherry why she had not pursued a career in fashion, she said, "Oh, I would never be able to make a living at it. I could never do that."

"Let me get this straight," I replied. "You make a prosperous living in real estate and you detest it. You love fashion, but you would never be able to succeed in it. That makes no sense."

Sherry was not living the joyful life that she deserved. She was only living a boring life, which was all Sherry believed was possible for her. Can you imagine what it would be like to wake up with excitement and thrilling anticipation for your day rather than dreading it? Once Sherry realized she had permission to follow her *Secret Spark*, she was so fired up about her new path that it was all she could think about. *Good-bye open houses. Hello clothes, purses and hats!*

I helped Sherry create a *Big Picture Vision*, a final picture of her biggest goal. She drew a picture of how her own fashion retail store would look, using magazine photos and her own stick drawings. (Note: *Blastation* software subscribers can create a *Big Picture Vision* at the website, www. InteractiveLifeCoach.com, using digital photo images.) I also asked her to write a detailed description of what her ultimate boutique would look like, and what it would feel like to work with clients to help them coordinate their personal wardrobes. (Note: The *Blastation* software also provides subscribers with a section for this type of writing assignment.) I told Sherry to spend the next two weeks envisioning herself buying merchandise for her store, stocking her shelves with beautiful, original designs, and helping her customers out the door with several shopping bags of her clothing. Sherry came to understand that by exporting her imagination, inspiration and intention onto paper, then expressing her vision out loud, she was already in cahoots with the energetic forces of the Universe to start the ball rolling. That was four years ago. Now Sherry owns two very successful fashion boutiques in San Diego, California. She no longer has just a job. Her career is an extension of her passion.

My heartfelt wish is that once you complete the *Blast Off! Program*, you will be living your dreams despite any perceived limitations in your current viewpoint.

Passion and Meaning: The Necessary Ingredients

Have you ever impulsively jumped on a great new idea to make money only to find that your enthusiasm dwindled after the first week or two? Have you started a hobby that a friend got you fired up about, dropping a big investment to get started, but soon after you completely lost interest?

In order for an activity or goal to sustain itself long enough to be successful through life's ups and downs, there must be meaning or a passion behind it. This love of your work, relationship, hobby or practice is the glue that will keep you cherishing your wins and picking yourself up after your losses as you progress on your path toward success. When an activity or goal has meaning to you, you're more likely to give your heart and soul to this cause, making sure that you stay focused, labor over every detail, and absorb yourself in every moment. When you spend time on efforts that really matter to you, it's much more probable that you'll make the commitment that's necessary to build a lasting entity.

The "If Only" Syndrome

Have you ever heard of the "If Only" syndrome? *If only I had a new car… if only I receive a big bonus… if only I lived in a different city…* then I would be fulfilled. And then you get that car or house, and yes, it's fun for a while, but soon you're back to *if only I had….* In contrast, when the purpose, the person, the message or the feelings matter to you on a deeper level, your efforts will endure. And when you reach your meaningful goals, success will feel like a shining glory. When you have built something you can be proud of, something you are completely passionate about, the satisfaction is not only in the outcome, it's in the day-to-day process. If you're only working toward the destination and not reveling in the journey, you miss out on the abundance of life. When you finally reach your goal, you may find yourself thinking, *"Is that all there is?"* while feeling empty, sad and bored, and once again, unfulfilled.

Two of my most successful achievements had absolutely nothing to do with money. When I decided to go back to school to study homeopathy, a friend asked me if I realized how much study time I was going to have to commit to school, and if I thought I would be able to manage it all. It was an interesting question because that thought had not crossed my mind. I was so excited to be learning this science that my biggest problem was finding the amount of time that I so desired to bury myself in my lessons. For several years I cherished every class, inhaling every page of each homeopathic book that I could get my hands on. Over time, my friends and family grew a little tired of hearing my one-track enthusiasm over my newfound knowledge. Never once did I find it challenging to stay focused because I felt so intellectually stimulated and absolutely loved what I was learning. Reading about and observing so many transformative cases was incredibly fascinating to me.

When I completed my homeopathic program and clinical hours, I applied for national certification. The certification process was arduous, including a presentation of several cases that I had worked on for over a year. In summary, this took a hell of a lot of time and dedication. However, because this work mattered to me, because it had meaning, it came so easily and so naturally. It was as if it were effortless, even though it took an incredible amount of time and exertion.

Once I completed the requirements, I had to do a phone interview with a board member of the North American Society of Homeopaths related to the final decision on my certification. I was incredibly nervous but I had confidence in the work I had presented. At the end of the interview, she said, "Allison, I want to congratulate you on your hard work. We are happy to announce you have qualified for certification." With a growing giddiness in my heart, while presenting a cordial and professional voice, I told her, "Thank you very much. This means a great deal to me."

> "There is one quality that one must possess to win, and that is a definiteness of purpose, the knowledge of what one wants, and a burning desire to possess it."
>
> ~Napoleon Hill, American author, and one of the earliest writers of personal success literature (1883-1970)

When I hung up the phone, I started dancing wildly around my apartment as I yelled, "I did it. I did it!" My daughter was laughing and jumping around the room with me. My eyes were soon filled with tears and my heart was exploding with joy and pride. I think you could rightly say that I had tapped into my passion.

Once you find your *Secret Spark*, your passionate energy will give you the momentum you'll need to move forward and make your positive changes, and it will provide that indescribable sense of elation, satisfaction and accomplishment.

Blast Off! PRACTICE 5: Accessing Your *Secret Spark*

The following four steps will help you access your *Secret Spark*.

1. **Inspiration Station:** Create an *Inspiration Station* in your home. An *Inspiration Station* is a special space that is quiet, uncluttered, relaxing and soothing. It can also be encompassed with inspir-ing elements that will trigger your imagination, creativity and ultimately your *Secret Spark* of passion and meaning. This space needs to reflect the results you are intending to create.

   Your Inspiration Station is a place to go to regularly in order to clear your mind so that inspiration will appear easily. To this end, find a quiet space in your home. Decorate it in a calming yet enlivening way that will assist in shifting you to a meditative or creative state, depending on what that visit is calling for.

2. **The *Secret Spark List*:** While sitting in your new inspiring space, make a Secret Spark List in your journal or workbook of all the things that you loved to do for fun in childhood. Also, list the things that you would love to try, but never have because of fear or lack of opportunity. These activities can be fun or career-related. You can even include intriguing activities that you have read about, seen on television or noticed others doing. Break out of the box and be bold in your list. Envision doing things you would never have thought possible. No limits due to money, time or capability need apply.

For example:

* Run in the rain
* Fly a kite
* Finger painting
* Go back to college
* Take hang-gliding lessons
* Write and record a song
* Write a book
* Start a Web-design business

* Get a patent on my great idea
* Practice meditation
* Go on an African safari
* Run a marathon
* Learn Italian
* Open a restaurant
* Play the clarinet
* Live part-time in another country

Take as much time as you need with this list until it feels complete. Visit a bookstore or do some career, adventure or travel searches online. Bookstores and the Web are both good sources of *Secret Spark* inspiration.

3. **The *Secret Spark* Meditation.** Prepare to sit comfortably in your Inspiration Station. To relax your mind, you might turn on some soothing music and light some candles. When you're ready to settle down, sit in a relaxed manner and close your eyes. Take a deep, long inhalation through your nose to fill your lungs with oxygen and expand your abdomen. As you exhale, feel any tension leaving your body from your head to your toes. To further relax your spinning mind, visualize all of your day's stresses or worries floating off in a bottle far, far away.

Once you're feeling quite relaxed and present in the moment, visualize yourself doing one of the activities on your list. Whether your vision is climbing Mount Everest, flying a plane, taking a walk on the beach, or playing with your dog, see yourself immersed in this activity. Feel the environment surrounding you. Hear the sounds and smell the scents of the landscapes. Feel the movement in your body. See yourself performing the activity as if it is really happening in this very moment. Feel the joy, peace, expansion or excitement that this activity brings.

Do this exercise once a week until one or two of the activities completely resonates with you.

4. **Immerse yourself further through writing.** After the meditation, write about the activity or goal in detail in your journal or workbook. Include what it would feel like to create, participate in and accomplish it. Be very specific in your description, such as, "I feel myself breathing under water as I am scuba diving in Hawaii. I am surrounded by hundreds of colorful fish, beautiful coral, and playful dolphins." Write in the present tense as if the activity is happening right now. Read it out loud. Also, feel it in your body as if it is already happening. Believe it to be true. Keep your journal or workbook by your bed and read about the activity or goal first thing when you wake up in the morning and right before closing your eyes to sleep. This will jump-start your unconscious mind into creating ideas and opportunities to make this fun activity or goal a reality in your life.

> "The more intensely we feel about an idea or goal, the more assuredly the idea, buried deep in our subconscious, will direct us along the path to its fulfillment."
>
> *~Earl Nightingale,*
> *Motivational speaker,*
> *cofounder Nightingale-Conant*
> *Corporation*
> *(1921-1989)*

By focusing your mindset on invigorating activities, you're activating your mind, body and soul in an inspirational vibration, your *Supersonic Gear.* You are also opening the channels for your *Secret Spark* to be revealed. ✪

The Front and Back End of Passion

For passion to sustain the long journey, it must have a front end and a back end.

The *front end* of passion is the blossoming intensity from which your passion is directed. This exploding energy is powerful, yet fits you so perfectly that it supports you with ease toward your goal. It is an energy that comes from deep within your life force and cannot help being expressed outwardly in an enthusiastic and contagious manner. The front end of passion is a positive expulsion of energy. However, if you are not prepared, this continuous momentum can deplete you in a flash. This is what happened, at first, to Mitchell.

Mitchell: On Finding and Sustaining Passion

Mitchell was a fifty-seven-year-old client of mine who had spent the past several years working at a career he was good at, but didn't enjoy. When Mitchell came to see me, his life had become a daily grind of routine and monotony. Mitchell knew he had the potential for more, but he was stuck in the fear of change and taking risks. Once we were able to identify and release the fears that had held him back from living his potential, Mitchell's life changed in a huge way. The fears he fed for years had been draining him of so much energy on a daily basis. Once those fears had vanished, Mitchell found the courage to take hold of a career he had always dreamed of.

Without expending so much energy toward his fears, Mitchell was surprised to find so much surplus energy to put toward his newly acquired passion as an inventor. In fact, he became so passionately focused on his ideas that he spent the next several months eating, drinking and sleeping his inventions. This was all very exciting for Mitchell, but when I saw him two months later, he looked happy but completely exhausted. He was heading toward imminent burnout.

For passion to sustain itself, it must have a *back end*—the exterior gas pump that will continually refill your internal production of fervor. The continuing cycle of importing and exporting passionate energy will keep your tank full and your motor strong, balanced and humming along. Simply put, you must continually support and rejuvenate your body and mind, the back end, so that your front end of passion, the expressed energy, will continue to runneth over.

This is similar to the art of love. If only one partner is infusing passion into the relationship and this dedication is not mirrored back by the other partner, the love will not sustain over time. The giving partner, even though they are in love, will end up feeling drained, sad, angry and resentful. They may end up shutting down, blaming the other partner, running out, or continuing to give while being self-punishing because of "everything they must be doing wrong."

In Mitchell's case, he had half of the equation spot-on. He tapped into his *Secret Spark*, an idea and a goal he could feel passionate and motivated about. His inventions were so stimulating that he never wanted to do anything else. Mitchell had succeeded with the most challenging component, finding a fulfilling purpose, yet his reserve energy, the back end of his passion, was dwindling quickly.

We worked together to develop his back end, the external juice that would nourish his body and mind so Mitchell could maintain this new soul-driven creativity. Mitchell learned how to balance his enthusiasm and support his body and mind so that his passion would continue to thrive.

> "Motivation is what gets you started. Habit is what keeps you going."
>
> ~Jim Ryun, American politician, former track athlete

Four Ways to Build the Back End of Passion

1. **Establish good nutrition**. It's easy to fall into fast food or snacking when you are so engrossed in your passion that you're not taking the time to eat right. (More detailed nutrition information can be found in Chapter Six.)

2. **Eight hours of sleep each night.** Sleep is one of the most healing, energizing medicines, and it is absolutely critical for a creative mind. Did you know that sleep deprivation is used as a brainwashing technique? Without sleep, you are living in survival mode, which is the opposite of a passionate life.

3. **Take a passion break once a week.** Most of my creativity comes when I'm not working. When my mind is clear and I'm exploring or having fun, the ideas have room to appear. Turn off your phone. Shut down your computer. Go spend the day outdoors in nature, go to a movie, take a bike ride, or visit some friends. Talk about things other than your passion. (For a few minutes, anyway.)

4. **Get physical.** Especially if your passion is of the intellectual persuasion, you must get into your body. If you're living from the neck up, your body needs

to be enlivened. Choose exercise that you can sustain by doing activities that you will enjoy, such as dance, running, swimming, biking or boxing. Mix it up! It's more beneficial to incorporate more than one activity to stimulate various muscle groups in the body. You will also stimulate the serotonin in your brain for more creativity and mood enhancement. You will prevent fatigue and burnout as you stimulate your cardiovascular system, get your blood pumping, and your billions of cells moving. Ahhhhhhh.

Five Principles to Support the Journey on Your Passionate Path

When each of these five elements is experienced separately, they are effective. But put them all together and you will have nothing short of soaring to the stars.

Blast Off! PRINCIPLE 1: **Find Your Purpose**

As you set out to find your purpose, or first commit to living a life of purpose, what drives you may still feel a bit elusive. Many people have no idea if they have a real purpose on earth. Ask a friend randomly what their life purpose is, and they may take a long pause before answering, "Good question. I'm not sure." Well, I'm here to tell you (and them) that you do have a purpose and it's probably not as mysterious as you think. Most likely it's right under your nose. Maybe your purpose is to feed hungry children, build a gigantic bridge, love your children, or just be in the moment. Your life purpose is most likely connected to the areas that create passion and meaning in your life. Here are some simple steps for accessing your life purpose.

★ **Get in touch with what really matters to you** in the world and in your life. What do you get passionate talking about, reading or exploring? Before taking impulsive action steps toward a new career, business opportunity, or new relationship, ponder what gives you that inner surge of excitement. This could be the most important key for long-term staying power and success.

★ **Gather your thoughts and focus your energy** toward these ideas. Find a way to involve yourself in this activity.

⋆ **Explore several possibilities before settling on one**. However, if one really moves you, then go for it!

⋆ **Connect with other people** on a regular basis who are passionate about these ideals or activities.

⋆ **See how you feel in this new arena**. Does it stir your *Secret Spark* energy? This is what we call "alignment," or "being congruent." When we are expressing our true inner thoughts, beliefs and ideals through external actions that match those thoughts, beliefs and ideals, we are operating in harmony rather than in conflict. The "practice-what-you-preach" philosophy.

⋆ **Not doing what you love could be very harmful to your health and your prosperity.** Most people think that doing what you love is a luxury, so they settle for something they don't enjoy. Someone who loves your career more than you do will no doubt perform the job better than you. This person will eventually be greatly rewarded because this work matters to them. Part of what you'll get from being out of alignment in your work is dissatisfaction and burnout. ✪

Blast Off! PRINCIPLE 2: Create Your Vision

To rev up your engines, you must first have a goal. Something that gets you fired up to jump out of bed in the morning. Goals can exist on many levels. It could be an "in-the-moment goal" to clean out your closet or go for a walk or run; "a loftier goal" to meet Mr. or Ms. Right or start a new career and increase your revenue; or "a magnanimous goal" such as healing world hunger or saving the Brazilian rainforest.

It takes tenacity to sustain a dream, and that comes from passion. It's true that fear is a big motivator; but if you're doing something out of fear, you will not be inspired to stick with it in the long run. Passion outlasts all fear and keeps you coming back for more. ✪

> "Goals give us a sense of direction. Direction gives us a sense of purpose. A sense of purpose gives us a feeling of well-being."
>
> ~*Unknown*

Blast Off! PRINCIPLE 3: Create Structure

Once you've created a direction, a structure needs to be developed to assist you in setting up a plan to stay on course and attain your new purpose. A structure helps to simplify your goals into a day-to-day, step-by-step roadmap. Structure gives us a feeling of stability and reliability. When you sway off course (which can happen from time to time), simply return to your daily structure and your plans will begin moving along your path again.

Here are some simple steps for creating structure to reach your goals:

* Create a *Big Picture Vision,* a long-range picture or vision of your larger goals, in any area of your life that you want to enhance or recreate. You can draw this visually or write it out in detail in your journal. There is also a form in the back of this book for written *Big Picture Visions*, as well as a sample. And we'll be doing some of this work in *The Blast Off! Workbook*. (Those subscribing to the *Blastation* software can create their *Big Picture Vision* on the www.InteractiveLifeCoach.com website.)

  Get as specific as you can about your vision. For example, write what it is, what you love about it, how it works, how it feels, how great you feel doing it, and how awesome you are at manifesting it. You'll find more information on how to create your *Big Picture Vision* in Chapter Three.

* Once you have created your *Big Picture Vision* in a particular area of your life, write out all the large steps that have to happen to make this vision your new reality. This could be five steps or fifty steps, depending on how big the goal is. These are your *Mile Steps*. (There's a *Mile Step Spreadsheet* in the back of this book that you can copy and use for this purpose. Alternatively, there are places where you'll do some of this work in *The Blast Off! Workbook*. Or subscribers can input their *Mile Steps* into the *Blastation* program on the www.InteractiveLifeCoach.com website.)

* You start with the *Mile Steps*, your bigger tasks in reaching your *Big Picture Vision*. Then break them down into small *Mini Feats,* the smaller accomplishments. (This process can be done on the *Mile Step Spreadsheet* in the back of this book.) These five-minute incremental tasks will help you overcome procrastination and overwhelm, and easily move you forward to completion and success. From your long list of all the things you need to

do to attain your vision and make your passion a reality, write at least three *Mini Feats* for each day. They need to be valued activities that will help move you toward your goals. You need not spend more than five minutes on each of the three *Mini Feat* tasks. You could schedule these *Mini Feats* on a copy of the *Mini Feat Calendar* form in the back of this book, in your personal calendar, or subscribers can easily input them in the *Blastation Calendar* provided in the interactive coaching program (see www.InteractiveLifeCoach.com). ✪

> "Accountability breeds response-ability."
>
> ~*Stephen R. Covey,*
> *Author of* The Seven Habits of Highly Effective People

Blast Off! PRINCIPLE 4: Be Accountable

Sometimes even the most motivated individuals need someone to keep them on track with difficult or challenging goals. It's also vital to create a support system of people you can come to for inspiration, wisdom and accountability. Make sure you choose and surround yourself with people who support your ideals, goals and lifestyle.

Negative energy can easily seep in and create fear. This low frequency can destroy your dreams and goals if you're not careful and aware.

★ **State your goals out loud to someone close to you that you can trust.** This proclamation of intention is a commitment to yourself, to your support system (friends, colleagues, only positive influences, OK?), and to the Universe that you are already in the process of attaining this goal. The act of declaring your goals, visions and dreams will be a powerful catalyst for your success.

★ **Make yourself accountable on this new path.** Accountability and support will keep you honest with yourself and help you stick with your promise and your plan.

★ **Hire a life coach or mentor who will help you connect with your dreams and create a winning plan to bring them into your reality.** A coach will keep you accountable to your commitments, as well as support and motivate you to make it happen. I have developed the *Blast Off! Life Coaching Program* to help bring direction, success and fulfillment into my clients' lives. Check out the 90-120 day program at www.MyBlastOff.com.

> ★ **Call on your support system for motivation** when you feel yourself slipping away from your *Blast Off! Program.* ✪

Blast Off! | PRINCIPLE 5: Take Action

Dreams are mere fantasy until action moves them into reality. It's time to take your idealist thoughts off the shelf and start taking action. I hear many people talk about putting their ideas out into the Universe and waiting for them to manifest. That sounds fantastic, and it's a perfect first part of the equation. But sitting around waiting for the perfect job to appear or the perfect mate to show up at your door will most likely not be enough. *The next step is taking action.* You have the power, the intelligence, and the capability to make anything happen. Pull out your *Mini Feats*, and take action today! Each small accomplishment will move you that much closer to attaining your dreams.

> "Success seems to be connected with action. Successful people keep moving. They make mistakes, but they don't quit."
>
> ~Conrad Hilton,
> *Founder of the international Hilton Hotels chain*
> *(1887-1979)*

Suggestion: With the practices in Chapter One, it will be much easier for you to become inspired, tap into your passions, and ultimately reach your goals. Before you move forward in the book, I have a suggestion for those of you who have not yet read the how-to section at the start of the book, I recommend that you go back and read through it now. In that earlier section of the book, I discuss the three phases that people typically go through when making changes in their lives with the *Blast Off! Program.* You'll also find Janice's story, which will show you how one of my clients used the *Blast Off! Program* to move through the various stages and on to success. In the Introduction, I also get you acquainted with the basic Daily Launch Tools (which I refer to on the very next page)—tools I designed to help keep you grounded and motivated. These tools include the *Sun-Up Scripts*, the *Rocket Words*, the *Mile Steps*, the *Mini Feats*, and the *Weekly Flight Assessments.* ✪

BLAST OFF! Daily Launch Tools

1. Each morning, write your *Sun-Up Script* and *Rocket Words*.

2. Read your *Rocket Words* to yourself and out loud as often as possible during your day.

3. Create and perform a minimum of *Mini Feats* each day. (These are the smaller steps for moving toward your larger *Mile Step* goals and your *Big Picture Vision*.) For example, today's *Mini Feats* might be:

- *Download a song I love to be my theme song for my life changes.*
- *Call to sign up for series of dance or acting classes.*
- *Buy an autobiography on Amazon.com of a person who will inspire me while I make my career changes.*

4. Choose one to two *Blast Off! Practices* from this chapter to do each day over the next week.

5. Fill out your *Weekly Flight Assessment Log* to review your week's progress toward realizing your *Supersonic Life*. (You'll find the log form in the back of this book.)

Summary of the Chapter Concepts

➤ At this very moment, ask yourself: *"Am I who I want to be?" "Is life full of things I want to do?" "Do I meet the goals I want to have?" "Do I want to be at this same place five to ten years from now?"*

➤ Where are you on your Personal Life Path? Are you stuck and frustrated or are you feeling successful and fulfilled? Take an honest assessment of your present status.

➤ Accept responsibility for your choice in creating each situation in your life, good and bad. By taking responsibility, you are no longer a victim, which gives you the power to make new and healthier choices for new and healthier realities.

➤ What anger and resentments are you holding onto in your life? What can you do to release them? What peace and positivity will you receive when you release this negative energy?

➤ Access your *Secret Spark*, the super-drive energy that comes into play when you tap into your passion, set goals, and stay focused on your path. Your *Secret Spark* will give you the momentum you need to move forward.

➤ When you are *in the zone*, you are completely connected and in sync with your purpose and your passion. You're in touch with the abundance of the Universe and cruising in Fifth Gear in the Supersonic realm.

➤ Passion and meaning are crucial for a successful, fulfilling and rewarding life. When you create an idea or follow through on an activity, goal, or vision with passion and meaning, the rewards run deep and are long-lasting.

➤ Create your *Inspiration Station,* a creative and meditative space that will be a catalyst for inspiration, and a haven for stress-free relaxation.

➤ What are some activities and/or hobbies that you love to do but have not done for years? What are some activities that you've always wanted to do but never tried? They are waiting for you to take action today.

➤ The *back end* of passion is the energy that needs to be rejuvenated regularly to make sure your passionate energy doesn't lose its edge or momentum. Eat healthy food, get plenty of rest, take a passion break weekly, and get your heart pumping on a regular basis through exercise.

➤ Get in touch with what really matters to you so that you can find your true purpose.

➤ Connect with others who have similar interests and passions to spark your inspiration.

➤ Doing what you love to do every day will give your body and mind an incredibly healthy boost for the rest of your life.

Summary of the Chapter Concepts (continued)

➤ Create Your *Big Picture Vision* (long-range goals), and then work backwards, from the end to the beginning, and break it down into the larger required goals called *Mile Steps*. From there, create even smaller palatable steps—*Mini Feats*.

➤ Be accountable to help yourself stay committed to your path.

➤ Take action. Success comes from the combination of the intention and the doing.

"The purpose of life is to discover your gift.
The meaning of life is to give your gift away.
An aim in life is the only fortune worth finding."

~*Jacqueline Kennedy Onassis,*
Former First Lady of the United States (1929-1994)

CHAPTER 2

BLAST Off!
to Soulful
Living

> "The Universe is constantly saying yes to us. It only says yes. It is our task to discover what within us it is saying yes to."
>
> ~Lenedra J. Carrol, *Businesswoman, singer, author, artist*

Your gut has been telling you that it's time to redirect your life for a while now. You feel the change calling to you from the core of your being. Every year, you give yourself the same rebuttals:

★ "Tomorrow I'll look into taking that design class."

★ "Next year I'll start looking for a new career."

★ "I'll stay in this relationship just one more year until I get on my feet."

★ "I'll write that book when I get some free time."

★ "I'll start going to the gym after I lose some weight."

Soon you'll open your eyes and five years, maybe even ten, will have flown by, and the only change you'll have made is that you're even more disconnected from your dreams than ever. Here's one of the reasons you may not have made any headway. For change to happen, you must first *slow down* long enough to figure out a few things, such as: (1) where you are, (2) what you've been doing all this time, (3) how you even got here in the first place, (4) what you're fed up with, and ultimately, (5) what needs to change.

The Slow Sweetness of Anticipation

Remember those times as a child when you were anticipating an event that was so unbelievably exciting, you could hardly stand it, such as your birthday party or going to Disneyland? Your enthusiasm would bubble up inside. Meanwhile, the days went by so slowly. I remember being ten years old and anxiously awaiting going to summer camp. It was only three days away and I was so excited. I was also perplexed at the sense that as the time grew nearer, the days seemed to be getting longer and longer. I told my mom, "I'm counting the minutes until Saturday and why is it taking forever to arrive?" I had figured out that once I went to sleep that night, I'd only have two more days and one more night left until I would be at camp. "What if I just stay in bed 'til Saturday," I said. "Then it would only seem like one more day until camp, instead of two." My mom responded with some advice that has stayed with me to this day: "Allie, never wish your days away. Cherish every single one... because if you wish them away, you may miss out on something wonderful."

> "Anticipation was the soul of enjoyment."
>
> ~Elizabeth Gaskell,
> *English novelist and writer of short stories in the Victorian period (1810-1865)*

As we age, time starts speeding up and those long anticipatory days happen less and less often. Instead of having time to wander in your backyard and dream of being an astronaut or a veterinarian, you barely have time to figure out what to cook for dinner.

The Truth Shall Set You Free

For change to happen, you must first learn how to slow down long enough to get acquainted with your inner wisdom. There are many names for this spiritual resource: *your inner knowing, your gut, your Higher Self,* or *the voice of your soul.*

Did you know that this wise voice always knows the right answers and the right choices for you in each and every moment? Did you know that you can access your truth anywhere, at any time? In fact, your inner counsel may have been trying to communicate with you for years, but perhaps you've been way too busy to listen.

If you're out of touch with your internal wisdom, I will teach you how to connect with this voice and access valuable information. And if you already access it, the information presented here will help you refine your practice. But first we need to address slowing down the pace of your life so you can better consult this inner knowing.

Living in the Fringe

Have you ever arrived somewhere and had no memory of the drive? If someone was to ask you what you had for dinner on Sunday night, would you remember? Do the days go by so fast that you can hardly recall all the things you do and say? This is called "Living in the Fringe," which means your reality is one big blur, just moving, doing, sleeping... waking up and moving, doing, sleeping all over again. This is the proverbial hamster wheel that eventually results in boredom, burnout, apathy or depression.

In my twenties, when I first opened my advertising agency, I would get jazzed about using my creative expression. I enjoyed brainstorming on new campaigns and seeing an idea develop into an end product. The process was very exciting and energizing. Unfortunately, I allowed these inspiring activities to consume my days. Over time, I made the mistake of cramming more and more accounts onto my list, without delegating any of the responsibilities to others. I thought I was the only one who could do the job right. *Wrong!* Eventually, because my body forced me to stop from time to time, tasks were slipping through the cracks. This ego-driven concept of running the show—and everything in between in my life—got the best of me, and I ended up spending most of my time putting out fires and making excuses about why we didn't make our deadlines. I eventually crashed and burned. My passion was ultimately smothered by the stress of way too many responsibilities and deadlines and not enough breathing room. (More details on my literal crash and burn later.)

> "The less effort, the faster and more powerful you will be."
>
> ~Bruce Lee,
> *Martial artist, movie actor*
> *(1940-1973)*

The Case of the Missing Invitations

I'll never forget one incident during my hectic life at the advertising agency. We had designed some invitations for a huge fundraising event, and had been waiting for days for the printer to deliver this already behind schedule job. I promised the understandably frustrated fundraising committee that I would personally hand them their invitations by two o'clock that afternoon. They were all waiting anxiously to address the envelopes and get them to the post office. At 1:45 PM, the printer finally delivered the invitations and they looked beautiful. The printing rep offered to put them into the trunk of my car because she noticed that I was hurriedly trying to wrap up ten other "to dos" before I could transport this job. I handed her my keys, and in a few minutes she returned, letting me know I was all set to go.

I got to my car and for some reason decided to look in the trunk. I'm really not sure what happened first... my body falling into a state of shock or feeling my heart splat on the pavement as I realized my trunk was completely empty! The invitations weren't there. After my first thought, "This cannot be happening. How much more can I take!" I panicked and called the printing rep. She swore to me that she put them in the black Ford Taurus. Come to find out, my car key happened to fit another black Taurus that was, of course, no longer there. (I later learned that this happenstance is nearly impossible, but obviously not in my case.) I had no choice but to drive to the committee meeting empty-handed while I was desperately trying to think of any excuse except the truth—that their invitations were riding somewhere in San Diego in the trunk of a black Taurus, other than mine. I arrived and there were twenty women sitting around a table with pens in hand. Feeling absolutely sick to my stomach with embarrassment and a complete sense of failure, I announced that the invitations had arrived but I was not happy with them and we needed to do a reprint. Needless to say, I had twenty-one new enemies in that moment—one being myself.

My life was going by so fast that I couldn't keep up. I had become so stressed and overwhelmed that I was totally disconnected from my true self. I had strayed off my Personal Life Path onto some crazy super speedway. My inner voice was calling out, but I was way, way too far gone to hear a peep. It wasn't until I hit bottom, and I mean complete emotional, physical and spiritual burnout, that my inner knowing voice started registering with me loud and clear.

Of course, my point is that those of you who have a crazy, hectic lifestyle are not alone. I've been there myself. Let's look at what was happening in Jerry's life and Jennifer's life.

Jerry: Overwhelm in the Fast Lane

I remember when Jerry first came to see me for one-on-one coaching. He walked briskly into my office with a tense and uptight energy. Jerry complained of feeling completely stressed from his jam-packed schedule as a project manager. It was easy to assess that his life had become one that was all about achieving. Jerry was so scheduled to the "nth" degree that he had forgotten why he was ever interested in his work in the first place. His days began to feel so overwhelming that he would literally fall apart inside if one task slipped through the cracks. (Men seem to fall apart internally and women externally. Same symptoms, different bodily approach.)

Project completion should have given Jerry a sense of pride and accomplishment; however, he was running on mental and physical overdrive just trying to make it through the day without self-combusting. He had become entirely disconnected from the process of each day, and any hope of fulfillment was buried underneath his computer, PDA and piles of to-do lists. It was as if Jerry were running his life outwardly, yet inwardly his soul and spirit had become comatose.

Jennifer: Running Ragged

Jennifer told me during her initial consultation that she had been non-stop busy for the last several years raising her three children. She also runs a part-time catering business out of her home that serves corporate lunch meetings and special-occasion business dinners. She said breathlessly, "I'm the official sandwich maker, diaper changer, chauffeur and all-around crisis manager. I feel like I'm running myself into the ground." That is exactly what would have happened if she had kept up that pace.

Jennifer kept everyone else running smoothly, yet the chaos was taking its toll on her health and her sanity. Her mental and emotional tolerance was low and lately she had been very irritable and impatient with her children. Jennifer collapsed around midnight and woke again at 6:00 AM to start all over again. When she had a rare moment alone, Jennifer would find herself in tears feeling physically drained and depleted, wondering how much longer she could keep this up. Jennifer was light years away from her inner self.

The Human Race

There have been studies showing that our birth name should be chosen carefully because it can influence the tone of our personality and how people perceive us. When I think of the phrase, *the human race*, our species' namesake, I visualize millions of people bursting from the starting gate and running through life with only one purpose—"Get to the finish line!"

> "Man can never
> be happy
> if he does not
> nourish his soul as
> he does his body."
> ~*Unknown*

A race is defined as a contest between two or more people seeking to do or reach the same thing first. Therefore, *the human race* does not embody the idea of getting in touch with the process of the "in between" stuff—the single moments that make up each day on earth. Life is not a race. The only finish line in life is our demise, so try to enjoy the ride. It's time that we leave the rat race and enter the human journey.

From the Rat Race to the Human Journey

The philosophy behind modern technology is that it's supposed to streamline and simplify our lives. But do you ever find that the more cool gadgets you have to make life easier (cell phones, PDAs, computers), the more complicated your life becomes? For instance, one time I returned from vacation to find over 2,000 e-mails! This is not simplifying life. It's amplifying more things to do.

It's easy to get caught up in the mania of the rat race in which life leads you instead of you leading it. The energy of our lives moves forward at an alarming rate. Just look in the rearview mirror while you're driving on the freeway. Everyone is heading forward in high gear to complete something. And many of the drivers are more focused on anything but being present in the journey. This is the "Living-Outside-of-the-Body Syndrome," a state of complete disconnection with the present moment.

> "Put the martyr in mothballs."
>
> ~Sue Patton Thoele,
> Author of
> The Courage to
> Be Yourself

The fact is, your life will be stressful if that is how you perceive the world. Plus the unexpected happens every day. Meanwhile, the more you attempt to live life to the fullest, the more you will expose yourself to diversified tones of energy and experiences. Well, *thank goodness for those surprises!* 'Cause let's be honest. If life were controlled and predictable you would be bored. This is the pace of our times. So how can we manage the "racy" ride in a calmer and more fulfilling way?

Is it even possible to live a full life while taking the stressful times in stride? Can you prevent burnout? Can you get everything done without losing your soul and spirit in the process? *Yes, you can.* There are many ways to slow down the pace without sacrificing your intent. Remember, productivity could be a waste of your precious time if your intention is to just get things done and off your list. I've had many people tell me, mostly women, that they cannot sit and relax until everything is done. But basically, everything is *never* done. So they spend their lives trying to accomplish the impossible, hoping that someday they can stop and enjoy their lives. This makes no sense, does it?

What to do about all the non-valued to dos? Well, here's a place to start. Let your people (friends, clients) know that you answer e-mails and calls certain days or times of the week. That way, you won't feel the pressure to respond right away. And when you do sit down to reply, you can handle it all at once rather than piecemeal throughout the day.

Balance or Bogus?

My feeling is that many of you can relate to Jerry's and Jennifer's harried lifestyles. The so-called state of "balance" has become an illusion that so many of us strive to achieve. All too often, people become stressed out and defeated in the journey to achieve this dangling carrot of harmony. For instance, women carry high expectations for themselves to play all their Superwoman roles, while the essence of their soul is yearning for help. (At least we have the benefit of girlfriends who listen and cry with us.) Men suffer with the same disease except they must keep moving forward while acting confident and strong, whether they are feeling that way or not. In fact, men just pile more and more responsibility on their shoulders, because that is what men are supposed to do. As the years play out, the essence of their soul is found six feet under.

> "The energy of the mind is the essence of life."
>
> ~Aristotle,
> Greek philosopher
> (384-322 BC)

Sorry to sound so morbid, but it's time to wake up, sisters and brothers! Here is the ultimate in irony... One of my clients was complaining to me that she received a speeding ticket that morning because she was running late to yoga class. What's wrong with this picture?

Initially your intentions may have been in the right place. There is an innate desire for balance in the body and mind. Yet when stressful situations occur, too many times people actually work against themselves and all of their inner wisdom flies out the window. If you can relate to these predicaments, it's time to slow down, reevaluate your personal path, and connect with that *Secret Spark* I've been writing about in this book.

Your Personal Energy Bank

Another preliminary step to reclaiming your true self is to find out where the energy leaks are in your life so you can begin to repair them. Then you can focus your energy in a direction that is feeding you—not draining you.

Everything is made of energy. This is the Law of Quantum Physics. If you look at a table or a couch under an electron microscope, you'll see that they are actually made up of atoms in constant motion—just like your body. And all of these things are always changing and never standing still. Therefore, you have the ability to create and change your reality in every moment.

Your thoughts and actions also operate from this precious field of energy, and thoughts are powerful. Just think… when you think to take a step, you take a step. When you think to raise your arm, your arm is elevated. Since thoughts are energy, it would make sense to choose positive thoughts and actions that will benefit you by replenishing and expanding your supply of energy—not draining it.

Blast Off! PRACTICE 1: **Plugging In**

Visualize your body attached to a cord that is plugged into a generator. Just pretend that you are receiving your morning dose of 100 kilowatts of positive energy, which is supposed to last you all day. You start the day with a full tank of energy. Let's see where you are at the end of the day after depleting your energy bank with negative energy-drainers.

Take a moment to consider how much negative energy you expend.

Here's an example of an overburdened tank.

Full Tank: 100 kW

Minus Negative Energy-Drainers

Dread concerning the meeting with your boss: 10 kW

Fear about not being able to do a good job: 15 kW

Self-reproach about not cleaning the house: 5 kW

Worry about how you're going to pay for the holiday gifts (three months away!): 10 kW

Saying "Yes" when you meant "No" and harboring resentment all day: 25 kW

Obsessing over your date and wondering if you'll ever get together again: 10 kW

Guilt about having that extra serving of mashed potatoes: 10 kW

Total Energy Left: 15 kW

You've already given away 85 kilowatts and that leaves you with only 15 left to make it through the day. No wonder you're so stressed and tired by 4:00 in the afternoon! You are emptying your tank through negative emotions and beliefs which are creating your reality. Just think what would happen if you replaced this negative focus with positive thoughts and actions.

Now try it yourself on your next full day. Start with 100 kilowatts again in the morning. But this time, whenever you feel a negative thought coming on, switch it immediately to a positive one, even if it is fake or forced. Eventually, positive thoughts will come more naturally and you'll end the day with lots of reserve in your tank. See how you feel!

That same night, write about your experience of doing this exercise in your journal or workbook. How did it affect your energy level throughout the day? ✪

Hollow Henry and Empty Ellen

Empty Ellen is running on fumes. There's no substance in her step. She's not experiencing any fulfillment or peace within her daily tasks. She drives off with a coffee mug on her car, cannot find her keys, and her glasses are lost sitting on her head. Meanwhile, Hollow Henry is losing himself in racing thoughts of what he has to do next. They are both preoccupied with "should haves" from the past, or the multitude of responsibilities that were not done perfectly or done at all. What a waste of precious time. The truth is, when we operate from a grounded internal space, we can be more efficient and accomplished without feeling overwhelmed.

> *"The soul, like the body, lives by what it feeds on."*
>
> *~Josiah Gilbert Holland, Editor and writer (1819-1881)*

If you have reflected on your day and realized that you were extremely busy, but accomplished little, it's time to assess your priorities. It's time to cut your list in half. You will finally have room to breathe, enjoy the view, and feel your spirit soaring again.

Mr. and Ms. Grounded

There is another way. What if you were able to stay grounded, no matter what your day threw at you? Take a look at the qualities and behaviors of The Grounded Woman and The Grounded Man.

The Grounded Woman

⭑ Knows how to take a deep breath and a little time to calm down.

⭑ Is forgiving of herself in every moment.

⭑ Has no problem prioritizing items on her to-do list, or even dropping tasks from the list.

⭑ Realizes that she was only given two hands, and is comfortable delegating responsibilities to others.

⭑ Knows the meaning of "one day at a time."

⭑ Puts herself up on a pedestal.

⭑ Gives herself the accolades due for a day well done, even if others are not recognizing her efforts.

The Grounded Man

⭑ Takes good care of his body and mind by making the commitment to exercise and eat in a healthy way.

⭑ Has learned to follow his heart in his career path and in love, rather than making choices to meet others' expectations.

⭑ Cultivates good friendships with other men and feels comfortable being open with his emotions.

⭑ Knows that feelings of sadness and fear are healthy and will heal faster when they are released rather than suppressed.

⭑ Balances his drive with fun and adventure.

⭑ Knows that laughter and balance feed his soul and therefore will feed his personal and professional life.

After reading about Mr. and Ms. Grounded, what changes do you want to make that would help you feel less frazzled? Can you think of any improvements that would help you feel grounded that were not on either of the above lists?

Mental Mania

We have already made it clear that, up to this point, you may not be living from your inner wisdom. If this is true, where are you operating from? Most people operate from their intellect, which can create fear or confusion in decision making (i.e., analysis paralysis). In fact, if you look back, many scenarios in your life may have been chosen out of fear, rather than peace or joy.

* ★ What if I can't find a better job? I could lose my house!
* ★ What if I can't meet the dream love of my life? I better stay with my partner, even though we aren't a match.
* ★ What if my daughter doesn't get accepted in this preschool? She may not start ahead of the game and get into a good college.
* ★ It would be so fun to pick up bike riding again, but what if I get hit by a car?
* ★ I have always dreamed of taking a year off and traveling around the world, but what if I can't find a job when I come back? I'd better not go.

So many of us end up not reaching for the dream career, the best relationship, the fun sport, or the big adventure because "what if" could happen. What if none your fears were ever realized, and you ultimately miss out on the most amazing life possible?

The Solution? It's time to get out of your head and into your heart and soul.

GO from the Heart

> "If I create from the heart, nearly everything works; if from the head, almost nothing."
>
> ~Marc Chagall,
> *Russian painter who settled in Paris, France (1887-1985)*

One way to begin moving from your head to your heart is to practice *gratitude*. For example, in a moment, we'll be turning your burdening or mundane tasks into an opportunity for feelings of thankfulness. Thoughts of appreciation will automatically shift the focus from your head to your heart. When you're operating from a heart space, your perception of life and its details will change immediately and dramatically.

I know what you're thinking. "How can I be grateful for this pile of work on my desk and overflowing baskets of laundry?" Before you throw in the towel (literally) on this idea, realize that the negative thoughts about your tasks are coming from the mental plane. No wonder your mind is on overload! By bringing the energy down to your heart, you'll experience a whole new world. *Just try it.*

Blast Off! PRACTICE 2: Heart Space

Here's a mini-meditation that you can do almost anywhere. It's an easy method to get you into your heart space.

1. Put your hand on your chest, over your heart. Hold it there for a few minutes while breathing in through your nose and out from your mouth.

2. Now visualize yourself in the process of doing a task or a bit of work (folding laundry, sitting in your department meeting). Try to generate a feeling of love or gratitude for this effort. If you're having trouble conjuring up the love, feel the warmth for someone you care about very deeply. (Perhaps not your mother-in-law.) Hold on to that loving feeling for a few minutes until it pervades your body.

> "Life is what happens while you're busy making other plans."
>
> *~John Lennon, Musician, peace activist (1940-1980)*

3. You might even feel a tingling in your body and lightness in your head. This is your energy shifting from a negative-mind space to an open-heart space. In a matter of minutes, your stress level (and blood pressure) will have dropped, your heart will be full, and your burdened feelings of carrying the world on your shoulders will have turned into feelings of weightlessness and gratitude.

4. Continue to hold on to that loving/grateful feeling while shifting your focus back to the task or work. Literally see it from your heart. Think of how much you appreciate having this opportunity, and how capable you are of doing your job well.

5. Now participate in the task or work. If you feel yourself losing this peaceful state, stop, cover your heart again, and access those adoring feelings once more. (I realize that you cannot cover your heart in a business meeting. Instead, take a moment to go inward and access being in the heart space. You might even catch yourself enjoying it.)

6. Take a moment during this exercise to breathe in a sense of pride and fulfillment. You're on course while fueling your positive energy meter.

Be patient. It takes practice. The more you operate from a heart space, the easier it becomes to go with the flow and get into the zone. The next time a crazed moment or heavy job calls your name, you'll be able to respond with strength and ease. ✪

Letting Some To Dos Go

You've already begun searching inwardly for your *Secret Spark* so you can lead a richer, more appetizing life. You may have goals that you would love to attain right now, but the thought of going for them so quickly feels a bit like jumping off a cliff. Diving right in has always worked for me, but testing the waters is a good method too. Although both methodologies work, let's start slowly with clearing the clutter in your life, so you can make space and time for your dreams to be realized.

> "Learn to always trust yourself more than you trust anyone else."
>
> ~*Mary Goulet,*
> *Author of* It's All About You
> *and* Go With Your Gut

Our days can often be filled with needless activities, commitments, and to dos that have nothing to do with our *Big Picture Vision*. You repeat them often because they have become habitual or a ritual, and for no other reason than this. Is it possible that by looking at this area, you could open up several moments, or even hours, in your week so that you could start moving toward your bigger life goals? My guess would be "Yes." Let's give it a whirl.

Blast Off! PRACTICE 3: True Choice Meditation

What plans have you set for this day, week or this month that you really do *not* want to do? To help yourself create a list, ask yourself, "What is the purpose of this task, activity or event? Is it serving me or my family? Do I feel good about the commitment?" List these unwanted activities in your journal or workbook.

Then write the answers to the following questions regarding your commitments for this week or the coming month.

★ What is the purpose of this activity?

★ Who will benefit from this task?

★ Am I doing it out of true choice or habit?

★ Is the action I'm taking working toward my *Big Picture Vision*?

Now sit or lie down in a quiet place and close your eyes. Take deep breaths until your body relaxes and your mind is clear. Visualize yourself first doing this activity, then imagine cutting this activity out of your life.

Consider the following questions for both of the above scenarios:

★ How does it feel in my body?

★ Do any emotions arise?

★ Do I feel fear, nausea, perspiration or shakiness when I think of deleting this activity from my life?

★ Does the activity work with or against my inner knowingness, personal beliefs or big-picture goals?

> "Cheshire-puss, would you please tell me, which way I ought to go from here?"
> "That depends a good deal on where you want to get to," said the cat.
> "I don't care much where—" said Alice.
> "Then it doesn't matter which way you go," said the cat.
>
> ~Lewis Carroll, *English author of Alice's Adventures in Wonderland (1832-1898)*

Your body is communicating something to you, and if you really take the time to listen, your intuition or inner wisdom will give you the answers. *Just listen.* You will often hear or feel, *"I don't want this anymore,"* or *"This feels right."* The trick is that you not only have to listen to your inner wisdom, but should also follow its lead. ✪

Blast Off! PRACTICE 4: Tasks to Trash

Now that you're clear about the activities you don't feel in alignment with, let's clarify which ones you definitely plan to keep and which ones need to be dragged to the trash. Then you can work on deleting them from your daily life so you can free up your ever-precious time.

1. **List the activities that you're presently involved in that fit within your** *Big Picture Vision*. This list could be written in a journal or in *The Blast Off! Workbook*. These activities should come from a place of true choice and fit into a positive frequency of energy that is propelling you to your goals. They add fuel to energize, support and uplift your new life launch. This is a revealing way to see how many activities throughout your days and weeks are really supporting your flight plan, rather than draining energy away from it.

   I'm not saying that you should never watch television or clean your house. And I understand that you cannot drop every unwanted responsibility. But do you really need to be on another committee? Is it serving your soul to have the best yard in the neighborhood? Does it give you true pleasure, or are you doing that to impress someone else? If it's for someone else's approval, delete, delete, delete.

   Examples of what might be on your "keep list:"
   - Training for a marathon
   - Taking an accounting class because you're starting your own business
   - Meditating
   - Standing on the sidelines at your child's soccer game

2. **Now list the activities that you're presently involved in that don't fit within your** *Big Picture Vision*. Which activities aren't coming from a place of true choice? If you're feeling drained and irritable around certain to dos and your inner self is screaming, "I hate this!" throughout the entire process, it's time to let it go.

Some examples of items that might go on your "let go" list:

▨ Babysitting for your neighbor

▨ Cleaning your teenager's room

▨ Handling work at the office that does not fall within the scope of your position

▨ Volunteering for another committee ✪

Add It Up

Once you've really taken a close look at how much time is spent weekly on non-valued activities, multiply that number by four for the monthly calculation, and by twelve for the yearly calculation.

2 hours x 7 days = 14 hours x 4 weeks = 56 hours x 12 months = 672 hours of wasted, or better yet, surplus hours per year

For example: If you watch television 2 hours per day, that calculates to 14 hours per week, 56 hours per month, and 672 hours per year. Do you have any idea how many of your dreams could be actualized in 672 hours? That is basically an entire month of every year sitting in front of the tube, brain-dead and passion-free. If that is your intention, go for it. If not, you just got a Get Out of Jail Free card. *Enjoy!*

This doesn't mean you must fill every moment working toward your goal. In an effort to slow down your pace, connect with your spirit, and feel more joy in your world, you'll also want to replace some of the time found in the unwanted tasks with rejuvenating or relaxing activities.

Just think of how much more enjoyable it would be to:

★ Take a nightly walk

★ Go to a movie with a friend

★ Meditate

★ Learn to salsa

★ Take a fun art class

What rejuvenating or relaxing activities would you like to add to your life?

It's Time to Say "No Go!"

You've established that you want to nix a particular task from the list. That was the easy part. Now it's time to speak up about the activities that you're deleting. In working with many clients over the years, men and women, I have assessed that the world is filled with pleasers. Not that making others happy is a bad thing; but if you're suppressing your true voice and losing yourself in the process, this is not a healthy behavior or practice.

Your ability to say "No!" can be measured by subtracting (**A**) how much time you were berated as a child for expressing your discontent from (**B**) the amount of time your parents encouraged your power as an independent person. Not that children should get everything they ask for, but encouraging them to have their own opinions and make true choices is teaching them to think for themselves. A home that allows children to be free to express themselves with love and boundaries is the most supportive and healthy environment for their emotional growth.

The "No Factor" is the ability to speak your mind, tactfully and kindly, yet clearly from a space of true choice. You don't waste your time and energy feeling guilty, and you're not concerned with what others will think about your choices in life. This gives you a feeling of confidence and freedom to actualize your dreams every day. If you were blessed enough to have experienced more of Scenario B than of Scenario A in your childhood, your No Factor will most likely be higher.

The reality is that many of you will relate to Scenario A. As children, you may not have been encouraged to express your feelings. And saying "No" was probably not viewed as expressing your individuality, but rather a display of selfishness, doing wrong and behaving badly—which ultimately may have resulted in punishment.

Remember Jennifer, the busy mother and caterer? She used to say "Yes" to everyone—responding to her mother's every whim, canceling her plans to go to the gym to instead baby-sit her neighbors' kids, throwing dinner parties on the fly for her husband's clients, and chairing every committee at her children's school. She was volunteering here, fixing there and running everywhere, except where *she* wanted to go. The result? Jennifer didn't know if she was coming or going, and she had drained her energy reserves. She had nothing left to give.

If you were admonished as a child for expressing your discontent or aversion to something, your reality became: "Saying 'No' is bad. I will be punished and the people I depend on will be disappointed or angry with me." The result is that we continue saying "Yes" for fear of being unloved or rejected. We continue to take on more and more responsibilities, smiling outwardly while inwardly boiling to the brim with resentment and anger. In reality, this does not make others love and respect us more. In fact, it often creates a pattern where you become even more unappreciated and disrespected. If your family, friends and coworkers know that you always say "Yes," they will keep asking you to do things for them. They'll have less and less respect for your time because they don't see you setting any personal boundaries. You do more and more for them, and because they have come to expect your willingness, eventually they will even stop showing their appreciation.

This is called living "incongruently," or working against your own spirit. Your true choices and feelings on the inside are not in line with how you live or what you display externally. Besides creating heavy emotional baggage, the repercussions of living this way over a long period of time can be disastrous to your health. By not speaking your truth or developing the courage to say "No," you've become a prisoner in your own world. You're choosing to live as an extension of someone else's life. And by suppressing your real voice and emotions, you could also be experiencing one of the many chronic conditions that arise from suppressed anger, grief, guilt or fear, such as bladder infections, cancer, chronic fatigue, fibromyalgia, migraines and a variety of digestive disorders.

> "Choosing to honor our truth is choosing to honor our authentic selves."
>
> ~Sue Patton Thoele, *Author of* The Courage to Be Yourself

For most of us, saying "No" is a learned behavior that needs to be practiced frequently. It's similar to working out your muscles at the gym.

It's a struggle at first, you will ache from the weight of it, but soon you'll begin to experience how alive, strong, vital and free you feel for reclaiming your true self. Now this doesn't mean that helping thy neighbor or getting involved in the community is wrong. It just means to choose wisely and make it a priority to take care of yourself first. This is just like when you're in an airplane and the flight attendant demonstrates that you should put your oxygen mask on first so that you can be of help to your children. You cannot be supportive to anyone else if you are drained and overwhelmed.

Blast Off! PRACTICE 5: "No Go" Exercise

Let's get to it once and for all. It's time for you muster up that "No Factor" and stand up for yourself.

First, practice the following mirror exercise at least four times a week and you'll be speaking your truth in no time!

1. Stand in front of the mirror and say, "NO!" *Say it like you mean it.* You may feel silly and awkward at first. *Get over it.* Feel your voice and demeanor strengthening with each "NO." Try pointing your finger at the mirror to give it more strength and power. (This doesn't mean you need to point to everyone that you say "No" to, but it gives some extra punch to the practice.) Do this once a day when you have some privacy until it feels comfortable to you. You can even do this in the shower (without the mirror, of course).

Also, take these additional steps:

2. The next time someone asks you to do something, respond by saying, "Let me get back to you on that." This gets you off the hook for the moment and prevents you from answering impulsively and possibly regretting it later. Take some time to get in touch with how you really feel about the request. Close your eyes and imagine yourself doing this task and see how it feels in your body and your heart. If you're getting an ill feeling, that is usually a sign that a good "No" is in order.

3. Now it's time to go for it. Keep that memory of the ill feeling in mind (so you won't cave) as you tell the person that you have decided to pass on

their request. If it's something you might want to do at a later time, tell them to keep you in mind at the next go-around. If not, just say, "I really cannot help you out at this time." Your stomach may be churning. *That is normal.* This is a new threshold that you're crossing. Guilt may be popping its ugly head up and saying, "You are so selfish. You're letting everyone down." Tell it to buzz off because there's no room for that wasted emotion anymore.

4. Revel in the achievement and freedom you own after releasing yourself from this unwanted task. Just think how you'll feel when you begin clearing your days of many unwanted yesses. All of that precious energy that has gone to working hard on tasks you didn't really want to do can now flow back to your inner being. And that's not even taking into account the energy that was being drained by the buildup of negative inner feelings.

Congratulations! You've just turned your negative output into positive input. Your health, self-respect and quality time have improved immensely. And much to your surprise, watch how others start to treat you and your time with more respect. ✪

Blast Off! PRACTICE 6: No More, No More, No More, No More

After completing Practice 5, make note of all the activities and tasks that you're ready to say "No!" to and start feeling lighter immediately.

Your list will look something like this (but with the blanks filled in):

I am choosing not to _____ anymore.

I am choosing not to _____ anymore.

I am choosing not to _____ anymore.

I am choosing not to _____ anymore.

No, I am choosing not to _____ anymore.

Go ahead. Erase all those unwanted activities and tasks from your to-do list and replace them (guilt free) with true choice activities. Your heart, mind and soul will thank you. Remember, this is not being selfish. When you're happy, those around you will be even happier. It's that simple. ✪

Perfectionism Syndrome

What's the point of "perfect" anyway? So many of my clients, especially women, tell me that they're striving for perfection and it's killing them. They want a perfectly clean house, to say the perfect words, and to do perfect work at all times. Pressure-filled expectations are a sure way to turn any goal into a ball and chain. Many people resist attempting new challenges or setting new goals because they're afraid they won't perform to their ridiculous expectations. The result? They give up before they ever begin. Then the feelings of disappointment and failure set in, because on a deeper level they feel that life is passing them by.

> **"Better done than perfect."**
>
> ~*Mark LeBlanc*
> *Speaker, author of* Growing
> Your Business! *and President of*
> *Small Business Success*

I started taking modern dance in my thirties. It was something I had always dreamed of doing and finally had the courage to start. On the first day, the room was full of young men and women who had obviously been dancing since childhood. I was aghast when the dance teacher asked us to repeat the exact dance steps she had just performed for us so eloquently. I knew I was in trouble as the class was spinning to the right and I was tripping to the left. (Picture a blend of Lucille Ball from *I Love Lucy* and the Rockettes.) As I was leaving the studio with no intention of ever returning, the Universe stepped in to encourage my dream to dance. One of the dancers came over to me and said, "You did terrific for your first day. I applaud your courage to start dancing. Just keep coming to class and you'll get the hang of it."

Through this experience, I learned to laugh at myself and let go of the notion of doing it perfectly. It wasn't realistic that I would be able to keep up with these experts, and having those kinds of expectations was putting way too much pressure on myself. I made the decision at that moment to dance for the *fun* of it. And wouldn't you know, once I lightened up, my confidence increased, my anxiety dissolved so I could remember the steps much easier, and I was able to perform in several dance presentations. Dancing became a healthy addiction and a true catalyst for my *Secret Spark*.

> "Man exists all the way down from his innermost Spiritual to his outermost natural."
>
> ~James Tyler Kent, Physician, professor at Hahnemann Homeopathic Medical College, and author of Kent's Great (Homeopathic) Repertory (1849-1916)

Creating a Soulful Journey

Now that you're beginning to slow down, clear your plate, and soothe your mind, it's time to start connecting with the essence of your soul. This is the inner core of your being that resides on a spiritual, emotional and energetic level. This is the energy that connects us to our true purpose and reason for being. When we're able to access this higher part of our being on a daily basis, we don't veer from our life path, even when our personal galaxy is fraught with unexpected twists and turns.

How do we bring spirituality into our everyday lives? How do we make a habit of tapping into our true self? It's one thing to find balance in a state of meditation or at the local ashram, but give me the steps to find inner peace in the grocery line or while paying bills. How do we find the smoothest route through life's tumultuous storms?

Once we accept that control is an illusion and learn to be mindful of each moment, we can start to flow within the innate rhythm of the Universe. By getting out of our own way, we can partake in the gifts that lay at our feet within every waking hour.

You are approaching some major transitions in your life. In the desire to reconnect with your true path, there will be many decisions to make. They will range from small day-to-day choices to huge decisions that will have a major impact on your life and others close to you. Getting into the practice of asking your soul what the best alternative is for you, then learning to decipher the answer, will be monumental.

When I had to make the major decisions about whether to stay in my marriage or continue running my advertising agency, I had many people telling me what I should and shouldn't do. Not to say that my friends and family didn't have my best interests at heart. But, I knew that I would be the one living with the result of my choices, so I needed to be clear about what was the best fit for my personal path. It wasn't a coincidence that both of these major sectors of my life were in flux at the same time. The real flux was the state of my soul. My relationship and career were the outward symptoms of this inward chaos.

> "I know when I have a problem and have done all I can to figure it out, I keep listening in a sort of inside silence until something clicks and I feel a right answer."
>
> *~Conrad Hilton,*
> *Founder of Hilton Hotels*
> *(1887-1979)*

Once I finally reconnected with the voice of my soul, I was able to hear the answer I was looking for. And once I knew what I needed to do, everything fell into place as it should be.

Blast Off! PRACTICE 7: Accessing Your Soul's Choice

I remember doing this exact exercise at that crucial time of change in my life. I also continue to practice it frequently in my life today. Just as we did the *True Choice Meditation* earlier in this chapter, we can utilize this same method in connecting with our Higher Self.

1. Get into your *Inspiration Station* or another quiet space and close your eyes. Inhale, taking a deep breath through your nose. Expand your lungs and feel your abdomen protrude with oxygen-rich air. Then, as you exhale, visualize any confusion, stress or fear leaving your body. Continue this breathing release method until you feel totally relaxed, calm and clear.

2. Now ask a question out loud that is currently on your mind.

   For example:

   - Is this the right career for me?
   - Is this relationship serving my soul and higher purpose?
   - What do I really want to be doing with my life?

- Am I happy in this situation? If not, how am I feeling? What do I need to do about it?
- Should I take this trip?
- Should I take this new job offer?

Listen to your inner voice and your long-awaited answers will come. It's a knowing that will permeate your entire body on a cellular level. If you experience pain somewhere in your body, ask your soul what this means. What are you doing to create this pain in your life and what can you change or do differently to release the pain?

Do you hear the words coming through? What is the message? If you listen closely, it will be ringing loud and clear. Later, in your journal or workbook, make some notes about the messages coming from your inner wisdom. ✪

The Miracles of Soulful Living

Now you have the answers. Life should be easy, right? Since we all can access the purest solution to how we need to be living our lives, then why aren't we all successful, joyous and feeling free? Well, even if we know the right answers, the most challenging part is listening and following through.

Have you noticed those red flags that appear when something doesn't feel right? You know the scenario. You want so badly for a certain object or situation to work out in your favor that you pretend you're momentarily blind and deaf when the red flags appear. Then you convince yourself that they were only a figment of your imagination. You continue to avoid your inner wisdom that is saying, "What the hell are you doing? You know where this is headed. Don't say I didn't warn you." And sure enough, one month, one year, or ten years later, you'll say to yourself, *I knew it, but I was too afraid to listen to myself.*

> "Living soulfully means to live one's inward, outwardly."
>
> ~*Allison Maslan*

You only have to do this a few times to know that the repercussions of avoiding your soul's true choice can cause so much unwanted and unnecessary pain.

This Is My Challenge to You

The next time you receive the calling of your soul, listen and follow it all the way through. Don't run, hide or avoid the truth of your Personal Life Path. It may be scary, even terrifying; however, walking through the fear will bring you miracles beyond belief. Your soul knows the truest path for you. Follow its lead.

BLAST OFF! Daily Launch Tools

1. Each morning, write your *Sun-Up Script* and *Rocket Words*.

2. Read your *Rocket Words* to yourself and out loud as often as possible during your day.

3. Create and perform a minimum of *Mini Feats* each day. (These are the smaller steps for moving toward your larger *Mile Step* goals and your *Big Picture Vision*.) For example, today's *Mini Feats* might be:

- *Before I go to bed read for five minutes from a spiritual or philosophical book that inspires me or helps me to reconnect with life's bigger picture.*

- *Listen to some guided meditation (see Resource section in back of book).*

- *Research, locate and sign up for a local yoga, meditation or t'ai chi class in my area to help bring some soul and sustenance to my days.*

4. Choose one to two *Blast Off! Practices* from this chapter to do each day over the next week.

5. Fill out your *Weekly Flight Assessment Log* to review your week's progress toward realizing your *Supersonic Life*.

Summary of the Chapter Concepts

➤ In order to hear your inner voice or get in touch with your purpose, you need to *slow down* the pace of your life so that the creative information can find space to seep in.

➤ "Living in the fringe" is when you're not present in what you're doing. If this is the case, life will become an unconscious blur rather than an experiential journey.

➤ Life is *not* a race. Taking on too much even of a good thing can create overwhelm and burnout. Slow down so that you can enjoy the process of living.

➤ Are you going non-stop, night and day, so that you will get everything completed now with the intention of enjoying life later? This approach will likely result in you missing out on the joy and the miracles sitting right in front of you this very moment.

➤ If you have only so much energy each day, where is it being allotted? Is it being depleted by energy-draining people and activities? Plug positive charges back into your personal energy supply.

➤ Take a deep breath, prioritize, delegate when possible, and take one day at a time.

➤ Getting overwhelmed now because of what may or may not happen in the future is a waste of energy. Whenever the situation does arise in the future, you will handle it as you need to then.

➤ Get out of your fear-filled head and move the energy into your heart space.

➤ It's time to clear your plate of unwanted and unneeded commitments.

➤ Make true choices in alignment with what you *really* want and need to do in your life, and you can create a ton of extra hours and extra space for the things you actually love to do.

➤ Practice saying "NO" now. Don't take on unwanted commitments because of fear, guilt or confusion. Get clear and practice speaking your mind. People will begin to respect you and your time much more.

➤ Perfectionism wastes energy. If you're waiting to do it perfectly, you may never get started. Do the best you can and then move on. As Mark LeBlanc says, "*Better done than perfect.*"

➤ Try doing your activity, goal or task for the fun of it, without the expectations or the pressure, and see how much better the whole experience feels.

➤ Get in a quiet, meditative state and ask the questions out loud to the Universe that you're unsure about, including decision making, your career, relationships, money, a certain confusing situation… then listen. The answers will come.

Summary of the Chapter Concepts (continued)

➤ The next step is actively listening to the answers and then following through. If you pretend you heard otherwise, or make up other conclusions so you won't have to take responsibility and face the truth, you'll pay for it later.

➤ Walk through the fear. It is much, much worse in your head than in reality.

➤ On the other side of your fear, your miracles are waiting!

*"Reach high, for stars lie hidden in your soul.
Dream deep, for every dream precedes the goal."*

~Pamela Vaull Starr,
Poet, artist and writer
(1909-1993)

CHAPTER 3

BLAST Off!
to Limitless
Living

> "The moment one definitely commits oneself, then Providence moves, too. All sorts of things occur to help one, which would never otherwise have occurred. A whole stream of events issues from the decision, raising in one's favor all manner of unforeseen incidents and meetings and material assistance, which no man could have dreamed would come his way."
>
> *~Unknown*

I once was told a story of a young boy who was collecting some small flying bugs for a science project. He would catch them in a little net and drop the net into a large mason jar. Once the winged insect flew off the net into the jar, the boy would quickly screw the lid on, entrapping the small creature. The lid had been punctured to make very tiny holes, big enough to allow air in so the insect could breathe but small enough so it was not able to escape. The boy repeated the capturing process until he had five of these flying bugs in his jar.

He provided the insects with food, plus a wet paper towel to keep the environment moist and comfortable. The insects would divide their time between flying around the jar and resting on the sides. After a few days, the bugs seemed content with crawling up and down the sides of the jar or remaining still rather than flying around. By this time, the boy was done observing the insects and decided to release the lid and let the bugs fly free. He unscrewed the top of the mason jar, and to his surprise, out of the entire group of five insects, only one gathered his strength and flew away. Even though the other four were finally free to escape, they decided to hang out in their small, enclosed universe.

The insects didn't want to be trapped in this jar. But once that lid was sealed, they had no choice but to make the best of their imprisonment. They had quickly adjusted to their new reality, becoming quite content with crawling rather than soaring. Once they were given the opportunity to escape bondage, only one of the insects went for it and succeeded in returning to its vast open space. Even though their lid was removed, the remaining four had adopted the illusion that they were still trapped and stuck inside that jar. Therefore, they never made the effort to fly free.

> "Our doubts and fears are not true in themselves. Our deepest beliefs about ourselves and the nature of our world are not true in themselves, but our thinking makes them true in our experience. We can change our thinking and change even our deepest core beliefs."
>
> ~Marc Allen,
> Author, speaker and cofounder
> of the New World Library

This story is a wonderful illustration of how millions and millions of people live their lives feeling entrapped, stuck, held back or indifferent, even though there is no lid containing them and they are not chained to any fixed objects. Their delusion is that a specific person, thing or situation is the cause of the stuck state of affairs, when in reality we cause our own limited life because we have chosen to be there in the first place.

Your personal universe has no bounds. If you're feeling stuck or trapped in one or more realms of your life, it's because you have enclosed yourself under an imaginary lid, then fooled yourself into believing that you are stuck or trapped in an unfulfilling or even miserable existence. The good news is that if you closed the lid, you also have the ability to unlock and release it. This move will open you up to a limitless Universe of opportunities, experiences, and the absolute ability to make your wildest dreams come true.

In this chapter, you'll learn how to identify where and how you are limiting your potential and what you can do to release your personal "lid." Then you'll have the power to completely transform every aspect of your limited world into a wide-open, abundant playground.

Stressed, Stagnant and Stuck

John walked into my office looking worn out and beaten down. During his consultation, he revealed to me that his job was filled with unending havoc and stress. He'd worked for this company for nine years, and a result, it was affecting his relationships with his wife, children and close friends. John believed that the unrealistic demands of his boss and the company's disorganized methods created a day-in, day-out situation that was leaving him feeling overwhelmed, angry and frustrated. By the time he arrived home, often after working overtime, John was irritable and exhausted, and he didn't feel like participating in family activities. His wife had expressed that she was considering a separation because she couldn't handle John's moods and lack of involvement with the family.

My first obvious question to John was, "Why do you stay with this job that is causing you so much agony?"

With a heavy heart, he responded: "I'm trapped in this company because I don't feel that I could get a better job. I have spent so many years forcing myself to do the work without much professional growth, that I feel I wouldn't be desirable to a better company. I should have advanced more by now, but my boss refuses to make any changes. I work hard for months on a project and at the last minute, my boss decides to change his mind about the company's direction or cancel the project altogether. Because I haven't been moving forward, I feel stagnant and boxed in with no choice but to stay. My mortgage payment and other financial obligations keep me from making any changes."

As I questioned John further, I found out that he had gone to graduate school and received his MBA while working at this company. He was the director of human resources and had thirty-five people who reported to him. John's belief that he had no qualifications to make himself desirable for a better-managed company was completely false.

John's Delusion of Being Trapped

John had created the delusion, or false belief, that he was stuck in this job because of his relentless, demanding boss, his financial responsibilities, and the misguided perception that he was not qualified enough to move laterally into a more fulfilling career. These delusional beliefs left John feeling immobile and depressed, with no escape route in sight.

The truth was that the idea of imprisonment only existed in John's mind—not in the unlimited possibilities of the Universe. John was suffering from low self-worth and a tremendous fear of taking risks. This client was projecting out into the world that he didn't deserve a career that he loved and was passionate about, and therefore life handed him what he *believed* he deserved. As time passed, his frustration and contempt for himself and his situation grew, making John harder and harder to live with. The more moody he was at home, the more his wife was dissatisfied, which made John feel like even more of a failure. And the cycle went on and on and on.

> "Be not the slave of your own past. Plunge deep into the sublime seas, dive deep, and swim far, so you shall come back with self-respect, with new power, with an advanced experience that shall explain and overlook the old."
>
> ~Ralph Waldo Emerson, Essayist, poet and 19th century leader of the Transcendentalism movement (1803-1882)

As John and I continued talking, I learned that his father had never told John that he was proud of him for any of his achievements in childhood. He would try and try to gain his father's approval, yet his dad would only respond critically with ways that John could have done the task better. John grew up under the delusion that he must struggle and struggle to feel accomplished, and even if he did a good job, it would never be good enough. In addition, his parents had always displayed their anxiety about not having enough money. His dad had complained constantly about his job. He once told John that he'd always wanted to own his own music store, but that most entrepreneurs fail in the first five years and it was just too risky. John's father frequently remarked that job security was the most important responsibility for a family man.

Now it made complete sense to me why John thought he had no other choice but to stay in this dead-end career. The fact was that John had more than enough qualifications to pursue a stimulating and enjoyable new career, but his fear and limiting beliefs had created an imaginary, yet powerful mental paralysis.

The Truth about Untruths

Many people give up on pursuing their purpose or passion, and then wrestle with the consequences of frustration, self-reproach, feelings of failure, regret and apathy. They cling to a negative belief system inherited from family or resulting from past traumas, societal pressures or present life situations. These ingrained unconscious beliefs, that I call "delusions," give many people the false perceptions of being trapped, held back, stuck and even lost. Making the effort needed to turn dreams into reality may seem much greater than it has to be. These delusions (that everyone has in some form) are just skewed misconceptions of the truth. Just like a dirty eyeglass lens that blinds your vision to a beautiful, sunny day, living with a false delusion can blind you to the abundant opportunities for joy and triumph.

You're not really trapped in your predicament, and unless you are literally chained to the floor (which is highly unlikely), your belief that you are stuck is truly an illusion, a creation of your misbehaving imagination. Yes, it may seem completely real. You can give me all of the evidence and circumstances that you can come up with and I will repeat the same answer. Whatever the data, know that your current situation is simply your own limiting belief that you must clear from one or more areas of your life.

I asked John to consider the idea of living his dream career. If there were absolutely no limits of capability, time or money, what would he love to do? Immediately, without a single breath or blink, John replied with a force of energy that I had not yet experienced from him, "I would move with my family to the mountains and open a bike shop with a coffee shop attached."

"Really?" I said, surprised. I was truly taken aback by John's surge of energy when he zeroed right into his deeply suppressed passion for biking, and his lifelong dream to own his own bike shop. John explained to me that he had always loved biking because it gave him an amazing sense of freedom and connection to nature. With the way his job and responsibilities had developed, he never had the time or energy to ride anymore. His creative idea of a companion coffee shop grew out of years of hanging out with fellow bikers before and after long rides.

So here was a guy who had a passion for being in nature and challenging himself physically, and he had created a life for himself where he spent most of his time indoors, physically inactive within a cubicle with a job description that fit a very analytical type of person. No wonder John felt so miserable! He had completely settled for the wrong path and totally given up on his dreams.

As I discussed in Chapter One, we all have some kind of passion, true calling, a potential for living life to the fullest, whether it be through our work, individual growth, relationship or spirituality. Yet because of personal misconceptions and an unawareness of their infinite capacity to manifest their dreams, many people settle for second best or far worse than that, desperately living in situations they don't even enjoy. Ultimately, their dreams become so deeply buried, that the once-passionate desire is now entirely forgotten.

Can You Relate?

Here are some other examples of how the core delusions of a few individuals have created negative patterns, and ultimately buried their dreams and passions. Do you relate to any of these scenarios? See how a shift in perception later changed the game from a losing battle to a winning celebration.

Fearful Delusion: I Must Control My Reality

Celia's Insecure Delusion was basically this, *"I might lose control if I step out of my comfort zone."* Holding on to this delusion resulted in her making life decisions based on fear or worst-case scenarios, rather than pure choice and gut knowingness. Celia always settled for the safe, unfulfilling job and the safe, unfulfilling relationship. She was afraid to take risks, yet knew this fear was keeping her from living a full, rewarding life.

Winning Truth: Letting Go and Embracing Life

When Celia finally became aware of her delusion, she learned to flip-switch it to polar opposite beliefs, such as, *"Change is full of excitement and an opportunity for growth and abundance,"* and *"Change is not the unknown. Once I change, that will be my new known."* And then she practiced walking through the fear. Once this illusory straitjacket was removed, Celia experienced a newfound sense of freedom and pride as she stepped into her true potential.

Because this insecure delusion has been removed, Celia's consciousness doesn't reflect on bad things happening anymore. She is trying new things, letting go of the control issues and taking risks. In fact, she is having fun for the first time in years. She feels that the Celia of today is the person she was always meant to be.

Self-Consciousness Delusion: What Will People Think?

Lisa's Image Delusion could be summed up as, *"What will my friends or my family think of me if I take a chance and reach for my dream?"* As a consequence of this delusion, she was living a life based on the opinion of others. The result? She was missing the opportunity to experience her unique and independent life-purpose.

Winning Truth: Speaking and Living Your Truth Is Liberating

When you stand up for your ideals, people will respect you, not shun you. Yet the fear of rejection was so strong in Lisa that she was afraid to put herself into a vulnerable position regarding her relationships, career or lifelong dreams. We flip-switched Lisa's trauma of childhood rejection so that she could began standing up for herself without the fear of being abandoned. She became much more at ease in her relationships, and with all this newfound strength and the help of the *Blast Off! Life Coaching Program,* Lisa opened her own business, a wedding cake bakery.

Perfection Delusion: What If I Make a Mistake and Fail?

Sean's Failure Delusion centered on thoughts like, *"What if I can't do it?" "What if I make a mistake?"* and *"What if it doesn't work out?"* This prevalent fear of failing is generally much worse than the reality of any possible failure in people's lives. Sean was so afraid of failing that he would only try things that he felt he was perfect at, so he didn't challenge himself at all. The result? Sean remained for years in a job that he truly disliked. In addition, he spent so much time trying to be perfect in his tasks that he could not live up to his own expectations. This is an incredible amount of self-induced pressure that would bog down, stifle and exhaust anyone.

Winning Truth: Completed Action, No Matter What the Results Are, Is Better than Living in Stuck Thoughts

> "Whatever you can do, or dream, begin it! Boldness has genius, power and magic in it."
>
> ~Johann Wolfgang von Goethe, German poet and dramatist (1749-1832)

Sean was taught through his childhood experiences that mistakes were bad. Instead of learning that mistakes are the ultimate learning tools, he spent his time walking a tightrope with the fear of making one wrong step. By clearing his negative core beliefs, Sean began to look at life in a completely different way. After four months, his life of fear shifted to a completely new perspective of healthy and fun challenges. He left his job, is in a new relationship, and has developed and sold an invention that he had ruminated on for years.

Did You Inherit Any of These Beliefs?

Do you remember a time when someone demonstrated, lectured about, or shared any of the harmful beliefs listed below? Whether you were told one or more of these negative thoughts directly or absorbed them indirectly, you most likely became influenced in some regard. Just living around people who carried one or more of these beliefs could be enough to deem you the lucky "winner."

★ "The world is a scary place."

★ "Better safe than sorry."

★ "Money doesn't grow on trees."

★ "Don't look at life through rose-colored glasses."

★ "True love only exists in fairy tales."

★ "Opportunities only come to the wealthy."

★ "I will not amount to anything."

★ "I can't depend on anyone."

★ "I can't do it on my own."

★ "I am not good enough."

★ "I am not smart enough."

★ "I am not beautiful enough."

★ "I am not thin enough."

★ "I am not successful enough."

★ "I am lazy."

★ "I am not capable."

★ "It's never good enough."

★ "It has to be perfect."

★ "You might end up on the street." (One of my family's favorites.)

★ "Life is hard."

> "You have powers you never dreamed of. You can do things you never thought you could. There are no limitations in what you can do except the limitations of your own mind."
>
> *~Darwin P. Kingsley,*
> *President of the New York*
> *Life Insurance Company*
> *during a period of*
> *tremendous growth*
> *(1857-1932)*

Does any of this sound familiar? What would life be like if these thoughts were not part of your brain's programming? How different would your life be if your thoughts were the complete opposite? *Hmmm…*

The Harm Is in Your Head

Believe it or not, your life could completely transform if you would only begin to walk through the fear or negative self-talk and make completely new and healthy choices. The only harm you're causing yourself with negative self-talk is that thoughts of fear are swimming in your head like a school of sharks. The mental doubts that grip you are the most painful reality of all.

Your biggest fears are merely figments of your delusional reality.

You either were raised in a home that shared fear freely, have adopted someone else's fear, or absorbed it from watching television or taking in other media. If each anticipated obstacle were faced pragmatically, like a child's first steps, you would find ease, even in your falls, because they are simply part of the learning curve. The attitude is, "Okay, that hurt my bottom a bit, but I can get up and take another step."

Living with self-judgment, fear of criticism, and fear of failure is a state of imprisonment that's holding you back from embracing life to the fullest. As an adult, you have the choice whether you want to continue living this way. You have the power and freedom to choose to live by doing, rather than fearing. **The reward?** *A brand-new life.*

Blast Off! | PRACTICE 1: **Name That Delusion**

Let's take a closer look at the negative core beliefs you have adopted. Then you can begin to undo the blockage and create magic, as you learn to shift the delusions to a completely new and limitless mindset.

Grab your journal or workbook. **Now, make a list of the strongest fears or negative beliefs that you live with.**

Creating awareness of your limiting beliefs is the first step in your upcoming release. ✪

> *"No one can make you feel inferior without your consent."*
>
> *~Eleanor Roosevelt, Humanitarian, writer, wife of President Franklin Delano Roosevelt (1884-1962)*

Blast Off! PRACTICE 2: Choices from Fear

Now that you've listed your core delusions, think about how they have affected the major choices in your life regarding your relationships, careers, financial state, hobbies and values. What are you living now as a result of these negative beliefs?

In a moment, I want you to list your present status in each life sector. But first, look at these examples:

Career: *I am so worried about financial security that I am not really pursuing my dream career. I am not mentally stimulated in my job. In fact, I am so bored at work.*

Relationship: *I have always settled for partners who I knew would not abandon me, even though I wasn't really attracted to them. Then I lose interest and leave.*

Now it's your turn. In a journal or your *Blast Off! Workbook,* write two to three sentences about where you are now in the following areas of your life based on any fearful choices you have made or limiting beliefs you hold: (1) career, (2) relationship, (3) financial, (4) personal fulfillment, (5) adventure and (6) spiritual. Take some time to do this now. How many of your life choices have been a result of a deeper fear?

Were you surprised to find how much your fears have played a role in your major life choices? Mind-boggling, isn't it? ✪

Blast Off! PRACTICE 3: Flip-Switching

Now that you've recognized your damaging beliefs and how they have shaped some of the circumstances you're experiencing in your present life, let's "flip the switch"—an exercise in deleting the negative sabotaging beliefs and thoughts and replacing them with limitless abundant thinking. Then you can begin to "remove the lid" on your life (as in the story at the top of this chapter) and allow the goodness to appear.

For example:

Core Delusion: *"The world has become so scary."*

Winning Belief: *"The world is safe and full of beautiful and exciting possibilities."*

Core Delusion: *"I must struggle to make money. I'm so tired of living paycheck to paycheck."*

Winning Belief: *"Money is always available to me and my bank account is growing every day."*

Core Delusion: *"I rarely try new things because I'm afraid to fail."*

Winning Belief: *"I enjoy challenging myself because I know that I can achieve whatever I set my mind on doing."*

Core Delusion: *"My friends seem to have the best luck. Meanwhile, I never seem to get what I wish for."*

Winning Belief: *"Opportunities are falling into my lap on a daily basis."*

Core Delusion: *"True love only exists in fairy tales."*

Winning Belief: *"True love is mine for the taking because I deserve it."*

Core Delusion: *"I am timid in gatherings and new situations."*

Winning Belief: *"I am dynamic."*

Core Delusion: *"I feel stuck. My life is boring and unfulfilling."*

Winning Belief: *"My life is fun and full of new adventures."*

"The mind can assert anything and pretend it has proved it.

My beliefs I test on my body, on my intuitional consciousness, and when I get a response there, then I accept."

~D. H. Lawrence,
*English novelist, short story writer and poet,
Author of* Lady Chatterley's Lover

Now, from the list of core delusions that you have listed in *Blast Off! Practice 1*, flip-switch each statement to a positive polar-opposite winning belief. **Hint:** Core delusions are heavy, dense and cumbersome. Winning beliefs are light, expansive and uplifting! ✪

Project Your Winning Beliefs to the Limitless Universe

Now that you have listed your new limitless beliefs, I want you to read them out loud every morning as you start your day, and each night before you close your eyes. Keep them with you so that when the negative beliefs start to seep back in (and they will), you can pull out your new winning beliefs and remind yourself of the truth.

Even if you don't fully believe these winning statements, you are creating positive energy every time you voice them. And the more positive energy you emit, the less those negative gremlins will have a chance to rattle your confidence. We are creating a new boundless mindset for you, so repetitive focus and expression of these positive high-frequency beliefs is key to the success of the *Blast Off! Program*. For added punch, write about them in your daily *Sun-Up Scripts*. Just like growing your garden, for your flowers to bloom and thrive, they need to be watered regularly.

Life Is an Energy Mirror

Your current reality is a mirror of your internal thoughts and feelings.

For example, if you believe that most new businesses fail, I don't suggest that you start one, because it will most likely fail. If you believe that it's hard to find your soulmate once you hit forty-five, you'll have a hard time finding your soulmate.

The internal energy that those thoughts and beliefs create is very, very powerful. I know that some of you are now thinking, "I don't express those negative thoughts; I just think them." Even if you're not voicing your fears or beliefs, you are emitting a negative frequency into the atmosphere every time you focus energy into the negative thought.

Now this doesn't mean that every single negative thought will create more negativity or lost opportunities in your life. However, if you continue to focus on your limiting beliefs, your life will begin to reflect that same internal energy. Very limited!

Once those internal negative thoughts are replaced with winning beliefs, your external world will begin to change in a dramatic way.

Luck Is Just Another Word for Good Vibrations

When I was ready to open up my homeopathic practice, I began looking for a new office space. I had a vision in my mind of what it would look like. I wanted to find a space that felt warm and cozy so my clients would feel comfortable. I envisioned sunlight coming through French doors that would look out into a garden. (Okay, I'm a romantic.)

My divorce had just finalized so I was also in the market for a new place to live. I wanted to have my office and my home close together so that I wouldn't have to spend too much time away from my daughter.

The next week, I was telling my friend about the kind of office space I wanted. Later that day, he mentioned it to his mom who was a psychologist. As serendipity would have it, she told her son that she had just visited a recently vacated space and that it was lovely, but too small for her needs. I was there within a few hours, and not only was it the exact space that I had envisioned (French doors and all), but also upstairs from the office was a beautiful two-bedroom apartment that had also just been vacated. I couldn't believe it. I thought, wow, the power of suggestion really works!

At the time, I chalked it up to being lucky, or being at the right place at the right time. I didn't really grasp how potent my thoughts were and how powerful the energy was that I was emitting behind those thoughts. However, life has granted me wonderful opportunities to practice envisioning my dreams, and they continue to be realized time and time again.

No, I'm not professing to have special powers like Jeannie in *I Dream of Jeannie* or Samantha Stephens in *Bewitched*. I have just learned, through years of practice, how to harness my energy and focus it in the direction of the wonderful thing that I want to emerge. (And no arm-crossing or blinking are required.) I realized that if my negative energy was creating my difficult relationships and stressful work environments, on the flip side, my positive energy should be able to create prosperity, harmony, peace and adventure.

I have used this method in every aspect of my life—to create new ideas for businesses, to find real estate properties to invest in, even to find my husband, the man of my dreams. It has been incredibly rewarding to teach my clients how to bring envisioning and actualizing into their lives and watch the transformations unfold. If being lucky means that you're the receiver of good vibrations, I'll take it.

Soaring to Bicycle Heaven

Remember John, our stuck project manager? Once John had the awareness that he was *choosing* to be stuck rather than merely being a helpless victim, we started flipping the switch of his delusions into winning beliefs. His outlook changed at work even though he didn't feel a connection to the job. Because John's mood became lighter as he realized he had the freedom to make positive changes in his life, his wife and children were thrilled to have the old John (or the new and improved John) back. And it happened just in time, because his wife was really ready to throw in the towel.

Next, I had John practice envisioning his dream of a bike shop with the coffee shop attached. I asked him to write in the present tense a very detailed picture (a *Big Picture Vision*) of what his complete dream looked and felt like, as if he were working there now. He began to read this to his wife on a daily basis and soon the bike shop even started seeping into his unconscious through his dream life.

> "We are what we think. All that we are arises with our thoughts. With our thoughts we make the world."
>
> ~Buddha,
> *East Indian spiritual teacher and philosopher*
> (563 BC - 483 BC)

Every free moment he had, John began researching bike shops for sale and what the financial commitment would be.

That summer, as he and his family were in Colorado on a family vacation, they drove by a bike shop for sale. Through his research, John found out that the bike shop had been very successful. However, the owner's parents were aging, so the man had decided to close up shop and move closer to his family in Florida. This bike shop was a mirror image of what John had envisioned. He knew in his gut that this was where his family needed to be. John's wife was completely on board. She also loved biking since she and John had met in a riding group. Within two weeks, the bike shop was theirs.

Well, that was four years ago. The delusion of being trapped is no longer a part of John's reality. He busted loose from his false view of the world and was able to truly see his limitless possibilities for the first time in his life. John and his wife love the new life they have created, and they're literally riding high in bicycle heaven.

Envisioning: It's a Beautiful Thing

Olympic athletes use visualization so that they can perform to their highest potential. They see and feel themselves in the process of their sport from start to finish. According to Albert Einstein, "Imagination is more important than science." Some professional athletes would whole-heartedly agree.

In 1984 a survey was done of 235 Canadian Olympic athletes who were preparing for the games—a whopping *99 percent* of them were using imagery. Basically, they were visualizing success in their minds—seeing their bodies deliver the performance they wanted to achieve. These athletes use visualization during training and also right before a competition.

> "Excellence is the gradual result of always striving to do better."
>
> ~Pat Riley,
> One of the greatest NBA coaches of all time

Olympic skiers use visualization and skaters do too. Figure skater Randy Gardner participated in the Olympics twice, skating with his partner Tai Babilonia. Before they would perform a complicated jump called the "throw triple Salchow," he would visualize the jump and landing in his mind. "Once you see it in your head, you can do it," he noted.

Dr. Robin S. Vealey, author of *Coaching for the Inner Edge,* believes that our muscles will respond as we rehearse a performance in our imagination—in a way that is similar to the actual activity! Thus a mental roadmap is created for the real thing. That's why athletes visualize their moves over and over again until their plan becomes part of their physical memory.

I'll take this idea even further. First, note that the body is made up of energy, and the Universe is also made of energy. If the body responds to what is imagined in the mind, think of how powerful the energy of your thoughts become once they leave your body and merge with the energy of the Universe. This marriage of energy is what actualizes your thoughts into being. So pay attention to those thoughts because they are way more influential than you realize.

The Wow Frequency

Envisioning takes visualization one step further. Once you visualize yourself doing or receiving the goal, then imagine the vibration of your own internal energy field shooting toward that goal and surrounding it with a vibrational charge or frequency. It is as if you were sending it a consistent stream of lightning. Just by imagining this and feeling your own internal energy field extend outwards, you are sending waves of energy that will begin to jump-start your dream. This is being in the *Wow Frequency*.

When you close your eyes and envision this energy flow, the physical sensation of it can feel as if you are vibrating or buzzing. This tremulous release of energy, which you could experience somewhat like an adrenaline rush, is called *streaming*. It's also been compared to what we undergo during laughter, physical exertion, sexual intercourse, artistic expression or a spiritual experience.

Because your thoughts are radiated with energy, you can use a version of envisioning to utilize their frequency to create the kind of day you want to have. Start your day by closing your eyes and visualizing with feeling your intentions for the day. See yourself going through the motions of each of your activities with your desired outcomes. Feel the quality of the energy involved in creating the day and the level of performance of your activities that you want, and send that out into the Universe. Repeat this throughout the day as often as possible. The more energy you give something, the more fuel it will have to succeed.

Yes, you have the power to create your desired outcomes. Whether you're planning your next day or long-term goals, you can utilize daily envisioning to manifest your desired *Wow Frequency* life.

Blast Off! PRACTICE 4: **Visualizing Your Short-Term Goals**

The following practice generalizes a process for realizing any short-term goal.

1. Write down exactly what you want to achieve regarding your short-term goals.

2. Visualize yourself going through all the motions as you make these goals happen in your limitless mind.

3. Take in the full experience of achieving each goal. See it, feel it, smell it as if you are experiencing it happening *right now*. Get in touch with the energy related to the experience. As you envision the goal, you may experience a reaction in your body and your mind that is like a buzzing or a warm feeling. Combine your wonderful energy with positive thoughts. *Wow, Wow. Wow!*

Commit this process to memory and then repeat it as often as possible. The more positive frequency your dreams receive, the more momentum they will have to take flight. ✪

Your Giant Goals: The Big Picture Vision

Not only can you use envisioning to achieve your daily tasks and short-term goals, you can also use it to create your *Big Picture Vision*—the intended end result. Your *Big Picture Vision* is the pot of gold at the end of your rainbow, and it can help you determine your desired goals in any and all areas of your life. Your *Big Picture Vision* should be the ultimate, most beautiful and satisfying end-result you could ever imagine. By defining and illustrating your *Big Picture Vision* through images, text or illustration, you will be creating a destination.

When you have a destination, even if you're not quite sure how to get there, you can experience some peace in knowing that you're not wandering aimlessly. Why? *Because you now have a plan.* This knowledge of your end-result will help you focus and target your energy in a clearer, more precise manner. Even if your *Big Picture Vision* is a gigantic undertaking, and it will take months or even years to create, having an illustration and description of your desired destination brings it to life. This process will make your large goals much more tangible, much easier to grasp, and that much closer to becoming a reality.

> "Dream lofty dreams, and as you dream, so shall you become."
>
> ~James Allen, Author of As a Man Thinketh (1864-1912)

For instance, if one of your *Big Picture Visions* is to redesign a room in your home, you could draw it on a big piece of paper. You'd imagine and draw what you want the furniture to look like. (It doesn't matter if you cannot draw. This would just be for you.) You'd position the fixtures where you want them, etc. Crayons or paint can be used to bring your *Big Picture Vision* to life.

Blastation subscribers can use www.InteractiveLifeCoach.com to create a *Big Picture Vision* of the room with photos and text. This way, it would be on your computer screen and you could access it at any time.

Blast Off! PRACTICE 5: Illustrate and Write about Your *Big Picture Vision*

It's time to use your artistry and creativity to set your *Big Picture Vision.* You need not be a Picasso or Shakespeare to do this exercise. Drawing, painting, photography, collage and writing open up your right brain, your imaginative and intuitive side. They're also great ways to release any pent-up emotions that could get in the way of envisioning and actualizing your dreams. If you need to take a red or black crayon and scribble all over a piece of paper first, be my guest. Feel better now?

1. **First, illustrate your vision.** Create images that represent your *Big Picture Vision* for any or all areas of your life, including career, relationship, health, wealth, personal fulfillment and spiritual. **Drawing and painting:** Whether it is a stick person (you) hanging out with the lions in Africa or dining with your lover in your Tuscan villa, get as colorful and as wild as you like.

When you have completed your masterpiece, hang it up in a spot where you will see it every day. **Desktop:** Subscribers can use the *Blastation* software at www.InteractiveLifeCoach.com to upload and combine digital photographic images to create an illustration of their *Big Picture Vision*. Visit the site as often as you'd like or make a printout and post it in a highly visible spot.

2. **Create your *Big Picture Vision* story (in other words, write about a day in the life of your *Big Picture Vision*).** Write the story in the first person and in the present tense as if it is happening already. You can use the *Big Picture Vision Board* form in the back of this book for this purpose. Also, note that the *Blastation* software has a feature, too, for this use.

   How does it feel to be there? What do you see? Who else is there?

   Example:

   I am standing outside the home we have built for foster children. There are kids of all ages playing on the swings or sitting inside at the computers doing homework.

   A little girl comes and puts her hand in mine as I walk into the beautiful stone and brick building that is adorned with lots of windows and vibrant greenery. My staff is qualified in child psychology and they are very well paid. They love their work and it shows in how they interact with the children.

3. Read your *Big Picture Vision* story out loud as often as possible, as if you are proclaiming it to the Universe. "Let there be light!"

4. Use your *Big Picture Vision* in the next *Blast Off! Practice*.

5. Now that you have more clarity about your *Big Picture Vision*, start envisioning it into being. ✪

Blast Off! PRACTICE 6: Envisioning Your *Big Picture Vision*

When you hook the cables to a car battery to jump-start an engine, you must connect the positive cable clamp to the positive battery charge and the negative cable clamp to the negative battery charge. This like energy ignites power in the dead battery, bringing it to life. This is similar to having high-quality thoughts and a positive vibrational frequency. To jump-start your dream, you must also send it like energy.

1. **First you must relax your body and mind.** The envisioning is going to be much more effective coming from a calm and peaceful energy, rather than a stressed-out, chaotic energy.

2. **Close your eyes and inhale deeply.** As you inhale, envision a glowing white light entering the spot between your eyes (your third eye). As you exhale, feel that rejuvenating energy move from the spot on your forehead and melt down through the inside of your system very slowly. See and feel the white glowing energy filling up every part of your body until your stress is replaced with clear, rejuvenating vigor.

3. **Begin to see yourself actualizing the dream** as if it has already happened. This can be done successfully in two ways. Envision yourself in the process of living your limitless dream, and also envision yourself as the observer of this dream (you observing yourself observing yourself). Both methods work. Seeing yourself inside and outside of your *Big Picture Vision* only creates more positive electricity around it.

4. **Dream big. Envision bigger**. When you visualize your *Big Picture Vision*, think outside the box. Bust through your limiting thoughts and think bigger than you ever imagined possible.

Example:

A woman named Karla came to see me for coaching when she didn't know what career path to take after a horse ranch, where she trained young riders, was closed unexpectedly. Karla had become distraught because she loved that job and now she didn't know what to do. She planned to go back to school to become a physical therapist, but just couldn't seem to get too excited about it.

We did some brainstorming and she said her big dream would be to own and operate a rehabilitation ranch for horses. When Karla first thought about it, her eyes instantly lit up with joy and a sense of relief. But once her newly accessed limitless thinking kicked in, I noticed that she became very overwhelmed and fearful at the thought of running a business like this. "I don't think I could ever do that," was her spontaneous limited-thinking remark. Karla said she could just work for another rehab ranch instead.

I knew that Karla was completely capable of actualizing her passion. Choosing to follow her fear, which many people do, would have caused her to settle for something less than what she really wanted. If she sold herself short, Karla's wonderful dream would vanish into Fantasy Land.

We broke down the general Mile Steps *that would be needed in order to open a small rehab facility. From there, we simplified the steps even more into palatable* Mini Feats. *(See the* Mile Steps Spreadsheet *in the back of this book which was designed to walk you through this process.) Through this technique, Karla didn't feel that the dream was too daunting to achieve. For the first time in a very long while, she felt excited and impassioned about her future. She now had a direction with manageable steps to follow. The biggest hurdle she overcame that day was breaking through her limiting thinking and then seeing and believing that it was really possible to realize her dream. Now she could envision and actualize the horse rehab center into her life.*

5. Not only do you need to see yourself in the process of this dream… you need to **feel it in every cell of your body**. Feel your senses open and your breathing deepen, as you allow your body and mind to feel this *Big Picture Vision* become a reality.

6. **Stay with that picture** and those thoughts as long as possible. The more time you emit those positive *Wow Frequencies* toward the life design that you have in mind, the more focused the energy will be in manifesting your dreams.

7. **Then let it go**. Remember that the best things in life come as a surprise. Think about it. When you consider the most wonderful happenings in your life, there's a good chance that they weren't planned, but were

unexpectedly dropped into your lap by Ms. Universe herself. So envision it, feel it, and then set your dream free. Allow the way that your dream comes to you to be a surprise. Remember, holding onto expectations too tightly will only cause them to slip through your fingers.

8. **Create a good mantra.** A mantra is a sacred word or phrase used as a repeated chant that helps to facilitate spiritual or personal growth. Create one for yourself now. In Karla's case, it could be on the theme of empowerment.

Here's an example of a **Phrase Mantra:** *My limits are dissolving at this very moment and my limitless life is already at work unfolding in a miraculous way.* Another could be: *All my dreams are coming true.*

> "It may be that those who do most, dream most."
>
> ~Stephen B. Leacock, Canadian writer and economist (1869-1944)

After working with this practice, you'll have uplifting thoughts and feelings about your *Big Picture Vision* that you will emit into the Universe every day. The next step, **Actualizing,** is a key element in the *Blast Off!* formula to launching your dreams into reality. ✪

Actualizing: The Art of Dreams Unfolding

Actualizing is the taking-part step in the process of realizing your dream. Once you project your energy field toward your dream, it is already in motion. *Now you can begin to plan the steps necessary for your dream to occur.* At this point, you may not have all the knowledge to understand how everything will come together. That is perfectly fine because the Universe is already conspiring in your favor. However, you can increase the momentum by taking action. Refer to *Blast Off! Principle 5*, "Take Action," in Chapter One to review the importance of actualizing.

The bolt of energy you have supplied is an initial step. Your intention through action will only further the pace of your success.

> "Pushing through the fear is less frightening than living with the underlying circumstances that come from a feeling of helplessness."
>
> ~Susan Jeffers,
> Author of Feel the Fear
> and Beyond

Use your *Mile Steps* and *Mini Feats* to break down your *Big Picture Vision* into palatable and attainable steps. (See forms in the back of the book.) You might start with the end in mind and work backwards, three small *Mini Feats* at a time. Three steps a day for one year equal 1095 steps closer to your dream life.

Here's how it breaks down:

Big Picture Vision

   divided into *Mile Steps*,

     divided into a minimum of three daily *Mini Feats*.

      Then the *Mini Feats* lead you to *Miles Steps* to achieve your *Big Picture Vision*.

Face the Fear and Go for It

On a final note, one of the most important philosophies concerning actualizing a limitless life is to acknowledge your fears and move through them. The only way to completely work through your fears about something you haven't done before is to just plain do it. Those two powerful words are widely used, so I will err on the side of being trite because there is no simpler way to put it to you. You will not be able to think yourself through the fear. You will not be able to feel yourself through the fear. You will, however, be able to overcome the fear through experience. The scariest part of do it is the mental anticipation and the first few steps. Once you blast off, your fear level will drop immensely.

When I first opened my advertising agency and started accepting jobs that I had no idea how to implement, was I nervous? *Unbelievably so.* When I first started practicing homeopathy, was I nervous? *Terrified!* However, I learned to breathe and to accept the panic as normal. On the bigger projects, I focused on taking one step at a time and I asked for lots of support from my colleagues, teachers and mentors. Before I knew it, I had moved through my self-imposed fear and doubt. As time passed, the challenges were no longer overwhelming and I began to develop a sense of strength and self-confidence that had not been there before. Initially, I could have allowed my fears to paralyze me from moving forward and realizing my dreams. But then you would not be sitting and reading this book today.

> "Only dreamers teach us to soar."
>
> ~Anne Marie Pierce,
> Author and editor

So the next time you focus on a heartfelt dream or a goal and you feel your adrenaline rise while your stomach drops to the floor, know that these are promising signs that you're headed down your right limitless path.

BLAST OFF! Daily Launch Tools

1. Each morning, write your *Sun-Up Script* and *Rocket Words*.

2. Read your *Rocket Words* to yourself and out loud as often as possible during your day.

3. Create and perform a minimum of *Mini Feats* each day. (These are the smaller steps for moving toward your larger *Mile Step* goals and your *Big Picture Vision*.) For example, today's *Mini Feats* might be:

- *Take one small risk every day this week, including, ask my boss for a raise, call a certain someone (who I have avoided) about getting together, and speak up and ask for something that I really want.*

- *Choose a certain action that I have avoided out of fear. (Make this your first* Mini Feat *of the week.* No more excuses!*)*

- *Research the new industry I'm interested in on the Internet.*

4. Choose one to two *Blast Off! Practices* from this chapter to do each day over the next week.

5. Fill out your *Weekly Flight Assessment Log* to review your week's progress toward realizing your *Supersonic Life*.

Summary of the Chapter Concepts

➤ We all have created or inherited delusions or misguided beliefs in order to feel safe and secure. These clouded perceptions are unnecessary and hold us back from realizing our potential.

➤ Negative beliefs can create a negative energy flow around us, which, in turn, can make it difficult for our dreams to be realized. Believing that you don't have what it takes to be successful will create a forever flow of doubt. This can compound your negative beliefs and leave more room for mishaps, or even worse, quitting altogether.

➤ The choices you make in life stem from these delusions. To begin to make positive, winning choices, there needs to be an awareness of your delusions.

➤ By recognizing these stifling beliefs, you can begin to flip-switch or reverse the negative idea to a positive one. Just by meditating and voicing the new ideas that result, even if you don't fully believe them or own them, you are already changing the frequency of energy that surrounds you.

➤ By changing your internal energy frequency from negative to positive, life around you will automatically begin to change. People will respond to you differently, opportunities will start to open up, and it will seem as if the flowers are blooming brighter than ever with your positive outlook.

➤ Create a *Big Picture Vision,* using an illustration and writing about the big picture of your dream.

➤ Add potency to your dream by envisioning powerful energy toward it.

➤ Take action through *Mini Feats* to break down the steps toward your dream.

➤ *Just do it!* Walk through the fear to capture your dreams and passions. What you fear is much greater in your head than what you'll experience in reality.

"When in doubt, make a fool of yourself.
There is a microscopically thin line between being
brilliantly creative, and acting like the most
gigantic idiot on earth. So what the hell, leap."

~Cynthia Heimel,
"Lower Manhattan Survival Tactics"
Playwright and author

BLAST Off!
to the Career
of Your Dreams

I was eighteen and embarking on my future, the big wide world of unknowns. After spending twelve years in primary school and having everyone but me make my decisions, I was supposed to figure out what I wanted to do with my life. I had absolutely no clue which direction to go in, much less how to do it. I thought about the things that I loved to do, what I really connected with. I loved gymnastics, but Cirque du Soleil was not in existence yet. I was also a cheerleader. Not a whole lot of potential for a career there. The extent of my cooking skills was macaroni and cheese, so master chef would be highly unlikely. I'd always had a deep desire to help people. Since I was very young, I would see people who were down and out and my heart just wanted to lift them up. But I really had no clue how I would do that either. Writing poetry was another passion, but most of the poets that I studied in high school had become recognized for their work only after they died. There was something about becoming successful while I was alive that intrigued me. Nevertheless, I did love to write.

I was rather shy when I was younger and writing was a way for me to speak up and out, even if I was the only listener. My parents divorced when I was thirteen and my world and my heart were crushed in an instant, in the midst of the teenage rollercoaster ride that was throwing me to and fro. When I look back, writing saved my little soul through a fragile and bleak period of time. Poetry was my friend, my emotional and sensual outlet, my do-it-yourself therapist. My parents thought I had nothing to say, but the truth was, I had too much to feel to be able to say it in a way that made any sense. Poetry helped me to get all that insanity on the paper so I didn't have to carry it in my head and heart. This expressive art helped me to turn my pain into beauty, and for that I am forever grateful.

My Dad and His Dream Career

My father was an amazing businessman, and he still is, at the age of seventy-nine. Interestingly, entrepreneurship goes back even further in my family history, so let me back up for just a moment…. My grandfather had a women's clothing store in Kansas City, Missouri, called Maslan's. It was founded in 1932. My father grew up working in this family business.

When my parents married, they moved from Missouri to Tulsa, Oklahoma, and over the next twenty-five years, my father renamed the company and expanded it to fifty stores throughout the Midwestern states. Stewarts was the women's ready-to-wear chain and Extension One was the trendy fashion hot spot. Because of his innovative vision, my father's company became the largest privately owned retail chain of its time.

My father had an eye for business and it was obvious to me that he loved every minute of it. So much so, that if he wasn't physically at one of his stores, he was probably on the phone talking to a manager or a buyer. Even though this was frustrating for our family at times, my father never appeared burdened, overwhelmed or tired, and he never complained about having to go to work, or about the obvious responsibilities and frustrations that came with his day-to-day business life.

I didn't understand it back then, but I do now. The business was his passion. He lived and breathed every aspect of those stores. The pitfalls only motivated him even further, and the victories kept him fired up for more. This was not his job, or his career. He was living his dream. He created a *Big Picture Vision* and he went for it. I was blessed by his example, to experience someone close to me who was willing to take risks for a vision, even though he may have had moments of fear or uncertainty.

One day I was riding in the car with my father on the way to one of his stores. As he was driving, my father asked me, "Do you know how to start a business?" After a brief moment of silence, I admitted, "No, not really." His joking response, which dripped with certainty and knowing-ness, was, "Just print up some business cards and make it happen!" I understood his point to be that if you want the business badly enough, put your name on it and do what it takes to succeed. He made it seem so simple that I grew up believing it was. And this has been the magic behind my success. I've never stopped believing that all dreams are possible. And although I have worked very hard, the results have manifested very simply. I admit that it wasn't easy having my dad away a lot of the time. However, through the process of osmosis, I would eventually inherit his zest for living a life of passion.

When it came down to me choosing a major for college, my dad said, "You love to write. How about being a journalist?" That sort of made sense to me, although I had no interest in writing about bad news, which seemed to be all that the newspapers contained. But I *was* into pleasing my dad for attention at that stage of my life, so I thought, "Why not? Journalism it is." As you can tell, I wasn't really emotionally connected with this career path, and once I started to write for the local newspaper, I realized my initial gut reaction had been right. I had no interest in writing about car accidents, robberies and other bad news. I had an affinity for more of the abundant side of life, even back then. That career path lasted about two weeks.

Except for my personalized poetry business back in college—which ended when I couldn't pay the bills with what I was making—I continued to choose career paths with the intention to receive my father's attention and approval, which I so desperately wanted. That's why my advertising agency, although outwardly thriving, was an inward disaster. It didn't come from the right place in my heart or my gut. As creative as it was, building ad campaigns did not ignite my *Secret Spark*. I didn't know it at the time, but I was also missing the more profound and inspiring connections that I found a few years later in the healing and coaching fields. And although I had the talent for marketing and advertising, it was not my passion. And that was a huge life lesson for me.

Dictionary's definition of success that I was raised with:

suc·cess [*suh* k-ses]—*noun*

1. the favorable or prosperous conclusion of attempts

2. gaining wealth, position, honors or the like

3. a person or thing that succeeds

Allison's evolved definition of success:

Suc·cess

To create ideas and perform activities that hold meaning to me. To offer services and solutions that help support people and their cause, and then receive positive results and monetary and emotional rewards.

Rewards that were generated solely through monetary gains would never be fulfilling enough for me to sustain the fortitude, courage, and faith necessary to be an entrepreneur. If my success back then had been measured by the attainment of social status or financial gains, I was the bomb. In my case, however, it felt like the bomb had just exploded inside of me, and success, as I had come to know it, just wasn't enough.

Destiny 101

What is your purpose? Your destiny? Have you known for some time what you are meant to do for a career, but you just aren't sure how to transfer it to real life? Are you still searching for that path you can call your very own? Everyone was blessed with certain gifts, talents and personality traits that can be transferred into a fulfilling, satisfying and financially prosperous line of work. Some people, as I discussed in Chapter One, know from the get-go what they want to be when they grow up. Others, like me, find their purpose through an evolvement of life's experiences and challenges. Either way, you come to find that it is perfectly right for you.

> "Work is love made visible."
> ~Kahlil Gibran, Lebanese-American writer, poet, philosopher and artist (1883-1931)

For some reason, which makes no sense to me at all, we were not offered any classes in high school or college on how to find your passion and purpose, and then turn it into a dream career, much less understanding the value of passion and meaning in a career. It seems like that help would take a lot of the guesswork and struggle out of the process.

I truly believe that you have the full potential to pinpoint, develop and achieve your dream career. *Yes, you!* One of the things that really saddens me is when I see someone with such potential for greatness, who is not allowing themselves to step into it and fully own it. I can share with you the important dos and don'ts and give you valuable tools and support; however, *you* need to be the one to take that first step. I know you can do it. After all, it's your greatness I am talking about.

The State of a Job

Did you know that from age twenty-five to sixty-five, we spend 73,600 hours at our work? And that 87 percent of Americans dislike their jobs? That means that 87 percent of Americans spend 73,600 hours in their lifetime doing something they don't like. What a massive loss that is! Because every part of our lives has an influence on every other part of our lives, this could make for a lot of unhappy people.

The reason I created my *Blast Off Life Coaching Program*, rather than doing career coaching alone, is because every part of our lives is connected. You cannot be completely at peace in your personal life and relationship if you're miserable at work. And, at the same time, it's hard to be supersonically flying in your career when your relationships are on the rocks.

My point is that job dissatisfaction affects our society as a whole on a much broader and deeper level than we realize. If you're stuck or burdened in your career, most likely you'll bring that pain home to your family. And just by sharing space with you, they'll experience your misery, too.

Society has taught us that the most important thing when entering the workforce is education and job security. However, there were a few minor issues left out of that concept, such as:

* Is this job inspiring?
* Does it help us to become enriched human beings?

Most job descriptions do not include these monumental aspects. Take a look at your current job situation and ask yourself the above questions. I personally believe that if your spirit is not growing and evolving, it is dying.

Can you imagine...

* Having a career that motivates you to get out of bed and off to work each morning feeling excited and grateful for the day ahead?
* Setting your own work schedule?
* Having time for vacations and adventures?
* Being paid for your special passions and gifts?
* Having no cap on the amount of money you can make?
* Taking ownership of your life and your future?
* Having a dream career that is prosperous in your heart as well as your bank account?

If these questions intrigue and excite you, then there is no time like the present to start moving forward with your dreams. If you desire to move these ideas from your imagination to reality, then let's start taking the steps to make them happen. The first step is to truly grasp the concept that once you have an idea, and you start to set it into motion, an energetic shift will begin to happen around you. Doors will start to open, opportunities will arise, and people will come into your life that will have the answers you'll need. The possibilities are endless. Your requirement—*intention and action.*

Before we explore what you might want to do, let's look at how my coaching client, Michael, learned to open up new career possibilities in his life.

> "Businesses are a collective consciousness of ideas, actions and relationships."
> ~Allison Maslan

Michael: In the Dog House and Loving It

Michael called me the week he found out about being laid off from his corporate job. When he came to see me for our first coaching session, Michael said he needed help to find new options rather than just going for financial security again.

I wanted to understand how Michael fell into this type of predicament. He shared that he tended to stand in the background at work and so he was overlooked for opportunities.

After a few sessions, we were able to determine what made Michael tick. I was interested in finding out the kind of things that were interesting, stimulating and inspiring to him. Michael loved animals, especially dogs. He also called himself a master gardener. Other fascinations were history, anthropology, studying other cultures, learning the flute and violin, cooking, traveling and writing.

We also noticed that a lot of what Michael did enjoy about his job was acquiring and researching information. We took at closer look at the many talents and traits that Michael was not recognizing, including working well independently, problem solving, attention to detail, being analytical, empathetic, and patient, the ability to sort through much information and making good decisions.

We began pulling each interest apart into possible careers. For instance, we discussed dog trainer and veterinary technician. He had a degree in anthropology so teaching was a possible avenue. Landscape designer was in the gardening realm. Travel writer and restaurant reviewer were possibilities. Another career idea, librarian, was discussed. In the end, I had Michael research careers in animal care, landscape design and librarian work.

The next time Michael and I met, we went through all of the options. I asked him, "Of all of these options, what gives you the most excitement?" He was interested in a two-year training program as a librarian because he loved having access to lots of information. This was also a program that could be taken while he had another job.

And when Michael talked about dogs, his face lit up. He had a lightness about him and he even laughed while telling me various stories about his dogs and those in his neighborhood. But he wasn't too thrilled about the vet technician or dog training ideas. I still thought for sure that we could figure something out that would bring all of Michael's gifts together. Then it came to me.

We'd had a conversation about the many people who have purchased or adopted dogs that did not match their lifestyle. This often becomes a nightmare for the owner and the dog. What about a dog matchmaking service that helped responsible owners find the right dogs? Michael was intrigued.

We started brainstorming the possibility of this type of consulting service and how it could really benefit dog owners and be personally and financially rewarding. Michael would do all the research and legwork for the owner. He would do a very detailed analysis of the potential owner's lifestyle to see what type of dog would make the best fit all around. He would also find the best breeders who were reputable and caring with the animals, refer to trainers and vets, discuss good diet and so on. He planned to help dog purchasers steer clear of Internet scams, too.

I asked him to create a *Big Picture Vision* about this business idea. I wanted Michael to see himself in this role and imagine how it would feel to create this in his life.

Michael left my office that day all charged up with a sense of possibility. He said it was the first time he had felt this way in years.

The next time I saw Michael, he handed me his business card with the name, *Connect the Dogs: Dedicated to Connecting Great Dogs with*

Responsible Owners. He'd been researching breeders, trainers, holistic veterinary services, and nutrition for dogs to provide the complete package to his clients. He had also began developing his website and a client questionnaire.

We discussed the large steps (*Mile Steps*) that were needed to launch this business successfully and then broke those down into daily *Mini Feats*. (Forms to help you do this are in the back of this book.) In our work together, I also had Michael practice flip-switching the negativity he was internalizing and projecting about his career.

> "The best ideas go unnoticed."
> ~*Allison Maslan*

In the meantime, other career developments were occurring. Michael was offered another job at the same corporation he had been with before. At first he was going to turn it down. But after much thought, Michael realized this would be the perfect opportunity for him to continue to launch *Connect the Dogs* on the side.

When I asked Michael how he felt about going back to this career, he said he felt really good about it: "I'm not the same person I was before I started the coaching with you. This is in a new department and I will have the opportunity to create a name for myself. I plan on using my voice and participating more in the work. I am so much more confident now and I also have this passion on the side that is fueling me."

Michael and I took the time to thoroughly explore his interests and talents. This made it possible for him to tap into his *Secret Spark* and added passion and meaning to Michael's life. Soon it was as if he had been reborn. Michael also stopped allowing the negative fear-based thinking to rule his life. This gave him the courage to speak his mind. And now he has so much great news to share.

The Right Brain: The Portal of Your Creative Side

Often when we try to think of an idea, it doesn't come. There are a few things you can do to connect with your creative side and stimulate the right side of your brain, the side where ideas are born. Science has found that the right brain is the more creative, emotional and intuitive hemisphere, and the left brain is the analytical and judgmental hemisphere.

Anything that's new or unfamiliar to an individual is right-brain dominant. Anything that's familiar is left-brain dominant. Most of what we are taught in school has strengthened our left brain—our logical, analytical, problem-solving and rational side. These are very important skills that you'll need to draw on in creating your dream career; however, they do nothing to help us creatively clue into our purpose or destiny.

Activities that can stimulate the right brain are emotional issues, the creative process, recalling memorized lists, participating in any unfamiliar event or activity, seeing unfamiliar faces and meeting someone new. By accessing and unleashing your right brain's potential, you can begin to spark new, exciting, fulfilling and profitable ideas to build your dream career.

Get Your Creative Juices Flowing

Here are some activities that you can do, either outside in nature or in your stimulating *Inspiration Station*, to facilitate opening your right-brain functions. Once your creative juices are flowing, make sure to write down any brilliant ideas that suddenly appear.

1. **Meditation** is a wonderful method to stimulate the right brain. Meditation practices can help you to reduce stress, birth creativity, or enhance your performance. The Dutch painter and sculptor Frederick Franck said, "We need a way to detach ourselves from an environment constantly bombarding us with noise, agitation, and visual stimuli. We need to establish an environment for recovering our unspoiled creative core, an oasis of undivided attention, and an island of silence."

(See the resource section for source of information on guided meditation CDs.)

2. **Art**: Any kind of art, such as crayon-drawing, painting or decorating, will stimulate the right-brain functions. Allow your ideas to come to you through your artistic genius.

A great way to stimulate your right brain is to take a crayon or pencil and start at the top of a blank white page. Then do a doodle without stopping and starting. So you're drawing one continuous line in whatever spontaneous direction your hand guides the crayon. Then finish back at the top connecting at the point you started.

Don't consciously guide your hand. Let it take the crayon or pencil where it thoughtlessly wants to go, back and forth, up and down and around until a pattern has developed. Then, and only then, guide the line back to its starting point. Next, take your colorful crayons and fill in all the doodling with as many colors or patterns as you like.

3. **Listen to Baroque music:** Why Baroque music specifically? Research reveals that Baroque music pulses between fifty to eighty beats per minute.

Baroque music "stabilizes mental, physical and emotional rhythms," according to music expert Chris Boyd Brewer, in order to "to attain a state of deep concentration and focus in which large amounts of content information can be processed and learned."

Music arouses your brain waves. Slower Baroques, such as Bach, Handel, Vivaldi or Corelli, can create mentally stimulating environments for creativity and new innovations. Once you're able to relax and detach from the stress of your day, you can fully move into your creative self.

> "Dreams are renewable. No matter what your age or condition, there are still untapped possibilities within you and new beauty waiting to be born."
>
> ~Dale E. Turner,
> TV and film actor

In general, music is a very powerful tool that stimulates thoughts, feelings and creativity. It can coax energy from a tired brain and body, and greatly enhance most experiences. So if you aren't able to connect with a Bach or Mozart, good ol' rock and roll will do.

4. **Physical exercise:** Get your blood flowing with physical activity, your heart pumping, and your brain will feel the effects, too. Thirty minutes of some cardio exercise a day improves the ability of the brain to learn. It also will decrease your stress, increase your energy, and uplift your moods. I often get my best creative notions while I'm running or biking. Not to mention that being away from distracting stimulation, such as cell phones and computers, will help calm the brain and make room for creative input.

"Everybody knows that exercise is good for your heart, but in recent years we've gathered compelling evidence that exercise is also good for your brain," says Fred Gage, Ph.D., of the Salk Institute for Biological Studies. "We now know that exercise helps generate new brain cells, even in the aging brain." What's the benefit of having new brain cells? This means that exercising not only helps us to stay in shape physically, but also mentally— helping to stave off memory loss and conditions like Parkinson's disease.

5. **Bodywork:** Massage is a perfect elixir for good health, but it can also provide an integration of body and mind. By producing a meditative state or heightened awareness of living in the present moment, massage can provide emotional and spiritual balance, bringing with it true relaxation and peace. Massage also increases circulation, allowing the body to pump more oxygen and nutrients into tissues and vital organs. Actor George Burns received a massage every day of his adult life until he passed at age 100.

   Energy work is also a form of bodywork that stimulates your brain. **Reiki** and **Jin Shin Acutouch** are therapies based on Universal life energy that serve to balance your internal energetic system, and bring healing energy to organs and glands. Both of these methods open up the energy meridians in the body to remove any physical or emotional blocks. Some practitioners incorporate visualization as a catalyst to stimulate the life energy.

6. **Homeopathy, Color Therapy, and Aromatherapy** are holistic approaches that balance and energize the body and mind. My site www. HomeopathicWellness.com is a good resource for homeopathy. (More on homeopathy in the health chapter.)

There are so many beneficial tools to stimulate, support and guide you much more smoothly to your destination. For some, it may feel uncomfortable to seek support. We often think we should be able to do it on our own and that reaching out for support is a sign of weakness. The opposite is true. Getting support takes courage.

Blast Off! PRACTICE 1: Ignite Your Right Brain

Choose from one of the tools above to stimulate your creative right-brain hemisphere: (1) meditation, (2) art, (3) listening to Baroque music, (4) physical exercise, (5) bodywork, (6) homeopathy, color therapy, aromatherapy and others. Try a new method each week and see which ones work best for you. Keep them in your repertoire for use at times when you're feeling stuck or in need of some creative inspiration and motivation. ✪

> "Success is not the key to happiness. Happiness is the key to success. If you love what you are doing, you will be successful."
>
> ~Herman Cain,
> *Radio show host, business executive*

Blast Off! PRACTICE 2: What Path Should I Take?

You know you want to make a change. You want to find a new direction that is inspiring and fulfilling. The following *Dream Career Questionnaire* can spark some ideas to help you get started. Write your answers in your journal, *The Blast Off! Workbook*, or within the *Blastation* software at www.InteractiveLifeCoach.com.

1. **As a child, what did you dream of being when you grew up?** It's helpful to get in touch with your earlier fascinations. In early childhood, it was easier to live from our imagination without all of the interference from our adopted limiting beliefs.

2. **What are some of your favorite hobbies or activities—in the present and in the past—and why?** Wouldn't it be great if you could turn your favorite pastime into your dream career? We choose hobbies and activities that most likely resonate with our unique personality as well as our physical,

mental and emotional nature. They are an extension of our inner voice and a blast off to your dream career.

3. **What do you do, or have you done, in your life that makes you the happiest? What is it about this that you enjoy so much? What does it mean to you?** When you are in a state of joy or bliss, you are in complete alignment with your purpose. And when you're in complete alignment with your passions, intention and actions, success is sure to follow.

4. **What things have you always wanted to do, but were afraid to try?** These could be activities or ideas related to your personal life or career that you have seen on television, in books, or heard of others experiencing. List anything that comes to mind that seems interesting, stimulating, exciting, meaningful or fun.

   As I outlined in Chapter Three, many people self-impose limiting choices and circumstances on themselves and their lives. Once those obstacles are removed, the possibilities are boundless! People often fear change, even if their current circumstances are not up to par with their capabilities. The hardest part of change is the first step. Once you get through that, creating your new and successful career becomes so much easier. The fear will be released the more you practice taking action.

5. **What is a cause that you could get behind?** Is there a cause or charity that you're passionate about? There may be some career ideas that will support and reflect the charities or causes that have meaning to you.

   One of my clients, Leslie, felt stuck for years in a job that offered no challenge or mental stimulation whatsoever. She was very over-qualified for the position, but stayed for the security. As the years went by, Leslie became more and more apathetic toward her work. In the meantime, she was taking classes in homeopathy for animals and volunteering at the local animal shelter. It was obvious that humane treatment and care for animals was a cause that she felt very strongly about. It never felt like work because she absolutely loved to connect with the animals. Over time, Leslie began practicing natural medicine for animals on a part-time basis until she developed enough business to take the leap in creating her full-time dream career. Now, instead of going to her boring job, she wakes up each day to a dream career that she is most passionate about. She successfully moved her professional status from the Floating Stage to Supersonic.

6. **What values do you hold most important in your life?** If you can incorporate some of the most important values of your character and your life into your work, you will be truly living a life of value and purpose. For example, I have always felt a calling to help people in need. At some point, I finally reconnected with my deeper values and life purpose to support and inspire others on their path. Life coaching was a natural evolvement because it matched my inner values and purpose.

7. **What are your strengths and talents?** By tapping into the special abilities that you were born with, you can consider translating them into your dream career. My client, Kenneth, loves parasailing, so he is creating a charity that will help trauma victims heal through this sport. He has found a way to combine his passion and talent to give back to a cause he feels strongly about.

8. **What movies and books have inspired you over the years, and why?** We are often drawn to books and movies that reflect our personalities and interests. For example, history books may reflect your interest in travel or research. Action/adventure books and movies may mirror your desire for a career in an outdoor setting rather than being office-bound.

9. **What does success mean to you?** As I discussed earlier, success can have many different connotations and can represent different things to different people. What does the picture of success look like to you?

10. **If you had plenty of money at your disposal to invest in your own dream career, what kind of business would you start?** Often the fear of not having enough capital, or an inheritance, or just-accepting-poverty thinking can dissuade people from reaching for their dreams. As I have mentioned repeatedly, just by putting your dreams on paper, sending your intention out into the Universe and following up with action, the necessary avenues to remove these supposed limitations will appear. This is intention in action. There are also many resources for small-business funding. Don't let the financial aspect stop you, because there will always be a solution if you

actively look for it. The secret is to profess your dream, and then start taking action toward it today. You may begin to receive checks in the mail. Stranger things have happened! The Universe has incredible ways of providing for us once we put out the intention, then *believe* that it will appear.

> "It is incumbent upon us all to raise the bar, whether you are a multibillion-dollar international corporation or a mom-and-pop selling blackberry jam."
>
> *~Howard Schmidt,*
> *Security expert and advisor to*
> *government and companies*

Upon completion of *Blast Off! Practice 2,* look at each of your answers to the questionnaire. Do you see a common theme throughout? This is a very good clue for your winning dream career. For instance, if all your answers have to do with creative activities, you may fit with a career in the arts, such as landscape design, interior design, fine art or graphic design. If you see travel dominating your answers, a career as a travel agent, excursion director, or editor of a travel magazine may be the fuel for your *Secret Spark.*

These answers will reflect your inner purpose. A dream career that expresses your values, hopes, loves and dreams is a winning recipe for victory. ✪

Blast Off! PRACTICE 3: Brainstorming Your Dream Career

Now get your journal or workbook, and write down all your common themes from the *Dream Career Questionnaire* on the left side of a page. From these themes, write down any dream career ideas adjacent to them on the right.

Here are some examples:

Inner Purpose Themes	Dream Career Ideas
Travel	Director of travel adventure company
Design	Interior design, architecture, landscaping
Networking, entertaining	Event planner, concierge
Cooking	Own a kitchen store, lead cooking classes
Psychology, nature, art	Healing retreats in nature, art therapy ✪

Allison's Story of Intention

When I completed my homeopathic and holistic education, I was ready to start my private practice. Was I nervous? Are you kidding? I was scared to death! But my determination, passion and dwindling bank account were thrusting me forward through the fear. My biggest concern was, "What if I don't get enough clients?" I believed wholeheartedly in homeopathy and my capability as a practitioner, but I was most concerned about getting clients to experience my work. And since I had no money, attracting clients was a huge priority.

I first thought, "I need to buy an existing practice." That way, I would already have a client base. I also had two other practitioners, a psychologist and a massage therapist, who wanted to join together with me to open a center. We were privy to a practice that had been in existence for a long period of time and was for sale. The three of us met with the existing business owners for a few meetings. During these meetings, issues came up between the three of us that brought up doubts about blending our work together. I realized that we each had different ideas on how the business should run and I began feeling a gnawing uneasiness in my gut. Also, through the negotiations, I realized that I was going to have to magically produce several thousand dollars that I didn't have to buy this existing business.

> "Control your destiny or someone else will."
>
> ~Jack Welch,
> Former Chairman and
> CEO of General Electric,
> Co-author of Winning

My mentor at the time referred me to a psychic. Honestly, I had never been to a psychic before, but I was willing to accept any insight I could find. It actually was a very interesting and validating experience. Whether he was reading me correctly or not, he said one thing that really stuck with me. And that was, "You have finally found your true path. All you have to do is hang your shingle and the clients will come."

I know what you're thinking. *If you build it, they will come.* Well, it was something like that. I hung my sign on my new office door and started with only two clients. Those two referred two more and those four referred more and, long story short, thirteen years later I have been blessed with thousands of clients. Did I just sit in my office and wait for clients to come? No, I did not. I set the intention, then took action by taking good care of my clients, and doing some good public relations, such as speaking engagements, publishing articles and teaching. My first blessing was that I actually listened to my gut saying, "The partnership is not the direction for you." Then I set my intention by opening an office and putting my sign on the door. I built it and they came!

Mission to Be Accomplished

Prior to starting your dream career, I find it imperative for you to write a professional mission statement. The mission statement will be a proclamation of the purpose of your dream career, and it will set your intentions. The statement should cover your professional identity, deeper purpose and loftier goals. It's important to refer back to your mission statement through the years to stay connected to your purpose. You can always change and mold it along the way as your business evolves.

Blast Off! PRACTICE 4: Your Dream Career Mission Statement

Now that you have some idea of what type of career you want to create or embark on, it's time to formulate the purpose of that dream career in your *professional mission statement.*

Here's an example of a professional mission statement:

Blast Off! Life Coaching (www.MyBlastOff.com) *is a consulting service that coaches individuals and companies on a one-on-one and group basis to inspire a vision, create a direction, and implement plans of action to meet and exceed long-term goals in all aspects of life.* Blast Off! Life Coaching *is committed to supporting its clients' dreams, personal and fiscal goals, human spirit, health and inner peace for a most abundant and prosperous life. As the Director for* Blast Off! Life Coaching, *I promise to be a catalyst for people to understand and reach their true potential.*

Now create your own personal or career mission statement. This can be done in your journal or *The Blast Off! Workbook.* ✪

Job Security, Job Schemurity

Now that you've discovered some palatable ideas for starting your own dream business, you may be wresting with inner demons that are screaming, "What about job security?" Yes, I do understand that job security is important. But let's look at it from the polar opposite point of view.

If you were to put a dollar value on your time, peace of mind, and happiness, how much are you losing every day that you are not living your potential at your dissatisfying job? If you place even $10 per hour on a forty-hour work week, you're losing $19,200 per year! You could easily launch your own business for that. Now don't panic. I'm not suggesting that you go to work tomorrow and hand in your resignation papers. You do have to consider your responsibilities. If you're single with no kids, I might say, "Go for it." (That was my approach and it worked for me. Poverty became a huge motivator to make my business a success. Failure was not an option.) Dipping your feet in to test the waters rather than diving into the deep end is also a very good approach, and this will allow you to reap the benefits of your financial security while you develop your dream. Let's put a plan together to make a smooth transition from your job to your dream if you would rather not make a spontaneous, *"I've had it!"* bolt for freedom.

> *"Expect your every need to be met. Expect the answer to every problem, expect abundance on every level."*
>
> ~Eileen Caddy,
> A founder of the Findhorn Foundation, Author of Flight into Freedom and Beyond

A good option is to develop your new dream career on the side, while you're still receiving a paycheck from your current job. Once you feel that the new business is developed enough to meet your survival numbers each month, then it's time to cut the cord.

If you would like to test-drive your dream career before taking bigger steps, you can actually mentor under a seasoned expert in a one- to three-day immersion dream career vacation. See what it would really be like to be a chef, interior designer, teacher, sports announcer and more. Check out Vocation Vacations for more information. (See Resources section.)

Face the Numbers

When I began my homeopathic practice, I needed to figure out how much money I had to make to survive. Once I had this number, I would be able to know how many clients I needed to see each week to pay my bills and stay in business. By seeing this clearly on paper, it made my goals much more tangible, practical and attainable, and much less overwhelming.

Consider this. If I had $4,000 in expenses per month (including taxes) and I was charging $100 per client visit, then I needed to see 40 clients per month, or 10 clients per week, to survive. Forty clients per month became a monthly marker that I called my *Blue Plate Special Number,* the absolute bare minimum number of clients that I needed to see to pay the mortgage, monthly house bills, car payment, food costs, taxes and so on. No extra dollars for frills. This was just enough to get by on and that was a good place to start. I was thrilled to be getting paid for something I loved to do. How cool is that!

Surviving was fine for a while, but to not have any surplus funds had its memorable moments—like when my daughter became fascinated with the art of shopping. I decided to set myself another marker to move myself beyond survival mode. I named this one my *Silver Platter Number*, at 17 clients per week.

I reached this number after one year. Setting the intention for this goal *by writing it down, stating it out loud, envisioning and feeling the goal happening, and then taking action* was the method I used for manifesting the clients and the dollars. Before taxes, that was an extra $450 per week and an extra $1,800 per month! This was enough for a little travel, and some extra for savings and emergency funds. Oh and, of course, the latest trend in blue jeans for my daughter. (She inherited her love of fashion from me, so I have no room to criticize.) When I accomplished this number, I was so proud of myself. In fact, I loved what I was doing so much that it wasn't unusual for me to have a restless night's sleep due to the excitement and creation of ideas tossing around in my head.

As time passed, and my skills and experience **increased**, I developed a new marker that I call my *Gold Platter Number*, at 22 clients per week. With dedication and determination, I was able to realize this goal within a few years. Over the past several years, I continue to raise my *Gold Platter Number* with each new project or business that I pursue.

Secrets of the Gold Platter

There are two secrets that have helped me to not only reach my *Gold Platter Number*, but increase it each year.

- ★ I *only* take on endeavors that I'm passionate about and that I stand behind completely. If I didn't care about the method and message of my work, then not only would I not make the *Gold Platter Number*, I would surely become bored, frustrated and burned out.

- ★ By reviewing my goals each year as my businesses have grown, I've seen time and time again that if I give my *Gold Platter Number* a new increased marker, write it down, and periodically profess it to the Universe, I always, always meet that goal. You can profess your intention to whomever you like. Just stating your goals out loud will ignite the energy flow around you. Then let it go and trust. All will conspire for your benefit.

Blast Off! PRACTICE 5: State Your Plates and Platters

Once you have developed your dream career idea, you'll want to take a hard look at the numbers so you can manifest more wealth into your life. The more aware you are, the better off you'll be. Review and check in with these numbers frequently. Adjust them accordingly. Hopefully upwards!

Blue Plate Special Number (Survival Number): This is how much money you need to make just to survive and pay the bills and taxes each month.

* ⭐ Make a list of all your monthly expenses, including your mortgage or rent, utilities, food, clothing, personal affects, other current bills, taxes and so on.

* ⭐ Total it at the bottom. **This is your *Blue Plate Special Number*.**

Silver Platter Number (Exceeding Survival): This is a goal that's higher than what you're reaching now.

* ⭐ Take the same financial budget from your *Blue Plate Special Number* and increase the numbers in areas where you wish to be able to spend more. For instance, if you spend $100 per month for personal care, such as massage or gifts, you may want to increase that to $500 or $1,000 in your *Silver Platter*. You can also add categories that you couldn't afford in your *Blue Plate Special Number*, such as travel or entertainment.

* ⭐ Total it at the bottom. **This is your *Silver Platter Number*.**

Gold Platter Number (Your *Blast Off!* Number): This is your ultimate financial goal.

* ⭐ Take the same financial budget from your *Silver Platter Number* and increase the numbers in areas where you wish to be able to spend more. For instance, you may want to add a category for your fantasy trip around the world. You may want to build your dream home. Figure your approximate total expense and break it into a monthly budget. Remember, this is what you are working towards. You do not have to know how or when this money will arrive yet. Be patient. Believe and take action. It will come.

* ⭐ Total it at the bottom. **This is your *Gold Platter Number*.**

I have written my *Silver* and *Gold Platter Numbers* each quarter over the past several years. By simply listing these each quarter or each year, you're setting an intention that you are expecting to achieve these financial goals. Then take action through your *Mini Feats* to bring these numbers into reality. I am always pleasantly surprised when I add up the income for the year and look back at my intentions. It works. I'm telling you, it really works! (The Plates and Platters exercise can be accessed on the *Blastation* software, www.InteractiveLifeCoach.com.) ✪

Most Important Rule in Business

Business 101. To succeed in any business,
you must bring in more income than you spend.

I cannot tell you how many times I consult with individuals who are about to launch a new company, and I find that they are spending a fortune decorating elaborate offices and buying expensive company cars. I realize the importance of loving the environment that you're working in, but this can be done on a more balanced budget. If you continue spending at this pace without your income growing beyond your costs, this is a disaster waiting to happen. Don't get me wrong; I'm not advising that you should be a miser. I am just suggesting that you stay within a reasonable budget so that your dream career will have plenty of breathing room to blossom.

> "To every man, there comes a time in his life-time, that special moment when he is figuratively tapped on the shoulder, and offered that special chance to do a very special thing, unique to him and fitted to his talents."
>
> ~Winston Churchill,
> *Prime Minister of the United Kingdom,
> Nobel Laureate
> (1874-1965)*

Learn to Discern

Once you have decided on your dream career, be cautious about who you share your idea with. This is a very, very important piece of infor-mation. When I decided to open a homeopathic practice, I made the mistake of telling all the wrong people who said, "You are making a huge mistake," or "What if you fail?" And then there was my favorite, "Have you lost your mind?" (It was actually even worse than that, but I'll spare you the gory details.) Luckily, I gained a piece of wisdom along the way that helped me deflect all the negative, doomsday energy. When you share your dream, and someone responds back with the reasons why it *won't* work, they're only speaking from their fear. Learn to discern who will be supportive and encouraging, and *only* share your dreams with these people. The risk you take by telling those people who don't believe in you or your dream is that you'll succumb to their harmful comments and begin doubting yourself and your quest.

Many of the inventors of the biggest discoveries of our time were criticized and even laughed at by others. Thank goodness their passion and determination were strong enough to keep them from giving up. The Wright Brothers received a tremendous amount of doubt and ridicule from the press as they professed to be building the world's first flying machine. The Paris edition of the *Herald Tribune* headlined a 1906 article on the Wrights, "FLYERS OR LIARS?" It was the Wright Brothers' passion, intention and determined action that sustained this duo through the backlash of skepticism toward their extraordinary goal.

When you have a great idea or a plan of action, then put your head down and keep moving forward. Your results will speak for themselves. Luckily, in my case, I just became more stubborn. I utilized the, "I'll-Show-Them" method. It worked for me!

Identify and Disconnect from Energy Drainers

You are about to embark on a new and exciting path. The last thing you need is to be drained by drama or negative people. You know the ones. There is always a crisis or something bad happening in their lives. It's not that I don't have compassion for these people. Otherwise, I would not be in the healing profession. However, if you're focusing on creating wealth, abundance, passion, and positive energy in your life, the fastest way to let the wind out of your sails and lose your momentum is to spend your valuable time with an energy drainer.

Like energy creates like energy. Have you had the experience of being in the presence of an energetic, uplifting person? Just by standing next to this person, you'll begin to feel uplifted yourself. By the same token, have you experienced your energy drop through the floor when you're in the presence of someone who possesses an intensely negative and heavy energy? Next time this happens, observe how you start to slump over and feel heavy yourself.

> "Talent wins the game, but teamwork and intelligence wins championships."
>
> ~Michael Jordan, Outstanding NBA basketball player (retired), businessman

Right now, you need all the positive energy you can assimilate. When you surround yourself with inspiring people who make the most out of life, it will only help to encourage, support and celebrate the realization of your *Big Picture Vision.*

Your Support Team

There's absolutely no reason for you to forge your new path alone. On my personal path in developing my dream careers, I have always sought out **mentors** and **coaches** who have blazed the trail before me. Through their support and experiential wisdom, I have acquired knowledge and valuable tools that have helped me immensely.

When I built my advertising agency, I called on television, radio and newspaper representatives to teach me the ropes and behind-the-scene workings of their industries, because I was completely clueless when my clients started asking me to buy media. They were happy to help me because I was sincere, and they knew I would eventually bring them business. They saved me valuable time and money. The other way to learn is through mistakes and failures. I had plenty of those, too, but working with mentors and coaches helped to keep those backslides to a minimum. When I needed to learn about the printing business, I asked printing specialists if I could come into their production rooms and watch them in action. They showed me how the printing jobs were run, and what to look out for in order to create a clean job. I even learned the lingo so that when I spoke to clients and printing reps, I didn't sound like a complete novice.

When I began my homeopathic career, I interned for a year with another established homeopath. I cannot imagine starting on my own without it. She was a priceless support system.

> "The path to greatness is along with others."
>
> ~*Baltasar Gracián, Spanish priest, author of* The Art of Worldly Wisdom

There are many successful businesspeople who would be happy to mentor and share their wisdom with you. Networking with people in your industry will educate you eons beyond your scope of information. They will teach you from their personal experiences, and you'll learn what to do and what to avoid. This is life wisdom that you can't find in a classroom or in a book. Make sure you respect their time and don't abuse the privilege. If they're living their dream, their time is valuable too.

A coach (visit www.MyBlastOff.com) is different than a mentor in that this is someone you hire as part of your support team. You can call on them as often as you need, and they can help direct you and keep you on track to develop and attain your *Big Picture Vision*.

I hired a business coach, Mark LeBlanc, when I wanted to expand my homeopathic college, Homeopathic Academy of Southern California. I was having trouble trying to manage and run two businesses at once, as you can imagine. He helped me tremendously. He was able to assess how I was running the businesses and give me ideas that I hadn't considered.

We often look at a problem over and over and see the same solutions. An outside support person, such as a life coach or business coach, who is not emotionally connected to your dreams, is an invaluable resource for you. That professional distance enables them to support you from a creative and innovative perspective without becoming clouded or enveloped by your personal stressors. They will be able to observe the problems and help you find solutions in a supportive and inspiring way.

More Dream Team Members

Here are some examples of Dream Team members who can support you in your new career.

* **Bookkeeper:** A bookkeeper can help you keep track of your income and expenses and help prevent you from going over your business budget.

* **Accountant:** Your accountant or CPA will support your business growth and tax preparation needs. I have had the same accountant for thirteen years and he has been a significant part of my advisory team.

* **Attorney:** A good business attorney can advise you about what kind of entity your business should operate as—whether it would better serve you to be a Sole Proprietor, or establish a C-Corporation, an S-Corporation or a Limited Liability Corporation. Discuss your business description and long-term goals and an attorney can set you on the right path.

* **Banker:** Get to know your bank manager. This relationship will become very beneficial when you're in need of business financing or account support.

* **Marketing/Advertising/Public Relations Specialist or Agency:** You have a great business idea. Now you need to let your potential clients know that you exist. This is a crucial aspect of any business. Interview three or four agencies or experts and see which one is the better fit. Start with a more modest advertising budget and then increase it as your business grows. Make sure you incorporate Web marketing into the mix. Internet exposure is key, such as an effective company website, website optimization, blogging and e-newsletters. There's a great deal of public relations that you can do on your own (free of charge). This includes sending press releases to newspapers and television. Also, send your articles and newsletter to Internet blogs.

* **Feng Shui Consultant:** Feng shui is an ancient Chinese practice of arranging objects in your work or personal environment to achieve a sense of harmony and equilibrium in your space. This helps promote health, balance and prosperity. I have used feng shui in both my home and offices for years. Simply rearranging your furniture and accessories in a way that allows the energy to flow around you, rather than a setting that feels blocked or obstructed, makes a huge difference in how you and your customers will feel.

There's no need to go it alone. With the foundation of a good team in place, you can focus on the most important part—*growing your business.*

Bring on the Competition

Many times over the years when I'm preparing to launch a new business, I hear the negative naysayers questioning, "Aren't you worried about the competition?" Besides following my own advice of steering clear of negativity, I respond by stating, "I don't focus on the competition. I focus on me and what my business has to offer."

Business owners who get intimidated by the competition are focusing too much on what's going on around them, rather than what they need to be focusing on most—their own product or service. I'm not saying to go into business blindly or ignore market research. However, I sincerely feel that if you focus on taking good care of your clients and offer a great and needed idea, service or widget, it doesn't matter what the competition is doing or not doing. In fact, the more the competition, the more people are hearing about your industry. And that just creates more demand. It's all good.

> "Life is a field of unlimited possibilities."
>
> ~Deepak Chopra,
> Pioneer in mind-body
> medicine, author of The Seven
> Spiritual Laws of Success

Abundant Thinking

My advice to you: Stay connected to your *Big Picture Vision* for your career. Don't forget your purpose and your passion. Read your *Big Picture Vision* often and proclaim it out loud. Set your goals higher than you would imagine possible and then take action. And the most important key to this Law of Attraction formula is to believe and act as if your goal has already happened. All will conspire in your favor once you think and live abundantly. Then watch the magic unfold.

I truly believe in my heart that you have what it takes to fulfill your dreams. *It's your time now!*

BLAST OFF! Daily Launch Tools

1. Each morning, write your *Sun-Up Script* and *Rocket Words*.

2. Read your *Rocket Words* to yourself and out loud as often as possible during your day.

3. Create and perform a minimum of *Mini Feats* each day. (These are the smaller steps for moving toward your larger *Mile Step* goals and your *Big Picture Vision*.) For example, today's *Mini Feats* might be:

- *Perform some market research. Research industry websites that pique my interest.*

- *Check out a local business networking group or chamber of commerce event. Ask people who share my interests about their careers. (You will be amazed at the good information you'll receive.)*

- *Sign up for Toastmasters to improve my self-confidence in speaking. (This will enhance your interviews, and sales, and of course help you to overcome the great phobia of public speaking.)*

- *Set a firm date that I will be making a change in my job or starting a business on the side. (Make that commitment to yourself. Start walking toward your* Big Picture Vision *now.)*

4. Choose one to two *Blast Off! Practices* from this chapter to do each day over the next week.

5. Fill out your *Weekly Flight Assessment Log* to review your week's progress toward realizing your *Supersonic Life*.

Summary of the Chapter Concepts

➤ **Success has many connotations.** In your career, if desired goals and rewards are only monetary, the fulfillment may not be lasting. By choosing a dream career you are passionate about, the rewards become much broader and deeper than money alone.

➤ **If you're dissatisfied with your job,** it can affect every other part of your life including your relationships, family and personal fulfillment. It's almost impossible to compartmentalize these feelings for an extended period of time.

➤ **Is your job inspiring**? Does it help you grow as a human being? Do you look forward to work each morning, or is that something you dread? Can you imagine having a career that excites you? How about being able to set your own schedule? What if you had no cap on the amount of income you could make?

➤ **Your right brain hemisphere** is your creative, intuitive side. Your left brain hemisphere addresses your logical, rational and analytical side. To access the creativity and inspiration of your right brain, utilize art, music, exercise, color therapy, homeopathy, energy work and massage.

➤ **To help tap into your purpose,** dreams, passions and destiny, play with the *Dream Career Questionnaire*. See what common themes arise and then brainstorm on some fantastic career ideas that fit you.

➤ **Write a professional mission statement** to proclaim the intention and purpose of your dream career.

➤ **How much monetary, physical, emotional and psychic value are you losing** in unhappiness and job security? Is the security costing you more than you realize?

➤ **Take a very direct look at your no-frills budget.** How much do you need each month in income to survive? How much would you need to sell in service or product to meet your survival needs, i.e., your *Blue Plate Special Number?*

➤ **Your *Silver Platter Number*.** What would your next higher goal, beyond survival, look like?

➤ **Look at your *Gold Platter*,** your ultimate *"Blast Off!"* number. Continue to reassess and increase these goals over time as your dream career builds.

➤ **The number one rule in business**: *Make more money than you spend.*

➤ **Be selective about who you share your dreams** and ideas with. Make sure they are supportive people so that you will not have to be vulnerable to their fears, doubts, negative comments or criticism. Only listen to and receive positive, encouraging energy.

Summary of the Chapter Concepts (continued)

➤ **Disconnect from energy drainers.**
Surround yourself with positive, inspiring colleagues, friends and family. If you spend time with negative people or energy drainers, your passionate energy will begin to drain, too.

➤ **Build your Dream Team of mentors**, life coaches, accountants, lawyers, physical trainers, spiritual counselors and health counselors. No reason to go it alone.

➤ **Don't be afraid of your competition.**
Whatever your career (even if it is similar to someone else's), it will be your own version with your own special twist. By focusing on yourself and your goals, you are creating a strong intention that will result in a strong actualization and results. If you spend your time focusing on what the competition is doing, you are giving your power away and draining all that precious energy.

➤ **Think abundantly**. Declare your *Big Picture Vision* and believe it will be arriving soon. And it will.

"Always bear in mind that your own resolution to succeed is more important than any other one thing."

~Abraham Lincoln,
16th President of the United States
(1809-1865)

BLAST Off!
to the "Love-of-Your-Life" Relationship

I met my soulmate, Mike, when I was forty-two. After twenty years of trying all the *wrong* ways to get it right, I finally figured out how to manifest the relationship of my dreams. *Manifest?* Yes, I called him in, and there he was. And I have many girlfriends who were witness to the magic. But before I share with you the secrets of my match-made-in-heaven, step-by-step process, you should know that in the relationship arena, it never, ever came easy to me. In the vein of hindsight is 20/20, I put myself through *way* too much drama and heartache than was even remotely necessary.

When I started thinking about manifesting this relationship, my life was radiant on almost every level. I had a beautiful daughter, a very inspiring dream career, lots of amazing friends, fun and adventurous hobbies and a growing spiritual connection. My love life, on the other hand, had its ups and downs. It was my weakest link.

You may be thinking, "She had everything else, though. Why wasn't that enough?" For some people, I'm sure it would have been more than enough. I had a great home life and growing finances; all of the other elements of a happy life were there. The challenge for me was that I am a relationship-oriented person and being alone over an extended period of time was just not my cup of tea.

Better Off Alone?

For some people, it's just easier to be single and alone. They experience less chaos, less tension, and life is plain simpler. On the other hand, when we're in a relationship, some of the not-so-lovely parts of ourselves and our counterparts have more of an opportunity to rear their ugly heads. That is because in relationships our unhealthy issues can be triggered by our partner, throwing all that dirty laundry out on the table. The positive side of this (which I appreciate) is that we grow spiritually and personally when that dirty laundry comes out and we learn how to face it, address it, embrace it and heal from it.

Now don't get me wrong. It isn't that I feel that I need to be with a man 24/7, but I longed for a life partner who I could eat jelly beans with, laugh with 'til I cried (that meant he would have to get my jokes), kick back with, dance and travel with, wake up beside every morning to start my day, and fall asleep with as I counted my blessings. Somehow, even though that was what I sincerely wanted, I seemed to attract and repeatedly choose everything *but* that.

When I refer to my love life as being the missing link, I mean that *amore* was the empty hole in my whole life picture. Now remember, in the career chapter, I mentioned that when your work arena is stagnating or frustrating, those feelings will most likely affect your personal life in some fashion? Well, the same is true for the impact of an underdeveloped relationship sector. Because my relationships ranged from boring to disheartening to outright crushing, my emptiness could not help but slip into my career and home life. Nonetheless, I had a daughter to raise amidst all of this searching, so my efforts to keep the search and my home life separate were close to heroic. Not by coincidence did I choose a career path of service to others. Healing people helped me to get out of my own way and focus on their pain, rather than dwell on my own.

Love Is in the Air and Yours to Inhale

From consulting with thousands of men and women over the years, I have been privy to it all—the good, the bad and the ugly. On the positive side, I have met couples who, after thirty years of marriage and raising families, are still madly in love. One of my male clients, after forty years of marriage, still calls his wife "his bride." I have witnessed many beautiful examples that demonstrate true love is alive and well in humanity, and absolutely and completely possible.

Two of my best friends have married their soulmates, and I have watched their relationships grow and evolve over the last twenty years. Observing their bliss always gave me hope that my true love was out there somewhere, and believe me, I was praying that my somewhere was not Tanzania or Iceland!

Another example is Karen and James, the very first friends we met when my ex-husband and I moved to San Diego. My daughter has grown up with their children. I always admired the natural flow of dialogue, love and just "beingness" between this woman and her husband. One day I was standing in their kitchen and James came in with the groceries. He realized he had forgotten the apples that Karen had asked for. While she was looking in the bag for them, James said in his fun-loving manner, "Darn it, I forgot the apples, but I so love you." And then he immediately went back to the store to get them. I remember thinking, "Wow! How thoughtful is the energy between these two." They adore and admire one another, and that is always completely obvious to everyone around them.

When I was experiencing a frustrating moment with a man of the hour, I would often give the situation "The James Test." *What would James have done in this instance?* Unfortunately, the men that I chose were never kind enough, loving enough, committed enough, or fun enough to meet such a standard.

> "Love and magic have a great deal in common. They enrich the soul, delight the heart. And they both take practice."
>
> ~Nora Roberts,
> Romance novelist

Allison's Search for Love in All the Wrong Places

I'm going to put myself on a limb by revealing some of my rather sorry dating and relationship moments, in the hopes that you will either resonate with them, or learn from my experiences.

My college days are a good starting point for this journey. Just before I left for school, I met a man who I thought was perfect for me—until I received a shocking call from his pregnant wife who informed me otherwise. Then there was Jeff, who loved to go out with me and have fun; however, when the evening was over, he never failed to return to his ex-girlfriend while I naively and pathetically waited around for the phone to ring. (That was before answering machines freed us from bondage.)

Then there was Barry, who ran for the door soon after I told him I loved him, and he never came back, leaving me feeling humiliated, and also angry at myself for being so vulnerable.

Another man, Stuart, was great at first, but thereafter he became so needy and suffocating. When I tried to break up with him, I had to escape through the window since he had locked me into his apartment!

There was also Thomas, who kept telling me how beautiful I would be if I only lost ten pounds.

Needless to say, after a few of these jolting attempts at love, my self-esteem had taken a beating and some torturous and dysfunctional relationship patterns had emerged. I was choosing men who would criticize me, abandon me or smother me. Sadly enough, even after four years of rejection and suffocation, I still had no awareness that I was attracting and contributing to each dismal scenario. Looking back, it was obvious that I was creating these abominable situations.

Attracting What We Fear the Most

I had such a fear of abandonment that I kept creating situations in which I *would* be abandoned. That may not make any sense to you, but here's why it was happening. As adults, we will keep repeating our childhood pain in our current relationships in an effort to work through it (if we haven't healed from our past hurts). They say the definition of insanity is repeating the same thing over and over, and hoping for a different result. Well, call it what you will, that was my story.

Being in the vulnerable state that I was in, with no understanding of my issues, I was a prime target for continued mayhem and madness.

Then came my ex-husband. He was fifteen years older, more mature and directed. And because I thought he would be my savior from an endless line of bad-to-worse relationships, at age twenty-two, I naively labeled him "my hero." However, as I said earlier, my true self, the one without all the scars, desired a life partner, someone to share the path with. Instead, I had chosen a parent.

By the time I reached age thirty, after both of us had tried to make a match out of a pairing of two misfits, the parent-child relationship wasn't working anymore. It was as if we started speaking completely different languages, which left us each feeling frustrated and inadequate. We decided to part ways after years of counseling and trial separations. It was a frightening time for me because I was somewhat dependent on that relationship. However, I knew that I couldn't rest my yearning heart until I found my soulmate.

Once again I was single and searching for Mr. Right. Six months later, I met Mark at a party. He was intelligent, witty, ambitious, sweet and romantic. He showed me that couples could talk lovingly and actually listen and respond to one another in a supportive way. We were together for three years and it was a very healing time for me. My self-esteem started to blossom again. Everything was terrific except for one major red spotlight. (In case you don't know, spotlights are more glaring than red flags.) Mark was six years younger than me, and literally terrified of the idea of marriage. In fact, he had openly expressed this to me many times. So the warnings were there, but I ignored them. I was sure that our love would overpower his fear and he would eventually change for me. *Can you relate to this experience?*

> "Life is one fool thing after another whereas love is two fool things after each other."
>
> ~Oscar Wilde
> *Irish playwright, novelist, poet and short-story writer (1854-1900)*

As three years came to a close, and with age thirty-four sneaking up on my horizon, I could finally see that my efforts to convince Mark into matrimony were not panning out. So I did a really wise thing: I ended the relationship abruptly and had an affair with a wild guy I met on a ski trip who had long hair and smoked pot all day. I was really making progress (not!). I even turned Mark's inevitable better-late-than-never marriage proposal down because I, once again, thought I was going to change my new man (the irresponsible partier) into the ideal mate. I must have been high myself.

It really didn't get any better for quite some time. I even got married at age thirty-six to someone I had known for only five months. Even though my sister and all my friends were begging me to reconsider, I refused to listen. Larry was a good guy and, in all honesty, I was tired of being a single mom. And my daughter liked him and they got along great.

Yet soon after the excitement from the wedding passed and Larry and I fell back into normal life, I suddenly realized that we had absolutely *nothing* in common. We would spend time together in complete silence, with absolutely *zilch* to say to one another. All my questioning, in an effort to open up a conversation between us, was responded to in one-syllable or one-word answers, such as, "Fine," "Good," "Okay" or "No." I even attempted to bridge the gap by buying books to read together, in the hopes of creating mutually enjoyable entertainment that would spur some commonality. Soon after, I revealed this communication challenge to a close friend and the friend said, "Allison, the word 'relationship' comes from the word 'relating.'" Well, Larry and I were in no way relating.

The crowning moment happened when we were at dinner one night. Following the shrimp scampi, as Larry was doing his usual staring off into space, I asked him, "Larry, what are you thinking about?" His response was simply, "Nothing." At that moment, with my stomach wrenched in knots, I knew I had made a huge, huge mistake, and all I could think was, "*How am I going to get myself out of this mess?*" I knew deep in my heart that even though I still had no proof that my true love existed, I could not condemn myself to live in another empty marriage.

After three months, and with no hard feelings from either of us, the blip of a marriage was over. Even though my daughter and I can laugh about it now, she had a really rough time with the loss back then. She wanted a family as much as I did, and I felt like I had completely failed her as a parent. I wanted more than anything to show her that it was possible for two people to live and grow in love and in harmony. Call me a dreamer, but I still believed that to be true, and I was not willing to give up until I found it.

Alexandra's Choice

During my searching-for-love years, I mentored many clients who were tremendously stuck in their love life and feeling very much alone.

Alexandra was one such client. This woman had a powerful and charismatic presence, but her body language revealed her inner tension and rigidity. Alex came to me because she was considering accepting a new position as a merger and acquisition consultant for a company in San Francisco. And at the same time, she had been toying with the idea of opening an art gallery instead. Alexandra didn't receive any personal fulfillment in her industry of mergers and acquisitions, but she was enticed by the fiscal opportunities this job was offering. Meanwhile, the dream of opening an art gallery was born out of her passion for painting and the art world. She wanted a venue to display her own artwork and the work of many other talented artists who she had come to know and admire. As Alexandra talked about the gallery, her demeanor expanded and softened. There was a lightness that radiated from her voice and I sensed excitement in her eyes.

Then Alexandra's demeanor tightened up again as she revealed to me that she was in love with a man who lived in San Francisco. I thought that was good enough reason to move, until I asked her if he loved her. Alex said she wasn't sure, since he hadn't called her for one month because he said he needed to work out some family issues. As she lowered her head, Alexandra told me that she was hoping to hear from him soon.

I responded very directly, "Okay, let me get this straight, Alexandra. You're considering taking a job you don't like and moving to another city to be with a man who cannot pick up the phone for a two-minute call?"

This made no sense to me, even though I wasn't doing much better in my own relationships. (It's much easier to define another's mistakes when you're not emotionally connected to them.)

Alexandra was a strong woman who was losing her identity to a career she didn't enjoy, and to a man who didn't love her in return. Alex revealed to me that she had a bad habit of choosing situations that gave less than she deserved, in her career and in her love life, because she wasn't really sure that true happiness existed. This client was also afraid that if she didn't settle, she might end up with nothing at all.

> "You will find as you look back upon your life that the moments when you have truly lived are the moments when you have done things in the spirit of love."
>
> ~Henry Drummond,
> *Inspirational speaker and author of* The Greatest Thing in the World
> *(1851-1897)*

Love versus Fear

Alexandra was shrinking her bright light to fit a career that was squelching her and an unavailable man who could not honor her greatness. In talking further, Alex admitted to being afraid that if she sought after and exposed herself to all that she really wanted, and all that she was fully capable of, she might intimidate others and then get rejected and abandoned by those around her.

I told Alex that she was already alone because the people close to her had never had the magnificent opportunity of meeting the real Alexandra. She was putting up walls and, therefore, receiving more walls in return. This was a huge light-bulb moment for her.

The Boomerang Principle

What you put out to the world, in any instance, is what you will most definitely receive in return. Throw the boomerang with a certain amount of force and it will come back to you with an equal amount of force. It may or may not appear on a conscious or external level that you are projecting grief, anger, sadness, resentment or fear. However, whether you are aware of it or not, your internal or unconscious energy is projected loudly to the Universe and everyone around you.

In Alexandra's case, she was giving love externally, but internally her fear had created walls that kept her heart at a distance. Her walls were saying, "You need to stay detached from me because I am too afraid to reveal what's inside." Therefore, she attracted men who stayed detached and noncommittal, which then only created more heartache and detachment. This is a vicious cycle that needs to be healed for healthy love to appear.

I asked Alexandra to meditate on and write about her true self, minus the walls. *No self-criticism allowed.* Once Alexandra was able to connect with her true self, she could see the truth and choose the right career path for herself, as well as the type of man and the relationship she really wanted to attract.

Blast Off! PRACTICE 1: What Inner Language Are You Projecting?

In my own situation, I kept thinking, "I'm not acting needy. I'm not clinging to these relationships. What's the deal?" I cried to the heavens, "Why is all this rejection happening?" Outwardly I was cool, calm and collected, and it was obvious that I was very independent in my career and completely capable of taking care of my child on my own. Nevertheless, the energy of my unconscious little girl longing for love was screaming out loudly and desperately.

To be able to finally draw in the love and relationship you desire, you must first recognize what energy or behavior you are projecting. What is your inner language expressing without saying anything at all? Get into a quiet space or your *Inspiration Station* and ask yourself straight out, "What is my inner language saying to the world?" Listen to your inner voice and the answers will come. Do not candy-coat them. The more honest you are with yourself, the more powerful and positive the change will be. Make a written record of the answers that come to you in your journal or *The Blast Off! Workbook,* and refer to it as you work on shifting and lifting your energy. ✪

Update on Alexandra

Alexandra and I continued to work together for the next six months. Once she stopped suppressing her wounded energy and began tearing down the walls that separated her from her dreams and from love, her true self was revealed to the world. Alex told me that she had never felt more alive.

Alexandra felt empowered after writing the San Francisco man a letter telling him that she was moving on. Over the next several months, as she was building her dream art gallery, Alex began working with a gentleman who specialized in advertising and marketing for the art world. Jonathon was drawn to Alexandra's strong, passionate character and they shared the same fascination with art and art history. This was the first time Alex did not suppress who she was, or put up any walls. One year later, she and Jonathon were married.

Blast Off! PRACTICE 2: My True Self Revealed

People often suppress their true identity and their needs in an effort to attain love and security. The truth is that the love and security you receive in this manner is most likely an illusion, because it is a result of self-fear, not self-love. Until we live our lives congruently, meaning our inner truth must equal outer action, we cannot find peace, love and happiness.

In your journal or *The Blast Off! Workbook,* make a list of all your glorious inner and outer qualities that you would want to be recognized and loved by a soulmate. ✪

Back to My Story...

After I left my second marriage, I took some time off from romance to try to figure out what the hell was going wrong. I obviously had not succeeded in figuring it all out by that point. After a year's reprieve from my soulmate search, I jumped back in the game and dated an alcoholic who left me at a girlfriend's wedding reception when I caught him with a rose in his teeth making a pass at a table of single women. Then I spent the next eight months trying to rescue a great guy who suffered from chronic depression. I ignorantly thought, "If only I could help him heal, all would be wonderful." *Yuck.* After that fruitless and exhausting emotional rollercoaster, I felt that what I really needed was someone calm and safe. *Be careful what you ask for.*

Then Taylor appeared. Thankfully, he was not melodramatic at all. He was neither up nor down. This was a definite improvement, but over time, it was obvious that I had, once again, chosen someone who was my complete opposite. No fault to Taylor, he was really a great guy. We were just *not* a match. And without the drama, it *finally* became glaringly apparent that my years of being the rejectee and the rejector stemmed from choosing men who I had nothing in common with, who I could surely rescue and change, who had different values or goals, and who validated any and all of my insecurities.

Taylor liked to stay home, and I enjoy that, too, but my passion for living craved occasional dining out and traveling to exotic ports of call. Basically, Taylor didn't want to leave town. I was a night owl; he went to bed at nine. He dressed conservatively and I liked a more carefree look. I am an entrepreneur, and he was a corporate guy who was unable to set a flexible schedule. I am a spiritual person who believes in karma, reincarnation and evolution of the soul. He was a left-brain pragmatist who thought my ideas were very "woo-woo," even though, in his favor, he attempted to go along with it.

We clearly didn't speak the same language. Seriously, there was absolutely nothing wrong with the guy. And for the right woman, he was a complete catch. But in our situation, for the relationship to soar, either

I needed to become a homebody or he needed to start injecting caffeine into his veins to keep up with me. Opposites attract, but unless there is some major compromise and or suppression of identity, odds are, the bond will not sustain. The only way to get a square peg into a round hole is to cram it in, and in a relationship, that makes for a painful fit.

Opposites Attract and Often Combust

In some relationships, opposite personalities appear to be connecting because one partner consciously decides to completely suppress an important quality or desire that they uphold until it reveals itself through resentment, disease or depression. For other luckier couples, this combination succeeds because one or both partners can fulfill that deep need or aspect of their personality through other avenues or relationships.

My best friend from college, Susan, has been very happily married for almost fifteen years. She is liberal, and her husband is conservative. She is open-minded spiritually, and he isn't really sure what his wife is talking about. However, Susan gets those needs met by sharing her thoughts on those topics with her friends. That works perfectly for Susan because she and her husband have a very deep love for one another. They also play a lot of tennis together, love to dine out, and share a similar sense of humor that keeps them laughing all the time. In their instance, they have enough shared interests to carry them through their differences.

The truth is that if the two people are not sharing some major interests and growing individually as well as together as a couple, they will inevitably grow apart.

In choosing a mate of opposites, we may be drawn to someone who has traits that we are lacking. We also may be drawn to someone who has traits that we need to work through for ourselves. Either way, unless there is a very deep connection, it's hard to sustain the harmony when friction forms between two opposite people.

For instance, if you're physically active and your partner wants to sit on the couch and watch television, you might try to convince yourself that this is good. My partner can teach me to slow down a bit, you might be thinking. But since you probably won't convert your partner from a couch potato to a go-getter that easily, this could cause friction on a beautiful sunny day when you want to enjoy the outdoors and your mate has a plethora of shows to watch. Or if you tend to get very excited about things, and your partner is very mellow, you could be overpowering him or her, and over time, this can create tremendous frustration on both parts. It makes life so much more enjoyable, and there's a huge reduction in stress, when the partners share similar views on life, interests, goals and values.

The Lightning-Bolt Moment

In my relationship with Taylor, the even-keeled one, my spirit felt like it was dying. I didn't laugh or cry anymore. I felt flat and numb. One afternoon, I was driving around my neighborhood thinking, "Why do I keep getting myself into these messes, and why do each of these relationships keep turning into a losing battle?" This time I said aloud in desperation, *"What am I supposed to do?"*

In a moment of silent confusion, it happened. I'm telling you point-blank exactly what I heard. My inner voice, Higher Self, my spirit, whatever you want to call it, spoke to me in a poignant, caring voice that I will never forget. It said, *"Why don't you make this a hell of a lot easier, Allie, by choosing someone who you are already attracted to and that has similar passions and beliefs? Then you won't desire to change anything about him. Why don't you open yourself up to attracting a man with a similar lifestyle, similar interests and goals, who also wants to find his soulmate, get married, and grow with a life partner?"*

I was stunned. First I looked around to see if anyone else heard it, but then realized I was still by myself in my car. Then I thought, "Really? Could it be that simple?" After all I had been through, I'd never really thought through what kind of man and what kind of relationship would be the best fit for me. By the expression on my face reflected in the car's rearview mirror, you would have thought that I had been struck by lightning. "You mean I don't need to fight so hard to make a relationship work?

Unbelievable!" Even though I knew this to be true with all the clients I had worked with, I hadn't been able to see it as an issue for myself until that point. I thought about how awesome it would be to find someone who wanted to live life to the fullest, like myself, and was drawn to and appreciated similar interests and beliefs. I also thought the messages that I received through the years that I was too strong, too passionate, too excitable, and too romantic were possibly false. Maybe there was someone out there who would appreciate and match those qualities instead of feeling barreled over by them.

> "Love is the life of the soul. It is the harmony of the universe."
>
> ~William Ellery Channing, Unitarian theologian (1780-1842)

Allison's Soulmate Shopping List

I immediately drove home and relaxed into my *Inspiration Station*, a corner of my bedroom that was devoted to invoking creativity, inspiration and relaxation. I lit some candles and turned on some soft music while I meditated on the type of man and relationship that I desired and—something I had not thought of before—what type of man and relationship would best suit my nature and my lifestyle. Below is my list. I wanted to attract a man into my life who:

- ★ Is close to my age.
- ★ Has an open-minded spiritual connection to God and the Universe.
- ★ Is good with children.
- ★ Enjoys life to the fullest through adventure and staying active.
- ★ Can make me laugh a lot.
- ★ Loves to travel.
- ★ Enjoys dining out.
- ★ I am visually and physically attracted to.
- ★ Is responsible with his words and his actions.
- ★ Is financially stable and able to support himself.

⋆ Is an entrepreneur, so that we can schedule time together at home and to travel.

⋆ Is encouraging and supportive of my career path.

⋆ Is passionate about the work he does.

⋆ Exercises and takes good care of his health.

⋆ Is easygoing, but also gets excited about life.

⋆ Is open-hearted and loving.

⋆ Is also looking for his soulmate.

⋆ Wants to get married to the right person.

After twenty years of hopelessly trying to manufacture the formula with the wrong guy, at that moment I had become clear on what qualities a man needed to possess to fit my soulmate status. Being the business woman that I am, I planned to spend the next two months searching for my soulmate. I was very confident that I would not settle for anything less.

> **Blast Off!** | PRACTICE 3: **Your Soulmate Shopping List and Soulmate Statement**

Think deeply and honestly about what's most important to you in a partner and then make your own *Soulmate Shopping List*. Record the list in a journal, *The Blast Off! Workbook,* or in the *Blastation* software at www.InteractiveLifeCoach.com.

What are all the qualities you want to have in a relationship, even if something might seem trivial to someone else? Only *you* know what you're attracted to and what your needs, desires and values are. It's time you get what you so beautifully deserve. **Do Not Write What You Don't Want.** By doing that, you would be still projecting energy out toward what you don't want. **Only List What You Do Want.** This will set your intention.

For example:

⋆ Is close to my age.

★ Loves to travel.

★ Is good with children.

★ Is ready for a relationship.

★ Etc., etc.

If you have already been blessed with finding your soulmate, your relationship can continue to grow and evolve. A tool to help you do this is the *Big Picture Vision* for your relationship, what I call the *Soulmate Statement.* Your Soulmate Statement will be a story about the two of you enjoying the current state that you would like to be in. By describing you and your partner in this ideal state, you will begin to make shifts in your relationship without having to do or say anything. Read your Soulmate Statement every day, see and feel yourself and your partner in this positive state, and watch the changes unfold!

If you're actively looking for your soulmate, your next step is to also write a *Soulmate Statement* in your journal, *The Blast Off! Workbook,* or in the *Blastation* software. (There is also a *Big Picture Vision Board* form in the back of this book that you can use.) Address how you would like to be together. Include how you would act toward one another, where the two of you would go, what you would do, etc. As mentioned above, this represents the *Big Picture Vision* of your relationship. ✪

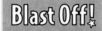 **Blast Off!** | PRACTICE 4: **Walk a Thousand Miles for the One You Love**

Write Your *Mile Steps* for Your Larger Relationship Goals

Review your *Big Picture Vision* (Soulmate Statement) for your desired relationship. From this broad picture, write out your major relationship goals (*Mile Steps*), such as marriage, children, values, and the activities you'd like to share (travel, archeology, rollerblading and bird watching). From these major goals, you will create your smaller *Mini Feats* steps. (There are forms in the back of the book that will help you chart this all out.)

Based on the *Mile Steps* above, your *Mini Feats* could be, take an archeology class, sign up for a bird-watching retreat, go to a bookstore and study the travel magazines, and enjoy an afternoon of rollerblading with a friend. (From experience, I recommend learning how to use the brakes on those things before hitting the road with a date. Just picture an out–of- control rollerblader crashing into a hot dog stand in Manhattan's Central Park. It wasn't pretty.) You are more apt to meet someone when you are partaking in an activity that you enjoy, rather than one you don't. So get busy. Your loved one is waiting! ✪

Settling... That Fateful, Yet Common *Faux Pas*

Can you relate to this scenario? A potential partner comes along who has some of the qualities you desire, but there are some glaring differences that raise those telltale red flags from the beginning. Still, you try to ignore them. I often thought that if I could blend a little bit of Jerry and a bit of Dennis I would have the perfect guy. Instead, I would settle for Jerry and spend time wondering why he wasn't like Dennis.

> "You don't marry someone you can live with—You marry the person you cannot live without."
>
> ~Unknown

I have many clients who come to me complaining about their relationships, and when we break down the issues, it's apparent that one or both individuals have settled for one reason or another. Below are the common reasons that people settle:

★ "There probably is no one better out there, so even though he forgets my birthday and criticizes me all the time, I better just stay."

★ "I would probably not attract anyone better so I should just stay even though I am so lonely."

★ "There's no such thing as a soulmate or an ideal match."

★ "He is only mean to me a few times a week."

★ "If my partner would stop drinking, she would be a wonderful."

★ "Maybe he'll change if I just keep trying."

★ "I get so frustrated that she doesn't like to join me. Oh, well. I guess I can give up enjoying the outdoors."

★ "I chose the wrong partner but now I don't want to deal with the up-heaval of leaving. So I just get my intimate needs met outside of the relationship."

I'm not saying that a relationship cannot grow and thrive if every single aspect of both partners is not a match. As I shared in the story of my girlfriend Susan's marriage, a relationship can work well with some important differences if many other core elements and attractions are present. However, if you have to convince yourself that you really don't need those elements that you honestly do need, then you may be settling for your second, third, fourth or even fifth best. I just know from my own personal experience, and from the experiences of my clients, we can talk ourselves into situations that we know are not right from the beginning because we feel, at a core level, that we either do not deserve someone better or that that person just doesn't exist.

Blast Off! PRACTICE 5: What Do You Give Up in Relationships?

Do you enjoy reading, but choose partners who prefer to watch television? Do you love boating, but you choose partners who dislike the water? Are you a romantic but choose partners who think romance is "Hey Baby, what's for dinner?"

In your journal or workbook, make a list of the desires, needs, interests and philosophies that you tend to give up in relationships and then regret later. By making a list of the things that you feel are important, you can start to be aware of your choices and actions. Then you can create new intentions for a relationship that fits your ideal picture. ✪

> "Joy is a net of love by which you catch souls. A joyful heart is the inevitable result of a heart burning with love."
>
> ~Mother Teresa of Calcutta, Humanitarian, advocate for the poor, winner of a Nobel Peace Prize (1910-1997)

Your Soulmate Needs an Open Door

Is it possible that your soulmate has not arrived because there hasn't been room for him or her to enter? You may think that you are open and ready, but is your heart wide open, too?

If you have experienced pain in past relationships, you may carry armor around your heart in an effort to keep it safe and protected. The truth is that the more you close your heart, the less love you will receive, and that will only cause you to close your heart even more. This is all well and good if you are content in living alone. But if you desire love, and I believe you do, then it is time to unveil your beautiful, passionate, lovely heart. Just because you were hurt in the past doesn't mean it needs to happen again. Especially if you're taking good notes now. Don't continue to bring a sad past into the future. It's time to attract what you deserve—*true love*.

Blast Off! PRACTICE 6: Open Your Heart to Receive that Supersonic Love

Get into a quiet space or go to your *Inspiration Station*. Sit down and then take some deep breaths until you are feeling calm and relaxed. If soft music and candles help you get into the mood, add these to your environment.

Now when you inhale, visualize a golden light coming into your body from the crown of your head and see it flowing all the way down to your toes. Feel it as the warmth and the sparkling light nurtures all the organs and systems of your body.

After a few minutes, focus on your heart area. Now put your right hand over your heart and continue to inhale and exhale this golden light. Then as you inhale, only focus on your heart area and visualize a soft, pink, loving energy coming into your heart. Feel your heart opening fully and allowing this pink energy to fill it completely and fully with love.

If you have had pain in your heart due to loss or heartbreak, visualize the tears of your heart pouring out as the pain begins to release and subside. Fill any emotional wounds with this pink loving energy. See your wound healing as your heart is surrounded with love. Continue to inhale and exhale deeply.

After another minute or two, visualize the pink energy turning into red, passionate, vibrant energy that is continuing to fill up your ever-expanding, open heart. Now feel that love and passion spread from your heart to the rest of your body, up to your head and down through your torso and legs, and through to the bottom of your toes. Feel how wonderful, light, free and uplifting this love energy feels. Continue to experience the opening of your heart.

Now I want you to expand this loving energy inside your heart and the rest of your body out to the world and to the Universe. See it expanding for miles and miles. Oh, how lucky the world is to experience your love! Now feel the love coming right back into your heart and hold it there.

Your heart is now open and ready to receive love.

Repeat this exercise at least twice a week to continue healing and opening your heart so that you may receive all the love you deserve. ✪

Whatever You Believe Becomes Your Truth

If you believe that your soulmate doesn't exist, then he or she will most likely not appear. If you believe that you don't deserve any better, then most likely you will not choose any better. Until I was completely honest with myself and gave myself permission to ask for what I wanted, the right match didn't appear.

* ★ **Awareness is key**.

* ★ **Making a list** helps you to focus on your ideal vision.

* ★ The most important element of all is: **To believe it can and will happen**!

I had come to my truth. I knew what I wanted and I was ready to manifest my soulmate into my life. The power came from a belief that I always carried in my heart and soul… *that true love was possible and would be mine for the taking.*

Proclaiming and Envisioning Mr. or Ms. Right

Once I finished my list, I spent some time reading it out loud with passion. I understood enough about energy and intention from the manner that I had used this before to attract all the magnificent elements into my career, personal life, financial state, health and spiritual life. I had witnessed in my own experience, time and time again, that if I projected my knowingness and deep belief that whatever I sought was out there somewhere, this "whatever" would be coming to me soon. So I projected this same energy out into the Universe in regard to my soulmate. I knew that if I transmitted any thoughts of doubt or pessimism, or if I continued to settle for not-a-match relationships, my dream man would not appear. It was crucial that I do the following:

> "Given the idea that we are all one, we should make a great team."
>
> ~Allison Maslan

* ★ Stay true to my list.
* ★ Send my thoughts of him out to the Universe as frequently as possible.
* ★ Set my intention by committing to a date that he would arrive by.
* ★ Take an action that would open me up to meeting him.
* ★ Believe, without a shadow of a doubt, that he would appear.

You know that meeting your soulmate is around the corner. Now it's time to proclaim it to be true to those you can trust to be supportive.

Sharing My Intention with Trusting and Supportive Souls

The day that I wrote my list of qualities for my soulmate, I also e-mailed the following note to seven of my closest girlfriends:

May 20, 2005

Dear Susan, Kelly, Mary, Cindy, Dahlia, Bara and Lori:

Just wanted you all to know that I am going to meet my soulmate by August 12, 2005, and we will be getting married one year from then.

Love, Allie

These were friends who knew me well and whom I trusted to support me in my quest. They also knew from my past experiences that when I set my mind and my intention to something, it almost always came true.

Remember to discern who you share your intention with. You want to protect your space from any negative energy that can be a catalyst for unwanted and unnecessary doubt or fear.

Blast Off! PRACTICE 7: Set Your Intention with a Letter

Write your Letter of Intention and set a deadline date for manifesting your relationship. You don't have to send the letter to anyone for it to work; however, it is a good idea if you can. That will keep you account-able to your word, and you will not only receive the rewards of your own intention, you will also receive the power of your support team. ✪

Action, the Mother of Intention

I never had problems meeting guys. Meeting *the right one* had been the challenge. This time, I decided to take action using a different method, online dating. I had always avoided the online dating services because I kept imagining that I would meet him in the grocery store, or smash into him on Highway 101. Since I don't cook that much and I'm not a speed racer, maybe those were the reasons these methods never worked for me?

This time I was seriously shopping for my soulmate. Therefore, the idea of reading the backgrounds of the men online before dating them sounded like a viable approach.

So I logged on and filled out a long and detailed questionnaire about my personality, interests, beliefs, values, shoe size, blood type and first pet's name. Just kidding. But the end result was a very honest, nothing-but-the-truth account of me, and what I absolutely, completely, totally, fully and finally wanted in a man and a relationship. I knew I would have a much better chance of meeting my match if I spilled my guts to all of hu-**man**-ity.

Then I waited....

Soon my e-mail box started to fill up. The responses ranged from marriage proposals, to, "Hey Cutie," to, "Looking for a Boy Toy?" I decided that the best way to go about this would be to meet the men who were interesting possibilities for coffee or a drink rather than for an entire lunch or dinner. My schedule was already pretty full between work and parenting commitments.

Over the next two and a half months, I met with nine different e-men. I know that this may not be the best practice, but I pretty much knew whether I was interested to pursue a next date after talking to them for thirty minutes or less. Others may dispute this, but I felt that if it deserved further exploration I would know. I told them all from the get-go that I was looking for my soulmate. I figured that if this statement scared them off, I would prefer to know now rather than later. The process was interesting, sometimes frustrating, but I met several really nice men. And what about the others?

Well, one of the e-men was still angry at his wife (who left him twenty years ago) as he talked about this the entire time we sat across the table from each other. Another one was ten years younger than me, which was flattering, but I really wanted a partner close to my age so that we could share a lot of the same history, music and nostalgia of our era. I also liked the idea of growing older *with* someone. Another man was really into me until I told him that I owned my own house and ran my own business.

One man talked the whole time about how he was lost in his life and trying to find his way. Another guy looked twenty years older than the picture he had posted on his profile.

I started getting extremely picky with each e-mail and profile that I reviewed.

If they had too many misspellings, delete. If I did not like how they dressed, delete. I know this may sound shallow to you, but these were issues that I knew might bother me later on... so why let it slide now?

I did start seeing one of the e-men, Jordan. He had a great personality, good sense of humor, was attractive, and kept very physically active as a volleyball player. After five or six dates, I realized that even though he had some wonderful qualities, and there was chemistry, there were many things missing from my list. Jordan was not very spiritual, he preferred to stay home rather than go out, he was feeling stuck in his career and he was a bit older. I did enjoy his company, but I knew if I continued to date Jordan, I might get too emotionally connected and end up settling. We all know that I had come too far to let that happen again.

The Energetic Art of Actualizing

I continued to meditate on my *Soulmate Statement* and I would visualize my dream man being next to me while I was working, riding in the car, out having fun, and going to sleep at night. I knew that I needed to continue to state my intention, feel and breathe his presence into my space, and believe with all the cells in my body that he would appear very soon.

Blast Off! PRACTICE 8: **Bringing Your Soulmate into Your Space**

Each morning and night, pull out your *Soulmate Statement* and read it out loud. Ask yourself if there is anything you are holding back or something that could be blocking your match from coming into your loving space.

★ Are you holding onto an unhealthy, going-nowhere relationship? Are you projecting self-doubt onto your intention?

★ Are you placing yourself into situations and places where you could meet new people, such as joining athletic activities groups, church groups, career networking groups, online dating services, alerting your friends that you are available, etc.?

Now see him or her coming to you and holding your hand as you do your daily activities. Come to know the feel of your soulmate's energy in your everyday life. See your soulmate with you as if he or she is already here. See them coming to you, feel their presence, and believe it to be true. ✪

In the Meantime...

By now, I had received two e-mails from a guy named Mike. His profile seemed very intriguing and he had a good sense of humor. He was an Aries, like myself, and seemed to have a similar zest for life. However, his profile was full of misspelled words! Being the writer that I am, seeing the spelling errors was like fingernails on a chalkboard. I am no perfectionist, and if you came to my house, you would see how easygoing I am. However, when it comes to grammar, I am a snob. I never responded to Mike's second e-mail, and two weeks later, around the first of August, I received a third e-mail from him. It read like this:

> "Love is composed of a single soul inhabiting two bodies."
>
> ~Aristotle,
> Greek philosopher
> (384-322 BC)

Dear Allie:

I really feel that we would make a great match. If you're interested, give me a call and we can meet for coffee.

Sincerely, Mike

Meeting "The One"

I have to say that I was pretty impressed with Mike's straightforward, no-nonsense, let's-get-together style. The fact that he had attempted to reach me two times before and had not given up-showed me that he had perseverance and determination. Also, in this e-mail, there were no misspelled words! Mike left his number so I called him about meeting.

We had a brief phone conversation and set a date to meet for coffee. Mike and I picked Thursday, August 4, 2005. On Wednesday (the day before), I was in the Starbucks that I had gone to every morning for the past four years. As I was waiting for my chai tea, I noticed a man in line who looked like the "Mike" who I was to meet the next morning. I wasn't sure, though, so I felt uncomfortable introducing myself. As I picked up my tea from the counter and turned around to walk out the door, this man looked in my direction at the very same instant. We caught eyes and for a nanosecond, our glance was locked. I kid you not, my breath stopped and my heart skipped a beat. At that point I was completely dumbstruck. I walked out the door in an unusual fog and drove off to work.

The next morning, I went to the Java Depot coffee house in Solana Beach and there was the guy that I had locked eyes with the day before. Mike said with a warm smile, "I knew that was you. I even walked outside looking for you, but you were already gone."

We talked for an hour or so, and Mike made me laugh several times. I was listening intently to every word. I enjoyed his demeanor, his smile, and his uplifting energy.

For the next month, Mike and I went out once or twice a week. Each time we got together, he would reveal another side of his personality. Once Mike began to relax around me even more, his sense of humor came pouring through. He was hilarious, and I found myself laughing out loud quite often. I also saw his spiritual side when, on one date, Mike told me how he loved meditating at the beach and that he loved the movie, *What the Bleep Do We Know!?* so much that he had seen it *three times*. This had become a popular movie about the energetic messages we project and receive. (My ex, Taylor, had fallen asleep in that movie, so Mike had just scored bonus points.) Mike was a total gentleman and loved to go dining, dancing, biking and scuba diving. He was extremely easy to be around, and the more time I spent with him, the more attracted I became.

As I relaxed around him, some of my quirkiness began to sneak out. Mike learned that, although I am completely focused in my work and responsibilities, I am a complete klutz and have absolutely no sense of direction. Whenever we were out together, I would inevitably spill something across the table, bump my head, trip and fall as we walked down the street, or get lost when I was supposed to meet him somewhere. He so aptly and lovingly named this embarrassing part of my nature, my "Allie-isms." The quality that I tried most to hide (because it really had annoyed other men) became one of my most attractive features *to Mike.*

He had operated his own wholesale office-furniture company for twelve years. Mike loved what he did for work and had built a good, honest reputation within the industry. His years of commitment now afforded him the time to travel, which he loves to do. Mike told me that he always wanted to go to Greece, visit South America, experience an African safari, and travel to Prague and Budapest, but he had been waiting for the right woman to share these experiences with.

He also revealed a darker side of his past. Mike told me that he had become sober from alcohol nine years before. He had been a functioning alcoholic, but the substance abuse had kept him from living the life he knew he deserved and was capable of. From the day he quit drinking, Mike looked forward rather than backward. After that time, he spent the next few years getting to know who he was without the shield of vodka. Mike said that he appreciates life so much more now because he knew what pain and loneliness felt like, and he was so thankful that he was given a second chance. He also felt that it was meant to be that we had not met back then, because it would have never worked.

Interestingly enough, Mike and I had lived very close to one another for the past ten years. We shopped at the same grocery story and even lived on the same street a few years back. The timing was just not right for either of us, until now.

Mike had to experience his "dark night of the soul," a time of going through the darkness, to ultimately experience the light. It was no coincidence that I had also done the same through relationships instead of a substance. I understood then that it had been necessary for me to go through all the heartache and angst to finally realize the power of my inner strength, embrace my passionate self, and learn that I held the key to my destiny.

Your Friends Know Best

For the very first time in my life, I experienced what it was like to fall completely and wholly in love with a man who was my match on every single level. I even introduced him to each of my girlfriends. He finally caught on after the fourth one that they needed to give their stamp of approval for this relationship to fly.

I know that may sound unnecessary, but I had ignored my friends' warnings in the past because I thought, "How could they know what's best for me?" Yet they did know me well and I had learned the hard way that, although ultimately it was my decision, their opinions carried weight. They were also tired of seeing me go through the rough patches.

> "I have learned not to worry about love; but to honor its coming with all my heart."
>
> ~Alice Walker,
> Author of The Color Purple and In Search of Our Mothers' Gardens

As I knew would be the case, they not only liked Mike, they loved him. In fact, my girlfriend, Dahlia, a very intuitive woman, turned to Mike after ten minutes of dinner and said, "I like you." Mary, another close girlfriend, said, "Allison, you completely manifested this guy." I replied, "Yes, I know."

Soulmate Manifested

The rest is history. One year later (as I had written in my intention letter), on August 27, 2006, Mike and I were married. These are the vows that we wrote for one another:

My Wedding Vows to Mike: *Mike, I've been searching for you, my one true love, for as long as I can remember. You are the one I have always dreamed of and more. A year ago, I finally became clear on the kind of man that could be my ultimate partner, and as fate would have it, you magically appeared. I have never felt so loved and experienced so much joy as I do with you. I love the way you appreciate all sides of me, even Allie-isms. And how you bring me back to center when my world goes a little sideways.*

When I am sad, you move my tears to laughter. When I am overwhelmed, you help me find the ground, and when I'm angry or frustrated, you help me get out of my own way to find the truth. To spend the rest of my days with my soulmate is a gift for which I will be forever grateful. Even though we are a lot alike in our Aries fire, I recognize and embrace our differences. I promise to walk beside you forever as a partner, your lover, your best friend and your confidant. I will hold your hands through the moments of bliss, and not walk away in moments of frustration or pain.

I give myself to you today, tomorrow, and through eternity.

Mike's Vows to Me (he calls me Boo): Boo, you have erased all doubts that there really is that one special person that could be my soulmate for eternity.

You continue to make me laugh, with your Allie-isms, and make me want to be a better person by the way you live your life. And you have opened my eyes to how to really love someone and be loved in return.

You're everything I've dreamed of; you're my best friend, my lover, my companion for life's journey. I will stand not in front or behind you, but by your side as equals in a loving and trusting partnership.

I promise, before all that have come to share this special day with us, that I'll be faithful, honest, forgiving, understanding, and will continue to love you during any troubles that life may present. I promise to grow with you spiritually and be the man you can be proud to say is your husband.

Will you take me with all my defects, to be your husband for the rest of your life?

Take It from Me...

I am living proof that true love and soulmates do exist. From the time I finally heard that message loud and clear, the path to a soulful relationship became easy. I had chosen relationships that were fraught with frustration and discord, because I didn't know any other way. Once I was with the right person, it was effortless, because we both wanted the same kind of love and relationship. No more coercing, convincing, or longing.

I could have chosen to ignore my *Soulmate Statement* and stayed with Jordan, the volleyball player. Then I would have been back at square one, kicking myself for not holding out for my match made in heaven. This time, I finally chose happiness.

I hope my story will save you from more grief than there needs to be. Just decide what you want in a partner and a relationship. It's important to consider both.

In summary, here are the steps to manifesting your own soulmate:

★ Have fun with the heart-centered practices in this chapter.

★ Set your intention by creating your *Soulmate Shopping List* and *Soulmate Statement* (this will be your *Big Picture Vision* for Chapter Five).

★ Envision yourself in the relationship of your dreams.

★ Set your *Miles Steps* for long-range relationship goals, such as marriage, travel with your partner, and activities and values that you want to share with them.

★ Take action by creating your *Mini Feats* (three a day takes the loneliness away) and bring that love to life. *Mini Feats* that match the *Miles Steps* above might be: (1) to work on a profile for an online dating service and make sure that the write-up includes your favorite activities and indicates your values, (2) join an activity group for one or more of your interests, such as golf, dancing, chess, scuba diving, politics, theatre, etc., and (3) buy some travel magazines with pictures of your dream ports of call to use in creating your Relationship *Big Picture Vision Board*.

★ Watch the energy shift and the love begin to flow!

For Those of You Who Are Already with Your Match

Intention and action can also be applied to an already existing relationship that may need some reconnection or sprucing up. You may have all the elements you need for a fulfilling, soulful relationship, but for one reason or another, the bond has lulled a bit.

You can apply the same exercises to your partner:

★ Focus on what you do want to manifest in your existing relationship.

★ Send an intention by visualizing and feeling the way you'd like your relationship to be, rather than focusing on what is wrong or not there.

★ Take action by treating your partner the way you would like to be treated.

If this is the right relationship for you, and it is meant to be, your bond will be renewed through intention and action. If your partner is open, and can feel and experience your *Blast Off!* frequency and effort, he or she will reciprocate with like loving energy.

> "We are all born for love. It's the principle of existence, and its only end."
>
> ~Benjamin Disraeli,
> *British politician and author*
> *(1804-1881)*

BLAST OFF! Daily Launch Tools

1. Each morning, write your *Sun-Up Script* and *Rocket Words*.

2. Read your *Rocket Words* to yourself and out loud as often as possible during your day.

3. Create and perform a minimum of *Mini Feats* each day. (These are the smaller steps for moving toward your larger *Mile Step* goals and your *Big Picture Vision*.) For example, today's *Mini Feats* might be:

■ *Check out the online dating service my friends have been talking about. (Online dating doesn't have to provide the stereotypically bad experience you might have in your head. It's a great way to get to know a person who you may never have had the opportunity of meeting otherwise. In fact, you can use the service to invite "The One" into your life.)*

■ *Put all my ex-partners' photos in a box. Write a* Sun-Up Script *about releasing these relationships to the past to make room for the new and improved one. (If you do this* Mini Feat, *describe all the appreciation you feel for having experienced these past connections and any life lessons you may have learned.)*

■ *Read a book on feng shui to create an inviting area in my home for love to arrive.*

4. Choose one to two *Blast Off! Practices* from this chapter to do each day over the next week.

5. Fill out your *Weekly Flight Assessment Log* to review your week's progress toward realizing your *Supersonic Life*.

Summary of the Chapter Concepts

➤ Relationships give us the opportunity to face our issues, and ultimately heal from them. This might not happen as much when you're alone.

➤ The Boomerang Principle: Your unconscious and unspoken energy is still projected to the world even if you're not expressing it outwardly. Whatever you project, whether you are aware of it or not, will come right back to you in some way.

➤ Get in touch with your inner language and look at what you are *not* saying with words, but are saying with energy.

➤ Who are you under all of your adopted or suppressive behaviors? What is your true identity? You want a Soulmate who is attracted to *the real you*.

➤ Opposites attract, but can they live happily ever after? It is so much easier to bond and grow with someone of like energy who has similar tastes, interests, values and philosophies.

➤ Write out your *Soulmate Shopping List* and *Soulmate Statement*. Who do you want your soulmate to be? What qualities are most important to you? What do you want in a relationship? Do not waver in your choice of your ultimate partner.

➤ Have you settled for less in a relationship because you were afraid that you would not find anyone better? In your heart, you may know that you settle, but you haven't found the courage to ask for more. What do you give up of yourself in relationships, and then feel resentful later? Once you make the decision to receive what you deserve, state what you truly want, and stop settling or suppressing your true desires. The Universe will give you what you ask for.

➤ State your intention regarding the arrival of your soulmate and send it to your friends as a statement of purpose. Set a date to make a commitment to yourself and your soulmate.

➤ Actualize your soulmate by projecting your intention and then breathing in his or her presence and love as often as possible.

"There is no remedy for love but to love more."

~Henry David Thoreau,
American author, Transcendentalist,
naturalist and philosopher
(1817-1862)

CHAPTER 6

BLAST Off!
to New Heights for a Healthy Body and Mind

"He who has health has hope; and he who has hope has everything."

~Arabian proverb

It was 5:30 P.M. and I was feeling harried and overwhelmed as I raced from my advertising agency, The Barali Group, to daycare to get my little girl. I had not eaten anything since that morning because I was on a major deadline to get an ad campaign ready to present to one of our biggest clients. Come to think of it, this routine had been just regular life for the past few years. If I wasn't at the office, I was running somewhere between home, daycare, client appointments and work, later arriving back home just in time to cook dinner and spend time with my daughter. Once she fell asleep, I was up into the night creating commercials and print ads. Sleep was an unnecessary luxury, while the career expectations I had set for myself were driving me into the ground.

As I write this, I feel sad for the twenty-something autopilot of a woman that I had become while I was running on a chaotic hamster wheel of life. What should have been a glorious coming-into-my-own phase was instead over-the-top serious, stressful and psychotic!

On that particular late afternoon, I was Empty Allie (see Chapter Two for background on this "Emptiness Syndrome"), with my body racing one way and my head spinning in the opposite direction. When I pulled into the driveway of the daycare center, I threw the car into park and jumped out of the driver's seat. My objective was cut short when I received a split-second wake-up call as my car began rolling down the driveway. This would not have been so memorable except that as my Ford Taurus was moving backwards, I was still between the inside of the car door and the seat. Without thinking (which is not a practice I recommend), I reached into the car to push the stick-shift back into park, but the momentum and weight of the car had another agenda.

> "Health is a state of complete physical, mental and social well-being, and not merely the absence of disease or infirmity."
>
> ~The World Health Organization's definition of health

It was like I was watching the experience from a short distance away. My mind was still thinking, "I've got to pick up my daughter," while my body was being pulled underneath the car. The car door, moving backwards, knocked me most of the way to the ground but trapped me in the corner where the door meets the car. My legs continued to be pulled under the car and the front tires literally ran over my thighs. But my torso was still caught in the door as the car continued dragging me backwards fifty feet down the driveway and into the street. In my terror, I could see that the next thing that was going to happen was that the bottom of the door would run across my face. I let out a blood-curdling scream like Jamie Lee Curtis in Halloween. And just as I was about to lose my career, my family and my life, the most amazing thing happened. The street abruptly inclined, which knocked my car to a screeching halt. I remember the strangest hush, quieter than silence, that permeated the neighborhood. An eerie vision of myself in a wheelchair popped into my head as I wondered, "Am I really alive? Do my legs still work?" I panicked and jumped out from under the car, and looked down to find my legs were still in one piece. I went running into the daycare center wearing my favorite suit from Nordstrom's Savvy Department, an outfit which was now ripped to shreds and covered in grease. The next part I don't remember. It is what I've been told happened. In complete shock, I barreled toward the doors of the daycare center scaring everyone as I burst in screaming, "I need pain pills!" The daycare director, Gracie, rushed me to the hospital, and as the adrenaline began to wear off, the pain set in. I had broken my collarbone in two places in the accident and adopted two new tattoos, lovely black tire-tracks embedded into my thighs.

As I sat in the hospital waiting for my then husband to pick me up, I remember thinking, *"What the hell am I doing to my body? What the hell am I doing with my life?"* I had completely taken my health for granted as I was racing after some meaningless, never-ending destination. This scene was merely the opening act for my one-woman show titled "Complete Breakdown," which ultimately led me on a search for wholeness.

Looking back, I realize that I needed a major wake-up call (maybe not such a dramatic one) to place me on my path to a healthy body and mind.

Over the past several years, I have had the opportunity to help many men and woman that were on this same one-way track to No-wheres-ville. By the time they showed up at my door, they were ready for a positive change.

The Blast Off! Principles for Health

We often take our health for granted until there is a reason to give it some attention. When acute pain or chronic symptoms arise, all of a sudden our health, which we may never have given a second thought, shoots to the forefront of our consciousness. If we are younger, and lucky enough to not experience any serious ailments, we may assume our good health will continue. And as we age, if we don't treat our body-mind with care, prevention and maintenance, the systems of our body can begin to break down and become more vulnerable and susceptible to weakness and disease.

Millions of Americans suffer from poor health conditions that can be prevented or improved.

* 13.5 million people have coronary heart disease.

* 1.5 million people suffer from a heart attack in a given year.

* 8 million people have adult-onset (non-insulin-dependent) diabetes.

* 95,000 people are newly diagnosed with colon cancer each year.

* 250,000 people suffer from hip fractures each year.

* 50 million people have high blood pressure.

* Over 60 million people are overweight.

There are usually many factors that come into play and contribute to the onset of these ailments, and that's why the whole picture of a person should be considered when addressing one's health.

The suggestions that I offer in this chapter are by no means a replacement for any current medical treatment by your M.D. However, these complementary healing modalities are very effective adjuncts to support and enhance your care. Refer to the resource section at the back of this book for further information on holistic adjunct therapies.

Your Body-Mind

When I discuss the body in this chapter, I often refer to it as the body-mind because I look at a human being (or an animal, for that matter) as one total unit, rather than separate parts of a unit. All of our organs and systems directly affect and influence one another. For instance, the gall bladder affects the liver, which has an impact on the endocrine system (hormones, thyroid, adrenals), which affects our moods and our energy level.

The *Blast Off! Program* incorporates a holistic point of view on healing because every part of your life affects and influences every other part of your life. For instance, financial worries can promote physical changes in the body that may lead to health issues. Meanwhile, it is clearly true that health impacts everything. When your body feels strong, it is much easier to focus, and your mood is uplifted and calm rather than frustrated and stressed. You are able to see and receive the abundance of life, rather than walking around seeing your life as that half-empty glass. By the same token, when your body is tired, weak and in pain, it's difficult to see and appreciate life's simple beauty and the opportunities that may be sitting right at your feet. When you're in pain, or feeling depressed, anxious, fearful or angry, it's hard to get motivated to find or connect with your sense of purpose and passion.

In Deepak Chopra's book, *Quantum Healing*, he explains that every cell in the body regenerates itself. The lifespan of red blood cells, for instance, is approximately thirty-seven days. Even brain cells have the capacity to regenerate. Nerve cells, he mentions, take the longest to renew. In fact, within a seven-year period, the body can create a completely new body of cells. Poor health is limiting, but the good news (as Deepak's observation suggests) is that we can improve our health and well-being at any time, at any age of our lives.

> "The time to relax is when you don't have time for it."
> ~Sydney J. Harris, Journalist and author (1917-1986)

In this chapter, I will share some powerful *Blast Off! Body-Mind Tools* that embody the essence of prevention and maintenance of your health and vitality, so that you can have the freedom to choose a full and vibrant life. The bottom line is that *health is freedom*—the freedom to move, to sing, to aspire and to grow.

Blast Off! Body-Mind Tools

* Eliminating and shifting your stress triggers
* Rejuvenating breathing techniques
* Energy work to remove blocks and open energy pathways
* Healing your vital force or chi
* Protecting and strengthening your energetic shield
* Exercise: health in action
* Homeopathy: energy medicine
* Releasing the negative drain of suppressed emotions
* Utilizing the power of good news
* Nutrition: heal your body with healthy food
* And a few of my back-pocket health secrets

"Don't Bother Me. I'm Stressed!"

Life can be stressful at times, no question. And too much stress with no support to counteract its often harsh energy can have detrimental effects on the body and the psyche. On the other hand, when your body-mind is feeling nourished, sound and resilient, the stress will not create such a serious impact or have chronic implications. In my harrowing car accident, my biological "fight-or-flight" stress response literally saved my legs. My stress hormones, including adrenaline, norepinephrine and cortisol, raced through my bloodstream, giving me the strength to uphold the weight of a 3,500-pound automobile on my 110-pound frame. (By the way, the tire tracks went away after one year.)

In everyday life, our bodies cannot make the distinction of whether the stress is a true life-threatening danger, just a work deadline, or a traffic jam. Repeated activation of the body's crisis-response system, without the support of consistent stress-releasing efforts and attention to rejuvenate and strengthen the body, can take a huge toll on our innate ability to heal.

In these times, stress is a reality of life for many people who face day-to-day challenges generated from a local to a global level. Our daily news should be more aptly titled, "What Went Wrong Today in Your Town and Around the World." If this is your reality and where you focus your attention, your body and mind are surely taking the heat.

Blast Off!	PRACTICE 1: **Take Your Stress-O-Meter Reading Down to Zero**

By taking a look at what triggers your stress responses, you can become more aware and actively prepared to take care of yourself in these instances. At those times, you can use your "Stress-O-Meter" (your inner sense of stress rising) to create strength, empowerment and resilience, and eventually learn how to avoid the trigger altogether.

Make a list in your journal or *The Blast Off! Workbook* of all the stress triggers in your life—those people, events or instances that take you from a calm, peaceful state to a condition of stress, chaos, agitation, or an array of negative emotions. For example, your boss, your workload, finances, your mother-in-law, the barking dog, your neighbor....

Once you have acknowledged your stressors, the next step is to examine your part in creating the stress. Taking responsibility will remove you from victim mode and empower you into choice mode. I realize that it takes two to tango, but you are 50 percent of the equation. **Is there something you can do to shift the energy?**

Some possibilities include:

> ★ Go to the gym on the way home from work to release your tension.
>
> ★ Journal your feelings to make some space in your crowded, spinning mind.
>
> ★ Start researching your dream career.
>
> ★ Go to the theatre to see a comedy movie.
>
> ★ Don't take your boss's ranting personally, since he most likely treats everyone that way.

> "Prana, the vital breath, is born of Self. Like a person and his shadow, the Self and the Prana are inseparable. Prana enters the body at birth, but does not die with the body."
>
> ~Prana Upanisad,
> a Hindu scripture of core teachings

I realize that it's not that easy to replace an overbearing mother-in-law, but you do have the power to decide how her actions and comments will affect you. If you can come up with some strategies to avoid, or initially reduce, your reaction to certain triggers prior to them happening, you'll be able to protect, deflect and shift your energy toward something much more positive. As a result, your healing energy will expand, rather than tense up and deflate. Whenever you take action, even a small step (such as a *Mini Feat*) to alleviate stress or change a negative circumstance in your life, you will begin to feel better *immediately*. Your positive intention and action create a universal momentum that will move you from feeling immobilized to back in the flow.

Now write down at least two possible strategies for each stressor in your life.

> **For example:** A difficult, complaining neighbor

> ★ Try to talk to them and come to a compromise.
>
> ★ If that doesn't work, before you completely lose your cool (which is pointless and will only create more stress), go deep within and conjure up some positive feelings and energy toward your neighbors, and then project this energy into the Universe.

Through the power of your intention, change will occur.

Breath: Your Connection to Life

You've heard it a thousand times, *"Breathe."* But are you doing it? Breathing is our first unconscious reflex as we enter this world, yet today we rarely notice our lungs expanding when we inhale oxygen (hopefully clean) and exhale carbon dioxide. You are obviously breathing to some degree, but most likely you tend to take shallow breaths. *Think about it.* Our breath is our connection to life. It is the most important food that we nourish our cells with.

Ancient yogis used breathing as a form of medicine called "pranayama breathing." This is practiced in the healing art of yoga. Prana means "life force" or "life energy." In the *Blast Off! Program*, breathing is compulsory. Meaning, to soar into the stars, you first need to be taking strong, clear and clean breaths from the depths of your gut. *Here we go.*

Blast Off! PRACTICE 2: Breathe, Baby, Breathe

When you find yourself under stress, overwhelmed, running late, dealing with conflict or in an emotionally challenging situation, your body tenses up. You start gripping the steering wheel or gritting your teeth while thinking about what terrible thing is going to happen because you messed up big-time. Panic may even set in. Heart palpitations, tension headaches, and stomach upsets are a few of the physical reactions that you might have encountered in a stressful moment. If this is your state much of the time, you can see where chronic physical conditions could arise. **Your first line of defense is to breathe.**

Here is a breathing exercise you can do first thing in the morning, at your desk at work, in your car, or during just about any stressful moment. (You might want to find a private space.) Basically, you'll be breathing the stress right out of your mouth.

1. Inhale through your nose.

2. Take the breath deep into your lungs.

3. Feel your chest expand, then your abdomen. (If you're only feeling your chest expand, you are not breathing deeply enough. Breathing more deeply may take some practice to feel natural.)

4. As you exhale through your mouth, feel your abdomen flatten again.

5. Focus your mind on the sound of your own inhalation and exhalation, and on the vital life energy replenishing your body, mind and spirit.

Squeeze in five slow deep breaths at a peak stress moment and your heart rate will drop significantly. Then your mind will begin to calm so you can focus and make clearer decisions.

Practice 2 Bonus: Sighing. The big *uhhhhhaaaaaa* is the sound that comes after taking in a much needed breath at a weary moment. If you find yourself sighing frequently, most likely you're not breathing deeply on a regular basis. It can also be a sign that you are suppressing some emotion right under your chest cavity. (That is where the heart lies.) Suppression is the opposite of expression. If you hold down your emotions on a regular basis, this can lead to an array of physical problems. I'll discuss emotional stuffing in just a bit. ✪

Release Your Energetic Blockages through Energy Work

"Energy work" is a general term for modalities based on the idea that the human body consists of energy fields which can be stimulated through various techniques in order to promote wellness. The concept of energy fields as a vital life force can be traced back to the oldest medical systems, and this life-force energy is known as *qi* (chi) in China, *ki* in Japan, and *prana* in India. There are many effective forms of energy bodywork, including:

* Acupuncture
* Shiatsu
* Healing Touch

* Reiki
* Bio-energetic Healing
* Jin Shin Jyutsu or Jin Shin Acutouch

During my major life transitions, such as leaving my marriage and changing careers, I explored many types of healing because of a newfound curiosity, wonderment and a personal quest to heal myself. My mentor at the time, Sid Wolf, Ph.D., a psychologist and gifted energetic and therapeutic healer, introduced me to the concept of energy work and told me about a powerful method of healing called Jin Shin Acutouch. One day, during one of our sessions, he said to me, "You have the energy of a natural, gifted healer. You need to be doing this work." It was at his urging, and from the introduction to different forms of healing modalities, including homeopathy and Jin Shin, that I was set on the course of being a healer.

Jin Shin is a form of Oriental medicine that evolved in the temples of Tibet, China and Japan. This powerful system of touch promotes emotional and physical healing. A Jin Shin practitioner will apply a light, gentle touch to specific points on the body to stimulate the body's own energy system. It is as if you are plugging into your electrical sockets to move the flow of energy that is stagnant in your body. By focusing on specific areas and organs, the energy opens up blockages that may be causing pain, stress or disease.

Energy work is so powerful and effective that many nurses in the Holistic Nurses Association nationwide are providing healing touch treatments to their patients.

Blast Off! | PRACTICE 3: **Jin Shin Acutouch Treatment**
(A Step-by-Step Self-Treatment)

Here's a treatment that you can give to yourself for immediate stress relief while sitting in your car or lying in bed at night. I use it all the time when I can't sleep, feel any physical pain, or just need to find calm in a stressful moment.

Jin Shin Balancing Exercise

1. Put your right hand on top of your head, palm down. Hold it there firmly until Step 6.

2. Put your left hand on your forehead. Hold it there for one minute.

3. Then place two fingers from your left hand under your nose so that the bottom finger rests at the top of your upper lip. Hold your fingers there for one minute.

4. Next, put your left hand on your chest for one minute.

5. Then position your left hand so that it covers your belly button and hold it there for one minute.

6. Then position your left hand so that it is on your pubic bone and continue to hold it there as you move your right hand under your tailbone.

7. Hold these last points for one minute.

You may already feel calmer by the time you get halfway through the exercise. Try it at bedtime and you may fall asleep before you finish. ✪

"I'll Take Ease Over Dis-Ease, Please"

The word "ease" means effortlessness, simplicity, comfort. The state of "dis-ease" is one of struggle, difficulty and discomfort in one or all levels of the body. The common denominators for most of my non-well clients are an ongoing internal suppression of emotions, such as repressed grief, anger, resentment, regret or fear; a toxic external environment, such as pollution, chemical exposure or substance abuse; or an acute

> "The important point to remember is that the concept of our body as a fixed, frozen sculpture in time is fictitious. What we think of as our solid body is really just patterns of intelligence briefly precipitating into tangible sensations. The reduction of reality to material properties is a myth. We are not physical creatures having intelligent thought; we are, in truth, the very intelligence which generates this physical experience."
>
> ~Deepak Chopra, M.D., Author of Ageless Body, Timeless Mind, *and leader in the field of mind-body medicine*

or chronic emotional stress that may stem from challenging personal or professional relationships, careers, issues of low-self esteem or loss.

Even though you may be predisposed to certain health issues due to hereditary factors, this does not mean you have to repeat the pattern. When the body-mind maintains balance and strength, you'll be a lot less likely to manifest disease. And if you do, the symptoms may appear on a much milder level.

Your Invisible Shield

Your body is your energetic temple. Imagine that you are a rare and precious container holding a complex combination of molecules and atoms. Surrounding your energy field is an invisible shield that protects you from negative outside influences, such as viruses, over-stimulation from loud noises, smells and bright lights, and outside emotional input such as criticism or anger. When your shield is strong, these outside forces may come toward you, and even surround you, but they will not enter your precious container because your healthy energetic shield is at work deflecting and protecting you from harm.

Your body also has its own self-regulators and protectors, such as eyelashes to screen your eyes from airborne foreign substances, perspiration and nasal discharge to release toxins, and fevers to give increased resistance to infections. When your resistance is weaker due to influences of an ongoing emotional or physical stress or a trauma, these self-regulators are not as responsive and protective, and you are more susceptible to the latest flu, or worse, the development of a chronic health issue. Also, in this compromised state, your energetic shield may be less likely to prevent any outside stimulus from entering your precious temple—creating unrest, chaos and illness.

For instance, with a vulnerable energetic shield, the following could occur. Loud noises may penetrate your body, triggering head pain or anxiety. Strong smells may be experienced in an intensified manner, creating nausea. Emotional upsets that normally roll off your back may impede you at a core level, throwing you momentarily off track or, worse, into a state of depression.

A good example: If you're a parent of a teenager who is rebellious—basically acting mean, rude and self-centered—you can react in one of two ways:

1. **If your shield is strong and grounded**, you will not take the teen's words and actions personally because you understand that this is part of their natural growth process, and you will be able to calmly and clearly set strong boundaries, letting them know that their behavior is unacceptable and will not be tolerated. As a result, your child will be more likely to respect you and abide by your rules and requests.

2. **If your shield is off balance and vulnerable**, you will take great offense to their teenage-itis and feel deeply hurt and offended. Then you will start screeching back at them in the same manner or worse. We both know where that leads. *Nowhere!* If this continues over a long period of time without practices to release and revive your emotional state, this ongoing low level of anger or sadness, with the occasional spikes of rage, may begin to weaken your immune system and create a whole host of not-so-fun stuff.

The good news is that your temple and your energetic shield can be fortified and healthfully maintained by implementing some simple yet powerful daily practices. Just because the Moroccan or Lithuanian flu is visiting a neighborhood near you doesn't mean that you have to invite it to dinner. A balanced body-mind can keep on doing its healthy thing, even when those around you are not quite so fortified.

Envisioning and Actualizing Your Health

There are many ways to protect and expand your healthy energy field. For instance, you can use the same principles of intention and action that we have utilized in previous chapters to improve your health. By closing your eyes and visualizing a healthy, happy body-mind for a few minutes every day, you will begin to vibrate at that healthy, happy level. And then to bring this healthy, happy energy into your physical and emotional being, you *must* move your intention into action.

"There's no easy way out. If there were, I would have bought it. And believe me, it would be one of my favorite things."

~*Oprah Winfrey,*
TV talk show host, actress
and philanthropist

Here's an example. It's great to envision yourself exercising, but it's obviously a much more powerful combination to see and experience your heart pumping, your lungs expanding and your body perspiring.

The benefits of exercise are numerous and I'm sure you've heard them many times. However, I cannot discuss the path of a healthy body and mind without stressing the importance of exercise and fitness. Remember in Chapter One, "*Blast Off! to a Life of Passion and Meaning,*" when I talked about rejuvenating the "back end of passion?" By integrating exercise into your routine at least five days a week, you will incrementally increase your capacity to be creative, and generate the surplus energy that it's going to take to develop your *Big Picture Vision* for all areas of your life.

Move That Body

As I mentioned earlier, I was very athletic as a child. When I got married and went through some rough times in my twenties, I stopped moving my body beyond what it took to get through the day. I worked long hours, and about the only exercise I did was to carry my daughter around, and walk back and forth to the car from wherever I was. One weekend, I went skiing with some friends—something I had not done in years. After three short runs, I was huffing and puffing and completely short of breath. I couldn't believe how hard it was for me to get my body moving. I remember thinking, "How pathetic is this!"

As I began to make drastic changes in my personal life and career, exercise became my physical and emotional therapy. Yes, it was hard to get started, but after a while, I couldn't believe how much more alive I felt. The next time I went skiing, I was all over those slopes with energy to spare. Over the years, my physical strength, bone density, lung capacity, posture and endurance have greatly improved, rather than slowing down. Getting physical has been a key ingredient to my creativity and business success. Now I cannot imagine a life without moving my body. I bike, dance, run, and do the flying trapeze! (More on my trapeze experiences in the adventure chapter.)

Hire a Fitness Coach

One of my greatest secrets is that for the past ten years, I have worked out with the same incredible fitness trainer, Markus Heon. Markus has trained many successful athletes, including Brad Dalusio (kicker for the New York Giants), Mark Philippoussis (a Wimbledon finalist), and Robyn Benincasa (a world-class adventure racer). I meet Markus at the gym three days a week, and because I know he is waiting for me, I cannot talk myself out of going. Markus's favorite saying is, "It is my duty to move your booty!"

If you don't have the resources right now to hire a trainer on a regular basis, hire one for just a few sessions. Have them put an exercise plan together that you can easily follow to help you reach your fitness goals. Meet with the trainer every few months to assess your progress and make any necessary changes in your program.

I treat my exercise just like an appointment with a client. I put it down in my appointment book so that I'm completely committed to exercising during that time. (Readers can log their exercise in the same way, and *Blastation* subscribers can keep track of their exercise schedule at the website, www.InteractiveLifeCoach.com.)

The results of this approach have been dramatic for me in so many ways. I may be in the middle of the busiest day, with the phone ringing and piles of paper on my desk. At 1:30 P.M., I close the door and get to the gym. Are there days that I would rather not go? Of course! But I know better, because when I return an hour later, my head is clear and focused so that I can calmly handle the rest of the work for the day. My body is relaxed and limber, and any emotions that needed to be released were punched into the punching bag or exhaled on the treadmill. All that is left is me, energized with a smile on my face.

You'll Be Surprised by What Exercise and Fitness Can Do

Before you picked up this book, did you think that exercise was only good for developing a lean body, strong muscles and a strong heart? Well, I want to remind you again that these are not the only benefits, and that exercise can do more. Specifically, physical activity has been shown to help the mental and emotional aspects of health, too.

While the majority of fitness research focuses on the physical and health benefits of exercise, there is a growing body of work demonstrating that exercise promotes mental health, too. Researchers at Duke University conducted a four-month study of people suffering from depression and found that 60 percent of the participants who exercised for thirty minutes three times a week overcame their depression without using antidepressant medication.

Don't get me wrong. You don't have to be suffering from a clinical or diagnosed mental illness to derive substantial mental health benefits from exercise and fitness. One study found that short workouts of eight minutes in length could help lower sadness, tension and anger (and it also provided improved resistance to disease in healthy people). Many people exercise to boost confidence along with reducing anxiety and stress, all of which contribute to psychological health and well-being. Exercise can be viewed as a preventative or wellness activity that may actually help prevent emotional conditions. As mentioned, even short bursts of activity help individuals feel better, and this means that you don't have to spend hours at the gym to gain real mental health benefits.

The Health Benefits of Exercise Are Astounding

Regular physical activity that is performed on most days of the week reduces the risk of developing or dying from some of the leading causes of illness and death in the United States.

* Reduces the risk of dying prematurely from heart disease.
* Reduces the risk of developing diabetes.
* Reduces the risk of developing high blood pressure.

- ⋆ Helps reduce existing high blood pressure.
- ⋆ Reduces the risk of developing colon cancer.
- ⋆ Reduces feelings of depression and anxiety.
- ⋆ Helps control weight.
- ⋆ Keeps your energy youthful and vibrant.
- ⋆ Helps build and maintain healthy bones, muscles and joints.
- ⋆ Helps older adults become stronger and better able to move about without falling.
- ⋆ Helps improve sleep.
- ⋆ Provides great thinking and creative time.
- ⋆ Promotes psychological well-being.

In my coaching and health-consulting work, I have many clients who tell me that they don't understand why they're not losing weight. When I ask them what they're doing for exercise, it is often "nothing," or "I exercise once or twice a week." I have to tell you that this is not enough. Studies show that just to maintain weight, you need to exercise five times a week. To lose weight, you need to add one more day. I know that this seems like a lot, but when you make exercise part of your daily routine, you will start to crave the physical release. You only need forty minutes of cardio three to four times a week, and a weight-bearing exercise forty minutes, three times a week, which is really important to promote strong bones. The weight-bearing exercise can include fast walking (sauntering does not count), weight lifting, stair climbing, racquet sports, biking, running (the treadmill is much better for your body than the hardness of cement), tennis and dance. If you get bored, mix it up!

A study conducted by the American Society for Bone and Mineral Research measured the bone density of athletes, and it showed that bone mineral density is higher across all sports, particularly weight lifting, gymnastics and soccer. These athletes' legs, hips, spines and arms demonstrated bone density that was, on average, 13 percent higher than non-athletes'.

I challenge you to make exercise a priority in your life. As I've already noted, it's an important element of *The Blast Off! Program* because a healthy motivated body-mind is more likely to have the energy and motivation you'll need to reach your dreams. If you haven't exercised in a while, it may take two to three months to start realizing some of the benefits—such as weight loss—even though you're likely to start feeling better emotionally right away. So don't give up after a month of little progress on the weight-loss front. Work out with a friend, hire a trainer, but whatever you do, stay consistent, and don't give up.

Longer term, regular exercise provides the opportunity for a longer, healthier and more productive life. Please remember that without health you'll never reach your true wealth. So turn off the television, stop making excuses, and get that body moving.

Healing the Cause, Not the Symptom Alone

Holistic medicine treats the whole person rather than the symptoms alone. This philosophy of healing not only looks at the symptoms the person is experiencing, but the possible underlying causes of these symptoms as well. If you remove the pestering symptom, you will most likely feel better for a short period of time. However, if you don't address and heal what caused that symptom, there is a good chance that physical or emotional pain will return. Over time, successively repressing your symptoms without healing the cause, the body may become less resilient and more susceptible to even deeper imbalances.

Imagine that a fire has just started inside a house and, consequently, the fire alarms start roaring. To stop the blasting roar of the alarms, the firemen could hit them with a hammer, destroying their capacity to warn you, but that will not squelch the inner destructive fire. In a similar way, to effectively treat the outer expression of an imbalance in the body, the healing must also address the inner source.

Classical homeopathy is a science of medicine that has been in existence for the past 200 years. It has literally changed my life and the lives of millions of other people around the world. Homeopathy's healing capacity is very broad and deep because it literally addresses every system of the body on the mental, physical and emotional levels. In this way, it's truly holistic. Homeopathy is also unique in that it works to heal the cause of an ailment, rather than treating symptoms alone. Because the homeopath targets the source of the pain or trauma, the healing capacity can be profound. In my case, it was literally life-altering.

> "I have had two revelations in my life. The first was bebop; the second was homeopathy."
>
> ~Dizzy Gillespie, American jazz musician, composer and bandleader (1917-1993)

Some of the proponents of homeopathy past and present are Charles Darwin, Abraham Lincoln, William McKinley, Ralph Waldo Emerson, Henry David Thoreau, Emily Dickinson, Ludwig van Beethoven, Frederic Francois Chopin, David Beckham, Boris Becker, Nancy Lopez, William W. Mayo (the physician whose practice evolved into the Mayo Clinic), Marlene Dietrich, Douglas Fairbanks, John Wayne, Leslie Ann Warren, Pamela Anderson, Jane Seymour, Suzanne Somers, Lindsay Wagner, Vanessa Williams, Priscilla Presley, Ashley Judd, Jennifer Anniston, Orlando Bloom, Paul McCartney, Cher and Hilary Clinton.

Jamie's Physical Expression of Grief

When Jamie came to see me, she had been suffering from migraines and insomnia for years. She was taking various medications that helped her function on a day-to-day basis, but they weren't healing her symptoms. When her migraines came on, she would be useless for at least three days. It was difficult for Jamie to take care of her children, go to work, and do the basic daily activities, just getting by. Jamie had struggled with this pain for so many years that it had become a part of normal life for her. Her neurologist supported Jamie's desire to seek other alternatives and referred her to me.

In an in-depth consultation, we talked at length about her life and I discovered that Jamie's migraines had started a few months after her mother had passed away unexpectedly from heart disease. Jamie was only nineteen at the time, and she had shared a very close relationship with her mother. Obviously this loss was devastating to Jamie, yet she did her best to push forward through the intense grief because she felt that this was what her mother would have wanted. Jamie went on to receive a 4.0 in college, a master's in business, and a law degree. By age thirty-two, Jamie had worked her way up to partner in a family-practice law firm.

In recent years, the migraines were happening more and more frequently and they were taking a toll on Jamie's energy level, leaving her fatigued and fragile much of the time. When I asked Jamie how she felt about the loss of her mother, she said she had tried her best not to think about her mom, because it was too painful. When Jamie shared this with me, tears were streaming down her face and her lip was trembling as she tried to hard to hide her pain. I told Jamie that I was amazed at her courage and ability to thrive after such a traumatic loss. It was obvious to me that Jamie's head pain was a symptom of the repressed grief she had carried so privately all these years, while she unconsciously pushed herself so hard to fulfill her mom's wishes. For Jamie's migraines to heal, she needed to allow her long-standing grief to surface and express itself, so that her body could once and for all release the pain.

I asked Jamie what she did for pleasure and relaxation. Jamie told me that she really didn't have time for such activity. After taking care of her law clients and her children, she was the last one on the list.

Besides releasing the grief, Jamie needed to reclaim some precious time and energy, plus learn to give back to herself, rather than only taking care of others. I understood that her practice of focusing on others' pain, rather than her own, felt safer for Jamie because it prevented her from feeling her own pain. That way, Jamie didn't have to face the mountain of repressed emotions that she lugged around every day.

The Benefits of Homeopathy

As I mentioned earlier in the book, I fell in love with homeopathy, and once I started studying it, I just couldn't get enough information on it. Here are some of the benefits that I discovered:

✴ Homeopathy treats the whole person rather than the disease alone.

✴ Homeopathic healing works at a very deep level in the body to heal the cause of the ailment.

✴ Homeopathy is energy medicine so it works deeply with the energy of the body.

✴ Homeopathy balances the mental and emotional aspects of a person at the same time that it balances the physical level.

✴ Each case is individually based on the person's needs.

✴ Homeopathy is gentle and non-addictive.

✴ Homeopathic remedies have been FDA approved since 1938.

✴ Homeopathy treats acute and chronic ailments gently and effectively.

✴ The client of homeopathy doesn't experience a drug-like effect; rather, they just begin to feel more like themselves before they were ill, or even better.

✴ Homeopathy works wonderfully on babies and animals, so it is not a placebo.

✴ Homeopathy complements Western medicine well because it doesn't interfere with allopathic treatment. In fact, it works well with it.

How the Homeopathic Physician Works

Through an in-depth interview, homeopaths trained in the classical method have the ability to ask questions and decipher the imbalance occurring within the client. The homeopath also observes the client's expressive body language and unconscious use of verbal language as he or she describes the complaints, sensations, feelings and experiences. Then the homeopath finds the common link that ties every symptom of their complaints together. The client's complete picture is then matched to the closest fitting homeopathic remedy.

By seeing and understanding the body's signals at a deeper level, the homeopath can also heal at that deep level. Rather than suppressing superficial symptoms with the Band-Aid approach, we can use homeopathy to address the core imbalance.

> "Homeopathy cures a greater percentage of cases than any other method of treatment. Homeopathy is the latest and refined method of treating patients economically and non-violently."
>
> ~*Mahatma Gandhi,*
> *Political and spiritual leader of India*
> *(1869-1948)*

If you'd like to learn more about homeopathy, go to the Resource section for Chapter Six in the back of the book or check out my website at www.homeopathicwellness.com.

Jamie's Healing Tears

In Jamie's case, her suggested remedy was one of the 4,000 FDA-approved homeopathics, Natrum muriaticum, which is sodium chloride (salt). In a homeopathic preparation (highly diluted energetic doses), Natrum muriaticum is able to act very deeply on the physical, mental and emotional levels of the body, and in Jamie's case, it targeted her suppressed grief and migraines in a safe and gentle way.

One week after taking the homeopathic treatment, Jamie called to say that she had the strangest weekend. She cried for the first time in years while feeling strong sensations of loss for her mother. Jamie was amazed to find that the release of emotions felt really good. Memories of spending time with her mother, which she had completely blocked out, came flooding back in a beautiful way. Jamie was able to recall and connect with the special love that she and her mother had shared, as she allowed herself to spend time thinking about her childhood for the first time in twenty years.

When her mom passed on, Jamie had made a decision to never look back because she'd been so afraid to truly face her traumatic loss. Now that Jamie had acknowledged her grief and allowed herself to go through the emotions, she began to feel lighter than she had in years. She didn't realize how much energy had been drawn from her in an effort to contain this grief. Once her pain was released, Jamie felt like she had been reborn. Over the next three months, with only two doses of her remedy, Jamie's migraines gradually dissipated, until they were completely gone.

Emotions Are Energetic Faucets

Emotions are like restrained or flowing energy. When they are released, we generally feel much better. When children throw a tantrum, they may fall to the floor, flail around, and scream for a few minutes, then move past it and get on with their day. They feel the upset, express it, release it and move on. This is a healthy release of emotion. In some cases, if the child is taught that it's not acceptable to express their feelings, they learn to adapt and suppress their emotions—all in an attempt to receive love and affection and to feel accepted. Over time, this suppressive habit becomes part of their normal behavior pattern.

As the child grows into adulthood, he or she begins to hold in feelings regarding relationships with friends, spouses, bosses and so on, until he or she is filled to the brim with stuffed-down emotions. Since the emotional energy doesn't simply evaporate into thin air, it builds up and is expressed in the body-mind through any number of symptoms.

If you tie a knot at the end of a garden hose and turn on the faucet, the garden hose will only be able to hold the water to its capacity. Soon the water will overpower the rubber hose and the water will begin to make its own crevices and bust through. The knot may suppress the water temporarily, but the pressure will be too great for the hose to maintain over time. Similarly, our bodies can only hold strong or ongoing emotions for so long before they begin to manifest in the shape of various possible symptoms, such as depression, irritable bowel syndrome, bladder infections, respiratory problems and, in Jamie's case, migraines.

I encouraged Jamie to journal about the relationship she had with her mother, and how their bond and this loss had shaped the decisions she had made in her personal and professional life. I also asked Jamie to examine how she was mirroring that same pattern of hiding emotions in other areas of her life—like in the relationships with her spouse, children and close friends.

> "When man is serene, the pulse of the heart flows and connects, just as pearls are joined together or like a string of red jade, then one can talk about a healthy heart."
>
> ~From the ancient Chinese medical text, The Yellow Emperor's Canon of Internal Medicine

Blast Off! PRACTICE 4: What Emotional Energy Are You Hoarding?

Emotions are a very healthy expression of energy, as long as they *are* expressed, not repressed. What unexpressed emotions are *you* carrying around in your body? As you lie in bed at night or walk about during the day, do you feel any pains or discomfort in your body? This exercise will help you get in touch with the emotions hidden behind the pain, and allow you to release them once and for all.

1. Go to your comfortable, private *Inspiration Station*. Close your eyes and use your breath to relax your body. Visualize any busy thoughts racing through your mind and then imagine them drifting from your brain off into the atmosphere. See your stressful thoughts or worries disappear into space.

2. Now that your mind is clear, focus on your physical body. Do you feel any pain, tension or discomfort?

3. Once you begin to connect with your pain, put your hand over the area that bothers you the most.

4. Now ask this pain what it's trying to express to you. If the pain could talk, what would it say? (You will be amazed at the insight and answers you receive.)

5. Start journaling the answers that have come to you. Don't analyze or judge your thoughts. Just keep your pen moving and don't stop to read what you have written.

6. Remember, suppressed emotions can hurt you and those around you. They create absolutely nothing positive for you or the world. Once you attain an awareness of the toxic energy that you have been carrying around, and then release and heal from the burden of these suppressed or pestering emotions, you will experience an awakening in your body that is expansive and freeing.

We don't realize how many emotions the body is holding on to, even if these feelings developed so long ago. Letting them go is like pulling up an anchor tying you to the past. To blast forward, you want nothing to hold you back any longer. ✪

Jamie Keeps Moving Forward

Now that Jamie was healing from her past, I encouraged her to start incorporating healthy habits and some fun and adventure into her life. Since Jamie's energy was not going to feed her migraines, she had the motivation to exercise and eat healthy foods. Instead of working late at the office, she took up piano again, something else she had quit at age nineteen.

Speak Up and Get that Energy Out

Did you know that when you express yourself, your body-mind is releasing energy? At the same time, if you stifle your voice for whatever reason, your body-mind is suppressing energy. Not that you need to run around screaming or crying all the time, but curbing your voice repeatedly in relationships and hiding your true self can actually create a health risk. Just like emotions, your voice is a powerful energy to be reckoned with.

Have you ever had the experience of needing to say your piece to someone regarding a particular feeling or conflict? You may have felt a charge in your body every time your mind wandered to your feelings about this person. Every time you focus on this person or issue, the intensity of energy keeps building up inside. You may experience the sensation of your chest tightening or stomach turning, as well as having shallow breathing and sweaty palms.

"Speak your truth" is a very powerful statement. The more you give yourself permission to speak and live your truth in all aspects of your life, the healthier and freer you will be. This doesn't mean you need to become an angry person, or someone who wallows in his or her sadness. It means taking responsibility, saying your piece, and moving on. Let it out, then let it go.

Here are some tips for addressing your internal volcano before it erupts.

★ Confront the person you're in conflict with if you feel safe to do so. Say your piece with "I statements." For example, "I'm not trying to upset you, but I feel

the need to tell you how I am feeling. I am feeling sad and angry because….
I am hoping that we can find a way to resolve…. " By avoiding "you statements," you generally defuse their desire to get defensive.

★ Remember that this is an exercise in releasing your emotions and standing
up for what you feel and believe. You will feel so much better because you'll
be getting these feelings off your chest, literally. However, you cannot control how this person will respond. They may not tell you or give you what
you're hoping to receive. If you understand this before your confrontation,
it will help to prevent you from taking on more personal disappointment.
It's about releasing and expressing—not controlling the situation.

★ If confronting the person face-to-face is not an option, then you can write a
letter. Sometimes this is helpful because it gives the receiver time to digest
your words and think through his or her response. The same rules apply
regarding non-blaming "I statements" if you really want your words to be
heard. Again, you may not get the response you desire. In fact, you may
not receive a response at all. However, you will no longer be carrying this
emotionally charged burden around. Your body and soul will thank you
immensely.

My Mom Speaks Her Truth and Heals

My mom is a truly amazing woman. She is seventy-six years old and
a survivor of cervical cancer, breast cancer and ovarian cancer. You really
see what someone is made of when you watch them go through illnesses
like this. I was literally in awe of her strength. As a healer especially, it was
very hard not to try to jump in and save her. The day she was diagnosed
with ovarian cancer, at age seventy, was one of the hardest days of my life.
I wanted to take her pain away, yet my mom made it very clear that she
didn't want to be rescued, and she didn't want anyone making decisions
for her. This was a huge lesson for me in letting go, and although I was not
in agreement with some of her choices, I respected her wishes.

During her healing process, my mom revealed more of herself than
she ever had. She shared with me that she had stifled her true voice for
many years because that was what was expected of her. It was not that

unusual for women of her generation to do what was expected, even if they were in complete disagreement.

As I just mentioned, suppressing emotions creates blocked or toxic energy in the body. Did swallowing her words cause her cancer? I cannot say for sure. Mom feels it might have. My mom was also on hormone replacement therapy (HRT) for over twenty-five years; we know from many reports over recent years that HRT creates an increased risk of cancer, especially for the length of time that she was taking hormones. What I do know to be true is that finally speaking her mind and making her own decisions on the direction of her healing process contributed greatly to my mother's recovery. Once she spoke up to me, our family, and to her doctors, my mom was a power to be reckoned with. It was an amazing sight to see.

My mother is not the same woman now that she was prior to her illnesses. Mom appreciates every day that she is alive. She laughs, loves and is truly happy. We have a better relationship now than ever before.

The Power of Good News

One of the major influences on our health (as I briefly mentioned earlier in this chapter) is the bad, even alarming news that we are inundated with every time we read the newspaper, listen to radio newscasts, or watch TV news reports. Besides being fed bad news, it seems that the more we watch it, the more difficult it becomes to ignore.

Look at the ongoing success of soap operas or the ratings increase when a well-known celebrity's heartache is aired on television. By watching another's misery on the big screen in your living room, you may feel that in comparison, your life is not so bad. Yet, after a period of time hearing and reading bad news, sad news, angry news and scary news, you're more likely to focus your attention primarily on the sad, angry and scary energy around you. And you may actually be taking on the energy that you're observing.

For instance, if someone watches television news each night before going to bed and continues to witness crime, trauma and disasters, how relaxed is their body going to be after their nervous system has witnessed and reacted internally to this intensity? What will their final thoughts of the day be like as they close their eyes, and why should they feel surprised if it takes a long time each night to fall asleep?

> "Laughter is the sun that drives winter from the human face."
>
> ~*Anonymous*

The good news is that there is an enormous amount of good news that happens every minute of every day. The good news may not be making the headlines, but we can find it if we turn our "good news radar" on. Imagine if all you heard all day long was wonderful news. You know that joyful heartfelt sensation you get when you see two people unite who haven't seen each other in years, or when the underdog team wins, or when someone realizes their dream after years of trying? Just think how much healthier our spirits and attitudes would be if we were exposed to more good news than bad news on a regular basis.

Blast Off! PRACTICE 5: The Good News Diet

When we think or hear of uplifting news and events, our energy and mood immediately experience a joyful lift. If you were to focus on one positive happening at least three times a day, and at the same time, turned off and tuned out the negative news, your nervous system would feel calmer and your energy would begin to radiate.

Try this…

★ In the morning, at lunchtime and before bedtime, write down one word or sentence that reflects some great news that has happened, recently or in the past, to you or someone you know. Or you can write something that you appreciate or are grateful for.

★ Be aware of the feelings that come up when you're focusing on this good thought. The more you draw your attention to the good news of life, the more you are putting that good-news intention into the Universe. And as I have discussed several times so far, that positive intention will be reciprocated with even more positive energy.

Here's to your great news! ✪

Healthy Stuff You May Know, Yet Are Not Practicing

Good nutrition is key to a healthy body, because it supports a healthy lifestyle. Here is some keep-it-simple information that can go a long way in supporting your body-mind through a healthy diet.

★ **Avoid fast food.** Too much fast food and too little exercise can wreak havoc on the liver, according to the results of a small Swedish study. In the study, eighteen trim, healthy adult volunteers restricted their levels of physical activity to no more than 5,000 daily steps and ate at least two fast-food meals each day for four weeks. The result? Their bodies showed clear signs of liver damage. The volunteers also put on weight.

At the end of the four weeks, the fast-food eaters had put on an average of 6.5 kilograms (14.3 pounds). That's a lot of weight for one month. Five increased their weight by 15 percent, and one person put on an extra twelve kilograms (26.4 pounds) in just two weeks! Moreover, after just one week on the fast-food regimen, blood tests showed sharp increases in a liver enzyme called alanine aminotransferase (ALT). ALT levels more than quadrupled over the four-week study period, which is often a sign of possible liver disease.

★ **Make several healthy meals in advance** for the week ahead so you won't reach for junk when you get hungry. Many people rely on junk food when they feel too lazy to make or buy something healthy, are short on time, or there is nothing else is in the house and they're starving. By making larger quantities or extra meals at the beginning of each week, such as grilled chicken, baked fish, veggies or salads, you'll be more likely to reach for them rather than the greasy or salty standbys.

★ **Keep healthy snacks on hand**, such as veggies, fruits and nuts (for example, almonds and walnuts). These healthy snacks will provide you with extra energy and nutrients throughout the day, and prevent you from binging on unhealthy food.

★ **Eat many dark green vegetables** such as broccoli, kale and spinach for extra fiber and nutrients.

★ **Eat organic as much as possible.** Based on 41 published studies comparing the nutritional value of organically grown and conventionally grown fruits, vegetables and grains, there are significantly more of several nutrients in organic crops. These include 27 percent more vitamin C, 21.1 percent more iron, 29.3 percent more magnesium and 13.6 percent more phosphorus. In addition, organic products had 15.1 percent less nitrates than their conventional counterparts. Nitrates and nitrites form nitrosamines in the body. Nitrosamines are carcinogenic. On top of the nitrosamines in non-organic produce, this substance is also found in many processed meats—like sausage and bacon. The heat that is used to cook these processed meats assists in the formation of nitrosamines.

★ **Avoid trans fats**. Trans fats can be natural or artificial. Small amounts of trans fats occur naturally in beef and dairy foods. Artificial trans fats are made when hydrogen gas reacts with oil. Cookies, crackers, icing, potato chips, stick margarine and microwave popcorn are major culprits for containing the artificial variety of trans fats. About 80 percent of trans fat in the diet of Americans comes from factory-produced partially hydrogenated vegetable oil. Trans fats contribute greatly to obesity and heart disease. Since 2006, the FDA has required food manufacturers to list trans fats on their food labels, so it helps to read the labels. Be aware, though, that manufacturer can list "zero" if there is less than 0.5 grams of trans fats per serving. Avoid food with labels that list "partially hydrogenated" ingredients or shortening, as this is a sign that the food has some trans fats in it.

★ **Eat the freshest food possible**. Food that lasts for months in your fridge is full of preservatives. An accumulation of these preservatives and other artificial ingredients can cause a whole host of unwanted side effects.

★ **Drink herbal tea instead of coffee**. I know how you love your morning ritual. But how about switching out that coffee to hot and spicy tea? Coffee can speed up your nervous system, much more so than tea. We are trying to calm down our nervous systems! Coffee is also very acidic. It is more beneficial for the body to remain in an alkaline state because an acid balance decreases the body's ability to absorb minerals and other nutrients. If you're having trouble giving up coffee, try Teeccino, an herbal coffee substitute made from natural ingredients. It's sugar- and caffeine-free. The added potassium in Teeccino will give you a natural lift without speeding you up.

★ **Avoid too much sugar in your diet**. Sugar can suppress your immune system, which can impair your defenses against disease. But you don't have to deprive yourself of sweets for the rest of your life. If you did try to abstain from sweets, what would be the first thing you'd crave? Sugar, of course. Try not thinking of sugar. What are you thinking of right now? Sugar, candy, chocolate and pastries! See how that works? Everything in moderation is a healthy rule. Just know that sugar is addictive and can cause hyperactivity and increased adrenaline surges. And the other side of the up is down. So after that sugar high, you'll be feeling drowsy and fatigued and maybe even craving more sugar. The more you eat sugar, the more you'll desire it. Eat fruit instead, which has fiber so the fruit sugar is more slowly absorbed, or give yourself the pleasure of one dessert on the weekend as a reward for a week well done.

★ **Drink pure water.** The benefits of drinking water are often underestimated and misunderstood. Water is not just a thirst quencher and a critical element for many of the body's biochemical processes. Water can help you and your body-mind:

- Get healthy skin.

- Flush toxins.

- Reduce your risk of heart attack.

- Cushion and lube your joints and muscles.

- Get energized and be alert.

- Improve your digestion.

- Reduce your risk of disease and infection.

- Regulate your body temperature.

- Burn more fat and build more muscle.

Here are a few more of my favorite healing secrets:

★ **Lavender oil:** A very gentle essential oil, lavender can be used in many ways. It is excellent for tiredness, tension and depression, and because it is so gentle, lavender may be utilized during pregnancy. It also helps maintains healthy skin and a drop or two can be a treatment for a burn or insect bite. When diffused, lavender's clean scent soothes emotional extremes, and when massaged into the temples and neck, it eases headaches and promotes feelings of calmness and relaxation. Colic, cramps, and nausea respond to a gentle abdominal massage of lavender. A couple drops of lavender on the pillow helps promote restful sleep.

★ **Bach Rescue® Remedy:** In any acutely stressful situation, Rescue Remedy can help immediately. Rescue Remedy is totally natural and non-addictive. It contains five of the 38 Bach Flower Essences: Rock Rose for terror and panic,

Impatiens for irritation and impatience, Clematis for inattentiveness, Star of Bethlehem for shock, and Cherry Plum for irrational thoughts. I carry it with me for stress relief in a pinch. When the pressure is on, put four drops under your tongue or in your water bottle, and feel your tension fade.

★ **Hot bubble baths:** There is nothing quite as soothing as a hot bath. The heat relaxes your tense muscles, drains your busy mind of unwanted thoughts, and helps your entire being loosen up. Taking a bath in the evening is a great way to unwind and to take time to review the day you just experienced. That way, the day doesn't pass without you appreciating every wonderful moment. A hot bubble bath also calms down your nervous system so you can have a sound, restful sleep.

> "I think we should leave no stone unturned in our search for better health. I also believe that you get out of your body what you put into it. Your body will respond to your efforts to improve your health. The time to start is right now."
>
> ~Bob Martin
> *Clinical nutritionist, health educator*

By making these simple changes or additions to your life, you could not only add years to your life span, but you'll feel so much better during this fantastic voyage you have been blessed with. To experience the best *"Blast Off!"* possible, keep your equipment healthy and countdown ready.

More Vitality, More Passion

There's nothing more humbling than to witness someone's life transform from illness to vitality, from apathy to passion. When that happens, everything changes. As individuals reclaim their health, it can positively impact the dynamics of their entire life. There's a desire to improve relationships, the motivation to reach for more in their careers, the incentive to be creative, and the inner peace to enjoy life's small but powerful moments.

You can improve your health at any age and at any stage. I went from huffing and puffing up the stairs to running 10k-run obstacle courses through the mud. If I can do it, so can you. The path to a healthy body-mind is an important part of the journey to the life of your dreams.

BLAST OFF! Daily Launch Tools

1. Each morning, write your *Sun-Up Script* and *Rocket Words*.

2. Read your *Rocket Words* to yourself and out loud as often as possible during your day.

3. Create and perform a minimum of *Mini Feats* each day. (These are the smaller steps for moving toward your larger *Mile Step* goals and your *Big Picture Vision*.) For example, today's *Mini Feats* might be:

   ■ *Do Internet research on water filters to find the best way to purify my drinking water.*

   ■ *Sign up for an ashtanga yoga class today.*

   ■ *Find the closest grocery store that carries USDA Organic foods, and meats that are hormone and antibiotic free.*

4. Choose one to two *Blast Off! Practices* from this chapter to do each day over the next week.

5. Fill out your *Weekly Flight Assessment Log* to review your week's progress toward realizing your *Supersonic Life*.

Summary of the Chapter Concepts

➤ To improve your health, you can use the same principles of Intention and Action that you have begun to use in your career and relationships.

➤ The "body-mind" is a term that represents the body and the mind as one.

➤ Too much stress, with no support to counteract its often harsh energy, can have detrimental effects on the body and the psyche.

➤ What are your stress triggers? Once you identify them, you can create a strategy to handle them in a new and different way.

➤ Your breath is your connection to life. *Prana* is the life force that is connected to the self. Learn to breathe deeper for access to more life force, while relieving stress and feeding your precious cells.

➤ Energy work is bodywork that balances and jumpstarts the energy pathways in the body, resulting in more energy, less pain and deeper healing.

➤ Health is freedom because when we are free of pain and disease, we can do anything.

➤ Your cells regenerate; therefore, we can improve our health at any age.

➤ Your invisible energetic field protects you from aggravating outside stimulation.

➤ Just because you're exposed to people with the flu doesn't mean you must get it. Keep your body healthy and rejuvenated and you'll be able take your sick days and change them to fun days.

➤ Exercise is mandatory for a long-term healthy body. It reduces the risk of so many diseases, including heart disease or cancer. *Move that body.*

➤ Research is now showing that physical activity is not only good for the body, but also your mind and spirit.

➤ For permanent healing, heal the cause rather than just suppressing the symptoms.

➤ Homeopathy treats the whole person effectively for most acute and chronic conditions. See the Resource section in the back of the book for a certified classical homeopath in your area.

➤ Emotions can be draining if they're running full-time to no avail. In addition, suppressed emotions can linger and create symptoms in the body. What emotions are you ruminating on or hoarding?

➤ You can tap into the intelligence of your ailments and find out what is driving them.

➤ Practice using journaling as an emotional release. You'll be glad you did.

Summary of the Chapter Concepts (continued)

➤ Good news keeps us vibrant and hopeful, yet we are often inundated with bad news. Learn how to deflect it and focus on what is wonderful around you.

➤ Our bodies are made up of water, primarily. We need to continually refill our tank with this vital fluid in order to detoxify, replenish and hydrate.

➤ Nutrition and exercise are the keys to your overall health and well-being.

"The groundwork of all happiness is health."

~Leigh Hunt,
British poet and essayist
(1784-1859)

CHAPTER 7

BLAST Off!
to Financial Freedom and Prosperity

"Take up one idea. Make that one idea your life—think of it, dream of it, live on that idea. Let the brain, muscles, nerves, every part of your body, be full of that idea, and just leave every other idea alone. This is the way to success...."

~Swami Vivekananda,
Spiritual leader from India, a
Hindu sage and social reformer
(1863-1902)

At age twenty-five, I had a husband, a beautiful daughter, a successful advertising agency, a gorgeous two-story park-side home and a new Lexus. Externally, life looked rather lovely. Internally, even though I was surrounded by all that stuff, I was completely miserable. At age thirty, I divorced, changed my title from "married with child" to "divorced, single mom." I sold my house, moved into an apartment, and turned in my leased luxury car for a used Ford. I was back in school, flat broke, and on top of the world. What does it all mean? Why was I happier after I stripped down my life? Was it because I didn't have money? Was it because I got divorced? The answer is *none of the above.*

As I look back, fifteen years later, the answer is perfectly clear to me. It wasn't until I found my true calling, my path of passion and meaning, that I could begin to heal and feel whole inside. And it wasn't until I felt whole in my internal world that I could receive pleasure from my external world.

Passion + Meaning = Wealth and Satisfaction

My passion has kept me focused and committed to a positive direction, and it continues to reward me with an incredible amount of personal satisfaction. This *Secret Spark* (an internal energy that ignites my passion, explained for those who jumped ahead to this chapter) has been the source of my continually growing fiscal wealth and prosperity, and it has influenced every aspect of my external world, in an exponentially rewarding way.

For instance, I had always loved being a mom. But you cannot argue with the fact that a happier person makes for a much better parent. Even though I was taking on the parental responsibility as a single mother after my divorce, my *Secret Spark* gave me the excess energy that was necessary to wholeheartedly enjoy the quality time with my daughter. In contrast, when you're unhappy, too much of your energy goes toward just sustaining your existence on a daily basis.

Also, even though I have worked long hours building my businesses, it has never felt like work to me. My passion is an extension of my true self, therefore, my work is an expression of me. The more I have expressed "me" through my work, the more people have responded in a positive way, because the energy behind it is natural and real, rather than forced or pushed. Over the years, this self-expression has grown through my creative and business endeavors. Through the ease with which my passion is expressed, and the mutual exchange of positive energy between myself and my clients, my wealth has grown emotionally, fiscally and spiritually.

Even though I earned a sizeable income in my first career as the director of an advertising agency, it didn't bring me satisfaction because that money didn't stem from my passion. To an outside onlooker during that phase I call my past life, it would have appeared that I had everything. In reality, I felt drained and empty because my soul was not being fed. Fast-forward to my present life, where I have earned the same material resources and more, and I can truly say that this time around, I am happy. *Why now?* Because once I found my passion, I stayed true and dedicated to actualizing my *Big Picture Vision* through intention and action. The *Blast Off!* process has paid off in every way. Now I deeply appreciate and enjoy all the good that surrounds me because it has blossomed from the voice of my soul.

The moral of this story:

> *Find out who you are and live from that place.*
> *Speak your truth, live your truth.*

The Door to the Big Unknown

After years of feeling stuck and unfulfilled, I officially hit a major impasse in my life path. I had no financial support, no inheritance looming, and zero in my savings account. The way I saw it, I had three choices:

1. Cave into the pressure, stay stuck, and allow life to continually overwhelm me.

2. Resort to the same habitual ways of doing a job (or making money) that continually left me feeling emotionally flat and worn out.

3. Step out into the big unknown world, face my fears, and aim for a life with purpose.

To this day, I'm so thankful that I dug deep, gathered my courage, and opted for Door Number Three. Many people stay immobile and stick with Door Number One or Door Number Two because they feel that nothing is worth risking the security and stability of a lifestyle that they feel familiar and safe with, even if they're

> *"I had to make my own living and my own opportunity. But I made it. Don't sit down and wait for the opportunities to come. Get up and make them!"*
>
> ~Madame C. J. Walker,
> *Hair care entrepreneur,
> philanthropist, first woman to
> become a millionaire by her
> own means according to the*
> Guinness Book of Records
> *(1867-1919)*

unhappy. I'm not criticizing this choice. Only you can determine the right path for you. There are realistic issues of responsibilities, the cost of living, education and retirement. I get it. Remember, I was there.

What I can say to help quell your fears is that when you're following your passion, the excitement and momentum you expel can create a financially rewarding outcome far above and beyond your survival consciousness. *The key is to move from survival thinking to abundance living.*

It's not about the Money, It's about Freedom

Money alone will not make you happy. It's what the money can do for you that can bring joy. It can give you leverage to capture a life-long dream. It can go to a family in need. It has given me the ability to buy this computer, my writing tool in sharing my *Blast Off!* concepts.

Money is often given a negative connotation. You've heard the idea that having wealth will make you greedy or give you an attitude of being "better than." How can this be true? Money is actually *an avenue for freedom of choice.* Just as a state of balanced health gives us freedom to move and be in the world, money gives us the freedom to do, or not to do, what we choose. When money is limited, your choices are limited. If you're struggling to come up with cash, your choices of housing and food decrease. The more money you have access to, the less you worry about survival, which frees up your mind from unwanted thoughts. There-fore, money is an avenue of liberty because it gives you independence to express your creative and individual voice.

What you want to spend your money on may not be what I want to spend my money on. Money is used to express your desires, whether you save it, invest it, or spend it. You may enjoy spending your cash on mystery novels and I enjoy spending mine on a vacation to Mexico. You may donate funds to the homeless and I choose to support a literacy campaign. Money gives us the freedom to express our passions. If you have money, you have more choices.

Money and Fear

Do you struggle with issues of fear around money? Have you ever thought that the fear and the action of holding onto your money or your safe job could actually be the very things that may be causing you to struggle in survival mode? This fear of losing or not making money will actually hold you back from creating more money.

*If your attitude tends toward the pessimistic, skeptical vein of life,
you are energetically closing off any opportunity or space
for your abundance to arrive. The result?
An even more pessimistic, skeptical life experience.*

Survival Consciousness

Survival, meanwhile, is doing what you have to do just to get by. It's more about existing or staying alive. It's similar to a predator/prey situation where an animal does what's necessary to survive or protect its pack. When you're struggling each day just to survive, there may also be a huge element of fear present that says, "If I don't do this job, even though I hate it, the rug will be pulled out from under me. Or even worse, the walls will all cave in."

Survival is "disaster prevention" rather than the creation of a new magnetizing prosperity. When you live to survive, you miss out on a whole host of opportunities waiting restlessly to be noticed and accessed. Survival thinking uses language like "stuck," "struggle," "effort," "hard" and "victim." Abundance thinking translates into language like "effortless," "in the flow," "passion," "dream," "is coming," "is happening," "fullness" and "feeling alive."

The Results of Survival Consciousness

When you look at your bank balance and the bills each month, how do you react? Do you feel a sense of anxiety rising up from your stomach to your throat, or a heavy, weighted pressure in your chest? Do you express your anxiety to your partner or do you hold it in and obsess about it? Do you have a dream that you continue to put on hold because you're waiting for your financial or personal situation to change?

As long as you continue to take the same survival actions that are based in fear, your results *will not* change. The reality in every aspect of your life is birthed from your belief about a particular situation, and the intention and actions you take regarding your situation.

If you believe, for example, that you will not have enough money by the first of the month to pay the mortgage, and you project that pessimistic energy out into the Universe with thoughts like, *"I just know I won't have enough money,"* or *"No matter what I do, I am always struggling for money,"* the Universe will grant you your wish. Or if, based on fear, you continue to take the same hindering steps of working in a dissatisfying job, you are limiting your possibilities for true fiscal and emotional wealth. Can you relate to either of these scenarios in some way? If so, you are supporting the probability that your financial circumstances will not change. And even if they do improve, a soul-deadening job will *not* bring fulfillment. In effect, by living through your survival thinking, you are literally blocking the arrival of abundance.

> *"Lack is simply the outpicturing of false beliefs."*
>
> ~John Randolph Price,
> Lecturer and author
> of the best-seller,
> The Abundance Book

Blast Off! PRACTICE 1: The Energy of Your Survival Words

Your words are an unconscious expression of your life force. This is an inner game. You may be saying or thinking negative language that you're not even aware of. If you are thinking these thoughts, you are creating an energy frequency, and therefore, a negative reality around them. Let's take a look at all the ways you are experiencing and expressing survival thinking, which consists of repetitive thoughts and language concerning money that limits your financial growth.

Do any of these statements resonate with you?

★ "Money never comes easily to me."

★ "I never have enough."

★ "I don't deserve to have money."

★ "People will think I'm greedy if I have money."

★ "Wanting money is a bad thing."

★ "Money comes to others, but not to me."

★ "I would love to travel, but I will never have that kind of money."

✴ "Money is dirty."

✴ "Whenever I try to make more money, I hit a dead-end."

✴ "Wealth only comes to rich people."

✴ "The economy is really terrible right now. It is a time of struggle."

✴ "I have a ton of bills coming up and no way to pay them."

✴ "I have to sacrifice important relationships and things in my life in order to receive money."

In your journal, *The Blast Off! Workbook,* or the *Blastation* software, make note of any of the above beliefs that you resonate with, and/or record your own additional negative beliefs and thoughts about money. Label this your *"Survival Thinking List."* ✪

> **Blast Off!** | **PRACTICE 2: Shift and Lift—Create Your Abundant Living Statements**

By simply changing your thoughts and action from a negative to a positive—as you did with the flip-switching exercises in earlier chapters— the energy frequency in your body will shift upwards. This will help you to feel more confident and empowered.

Try this experiment. Say the words, *"I am stuck, broke and frustrated."* Repeat this statement five times.

✴ How do you feel in your body as you repeat this phrase?

✴ Do you feel your shoulders slump forward?

✴ Do you feel heavier, as if there is a weight on your chest, shoulders or back?

✴ Do you feel tired or anxious?

Now repeat this sentence five times, *"Money is flowing effortlessly and easily to me, and the Universe is taking care of all of my financial needs."*

✴ Do you notice an energetic shift in your body?

✴ Do you feel lighter and more uplifted with a sense that change is on the horizon?

Next, take the *Survival Thinking List* that you just compiled and flip-switch the sentences to positive *Abundant Living Statements* that have the polar opposite message and feel. (Do this in your journal, the workbook or the *Blastation* software.) The more specific you are about your needs and desires, the better.

For example:

"Wanting money is a bad thing."

Flip-switch it to:

"Money is a wonderful expression of energy."

"Money gives me a sense of freedom and choice."

"Money is a very positive asset because it gives me freedom."

"Money helps me to help others."

"The money I am receiving now will cover the cost of my tuition to culinary school." ✪

> "Lack of money is the root of all evil."
>
> ~*George Bernard Shaw, Irish playwright (1856-1950)*

Once you've completed your new list, start reading your *Abundant Living Statements* out loud each day. They'll be especially helpful when you feel any of the manipulative survival thinking energy beginning to play tricks with your brain again. Keep repeating your abundance phrases throughout the day, and you will begin to feel a shift in your energy, mood, spirit and motivation. Memorize the ones that seem to give you the biggest shift and lift, then incorporate them into your everyday language.

Money Is Energy

When money is flowing in your life, and you are directing the money into and through your passions, or outward to help others, you are actually creating a reciprocal flow of money energy. By spending money, we create flow and freedom in someone else's life or business, and as a reaction, money will flow back to us. I'm not saying that you should go empty your savings account and have a free-for-all. However, if you hold on to your money too tightly, you will not be creating a flowing stream for money to swim back to you.

Movement is also energy, and money can be the catalyst of that energy. Money creates movement as it gives us the opportunity to do things. In this way, it creates energy by connecting us to others through lunch meetings, vacations, coffee-shop talk, parties, business meetings, hobbies and more.

If money is energy, why not create the momentum for that green energy to flow right into your wallet?

Make Room for Money

In earlier chapters, I've discussed clearing out negative energy by ending unhealthy or toxic relationships and releasing draining behaviors such as perfectionism and people-pleasing. You have also been clearing negative energy by flip-switching stifling emotions such as fear of failure, or low self-worth. By setting boundaries and refusing to settle, then flip-switching your intentions from the negative to the positive, you'll begin to make room for the relationships and results you desire. The act of space-clearing works well in the money arena, as it has in other sectors of your life.

If you surround yourself with people who have negative feelings towards money, by osmosis you'll operate at their same negative energy frequency. The best way to keep the flow of money circulating freely around you is to surround yourself with people who know how to spend, invest, save and create money in a healthy and positive way.

Another form of negative money energy is debt. Bills, on the other hand, are not necessarily negative because you're getting something in return for your payment, which stimulates positive money energy to flow. Debt is different. It's a buildup of energy that is not being released, so it gets backed up. And the more it gets backed up, the harder it will be to see your way out. This is similar to a clogged shower drain with no room for the new water to enter. Debt clogs the energy pathways, creating resistance for your money to flow in. I know this is counterintuitive. Obviously, if you had more money, you would be able to pay off more of your debt, creating more room for more money. The truth is, if you're not careful with your money karma, more money may just bring in more stuff, and ultimately more debt. The cleaner your money closets are, the bigger your positive cash tree can grow. Also, if your debt is mounting and you're not taking action to clear it out, there may be a great deal of emotional energy in the way of worry, stress, and burden that is draining the abundance-maker in you. By making arrangements, even if they are small weekly or monthly payments toward clearing your debt, you're creating a movement of energy and room for new wealth. And in *Blast Off!* language, this is a good thing.

Here are some ways to open up your money pipes:

* **Pour all your debt into one money jar:** If your debt is on credit cards, try to find the lowest-interest rate credit card you can find, and if possible, consolidate all the debt you owe onto one card. That will reduce the amount of emotional energy you extend by reducing the number of bills you receive each month. There are cards that offer low interest for a short period of time. Prior to the date of the interest increase, transfer once again to a new low-interest card until your debt is resolved.

* **Auto-pay will brighten your day:** If you have a large debt you're paying off, set up your Internet banking so it will send one check per month larger than your minimum payment in whatever amount you decide on. That way, the balance will begin to shrink without you having to think or worry about it. Over time, the debt will dissolve.

* **Stick $30 in the kitty:** Put a certain amount of cash aside each week. For instance, if you put $30 per week in your piggy bank, that is $120 that can go to cover your finance charges. Then the rest you pay toward your credit bills will be above and beyond the interest-only payment that is keeping you stuck and trapped, where no energy can flow.

* **Prosperity networking:** Ask your successful friends, neighbors or mentors who they use for financial planning. Always get a few referrals when hiring someone to support your wealth-building.

★ **Create a** *Big Picture Vision* **for your money:** Create a financial plan or monetary *Big Picture Vision* for the next five, ten, fifteen or twenty years. Write down your financial goals in detail. What you plan to make, how and why. (This information can change and evolve along the way.) By putting these figures in writing, you are setting your money intention to actualize your plan and receive fiscally.

★ **Face the music:** You may find that you spend less (or more) than you realize. By taking an honest look at what you spend, owe and receive, it becomes a tangible thing rather than something swimming in your head. Then you can create intention and action with the numbers. *The goal—less debt, more income.*

> "The only way not to think about money is to have a great deal of it."
>
> *~Edith Wharton,*
> *Pulitzer-Prize-winning*
> *novelist*
> *(1862-1937)*

Blast Off! PRACTICE 3: Just the Fiscal Facts

You may feel that a budget is a six-letter dirty word. However, a budget can help in many ways. It moves the anxiety about money out of your head and onto the paper. Once you know what your bottom line is (basically what you need to make in order to survive), then we have something to work with.

★ Look closely at and write down the total amount of monthly expenses that you listed in *Blast Off! Practice 5* of Chapter Four. I recommend averaging the past four months of expenses for a broader perspective. This is your *Blue Plate Special* Number, the amount of money that must be actualized to cover your expenses. Now you know that after these expenses are paid for this month (including any investment income and taxes), the rest is surplus. You can save the surplus, which I recommend, or spend it and make the world go round.

★ Now that you have your survival number, you can start to move beyond that. Way beyond that.

Knowing your bottom line will help you feel more in control of your finances so you can take action for growth and abundance. ✪

Abundance Consciousness

The definition of *abundance* is a high degree of fullness and prosperity that transcends through each area of life. It is a word that mirrors an energy of growth and limitless living. Abundance is displayed in our world on every level. You witness an abundance of spirit as you observe children playing together, running and laughing; an abundance of joy as you share a tender moment with your loved ones; an abundance of giving as you help an individual, family or a community in need; an abundance of passion as you actualize your true calling; an abundance of health as you move your body freely; and an abundance of wealth as you create opportunity and space for money to flow to you and through you. Abundant thinking is a language of consciousness that translates into the following statement:

> *"I believe and see that we create our own limited world,*
> *therefore we have the ability to create an infinite reality.*
> *All we desire is possible."*

As I discussed earlier in the book, if you believe that all is possible and make room for these possibilities to appear, abundance will arise in many levels of your life. You'll find more on moving out of limited thinking in Chapter Two.

The Power of Money Knowingness

In my life, whether I had surplus cash or was flat broke, I've always known that the money would come, and that I would live in prosperity. I am not a psychic, nor a fortune-teller, and I haven't inherited a trust fund. How do I know that the money will always be present in my life when and where I need it? And where did this belief originate? Whether this developed from watching my father build his business, or just plain denial of my bank balance, I cannot say for sure. I do know that what I project out into the Universe will come back to me. Faith in abundance has become a part of my cellular makeup.

The biggest asset towards creating wealth and prosperity in my life is this deep belief that all things are possible, no matter what.

This *money knowingness*, a state of mind and "beingness" that the money will undoubtedly arrive as needed, has been one of the major factors of my business and financial success. It has also gotten me through my roughest financial times. Because I believe that my sense of the money coming is accurate, the Universe supports this belief, too.

Money Synchronicity

When I was going through my divorce, I remember scouring the house looking for enough change to buy a cup of coffee. I was almost laughing to myself because I hadn't been willing to believe it had gotten that bad. A latte at the time was $2.10. I pulled every purse out of my closet and poured all the contents onto my bed. I started counting pennies, dimes, nickels and quarters. No dollars. *Not a one.* After I had counted $1.90, I looked at the remaining money that was left on the bed and I couldn't believe my eyes. In my scattered scouring, I had found the exact amount of money that I needed, $2.10! The thrill in my heart didn't emerge because I could afford a cup of java. I was high on the synchronistic message that I had just received from the Universe.

If I continued to believe in my dreams, and continued to take small steps in that direction, wealth and prosperity would arrive.

Finding the exact amount of money that I desired in that particular time of need (at that moment, coffee was the need) was the validation that my *money knowingness* was in working order. In my journey, this deep belief coupled with intention and action (in this case, the action was scouring through my purses) would fulfill all my goals, desires and dreams.

The Divine Collision

Here's another story about *money knowingness*. During that same time period around the divorce, I had some bigger bills that were due, and I was trying to figure out how I would pay them. One major bill was the final payment for my school tuition, totaling $2,400. I wasn't worried, because I knew the money would come somehow, especially since I was finally following my true calling and had found the right path. The educational program was coming to an end, and I was about to start my internship, so I wasn't bringing in any income as of yet. I was also still waiting for my child support agreement to be resolved.

It was a gorgeous sunny day and I took advantage of a surplus half-hour to drive down to the beach in Del Mar to meditate. I parked on 9th Street and looked out my open car window at the never-ending ocean. As I often did, I closed my eyes and inhaled the peacefulness of the ocean breeze and visualized myself working in my private practice, helping people get healthy, and motivating them to reach their potential. (Some-how I always knew I would do this kind of work.) At that very moment, out of the depths of the brazen blue sky, I heard, "Bang! Crunch!" as my car jerked abruptly to the left. I turned my head to get a clue about what the heck had just happened, and I saw that a young man in a white BMW had just smashed into the back left corner of my car. Needless to say, that quickly yanked me out of my meditative state.

The gentleman was very apologetic. He said he was driving slowly while looking out at the ocean, and somehow had not noticed my car. Luckily, the damage didn't look too bad, and I felt fine. We exchanged insurance information and he was on his way. I immediately called my insurance company and they set an appointment for me to bring my car in for a damage appraisal.

The next week, while I was waiting in the repair shop that my insur-ance company had recommended, I did a bit of multitasking and decided to pay some bills. I pulled out my checkbook and wrote a check for $2,400 for my tuition, setting an energetic intention for that amount, even though the funds were not yet in the bank. A few minutes later, the insurance adjuster came out to talk to me. He told me that the car would cost $2,400 to repair and that his company could handle the repairs, or he could just give me a check for that amount and I could handle it myself. "Of course," I thought to myself, "how appropriate." I smiled and said calmly, "I'll take the money and handle the repairs myself, thank you."

When I got to the car, I burst out with the biggest laugh. Talk about, "ask and you shall receive!"

There I was, meditating at the ocean about building my private practice, and a gentleman in a BMW drove up and basically provided the situation that would deliver the exact amount I desired to pay my tuition! You may be wondering, "What about her smashed car?" So I had a dent on the back of my car. At that point in my life, I really didn't care about material things. I was on a mission to create a life for myself doing the things I loved to do. I knew the money and stuff would come later.

> "We make a living by what we get, but we make a life by what we give."
>
> ~Winston Churchill,
> *Prime Minister of the United Kingdom, Nobel Laureaute (1874-1965)*

The challenging part is that deep belief often comes from personal experiences. It is not so simple to believe the check is in the mail when it has never arrived before! The trick is to fool yourself and pretend that the money has arrived, even if it hasn't happened yet.

The Karma of Money

Karma is an action that determines your future. Put simply, "You reap what you sow," or, "Your actions create a reaction, so choose them intuitively and wisely." The freedom of choice that money offers doesn't come without consequence. Just as you're creating intention toward your *Big Picture Vision*, you are creating intention with the money you spend. If you're a wild spender, you may have fun in the impulsive moment, but you will most likely pay later with regret or more debt. Freedom does not mean being irresponsible.

Money is energy and it just keeps traveling down the line. Once you realize that you're part of that line (because we are all connected in some way), you will begin to think about the effect your money has once it has left your wallet.

Blast Off! PRACTICE 4: Magnetize Your Money

Have you ever thought about someone you hadn't thought of in ages, and within the next day, they called you or sent you an e-mail? Have you talked to a friend about a venture or activity you wanted to be involved in (but didn't have the resources or contacts to get started), and all of a sudden, someone came along with all the answers you were looking for or they were the perfect person for you to talk with?

Your thoughts and words are powerful. You project them outwardly without even realizing it, and out of the blue, you receive. You can create the same response with money.

Set your financial intention through meditation on abundant thoughts and feelings, and watch the money roll in through unexpected checks and financial opportunities, inheritances, dream careers, windfalls—*you name it.*

* **Practice with coins and work your way up to your treasure chest.** Focus your energy on finding fallen coins wherever you go. Start your day by projecting a powerful "feel good" desire and intention for finding coins. Meditate for sixty seconds each morning on this feeling, and see yourself finding these coins throughout your day. Keep your eyes open and make sure you have room in your pockets.

* **Once you're comfortable and confident with receiving coins, shift your intention to dollars.** The money will appear on its own or by way of fiscal opportunities. Once these opportunities appear, see how you feel about them intuitively. If your gut says "go," then take action. *Intention and action are the most powerful duo in the cosmos.*

* **Write the amount you want to receive in your check register**, as if that is your actual bank balance. Just by writing that number down and telling yourself that the money is really there, you are setting your mental intention and projecting it outward. Your intention and action can change your make-believe vision into reality.

* **Write a check for a major purchase that you plan to make in the next ninety days.** Whether it is for an upcoming vacation, a new computer, a house remodel or a business loan, write the check to "you" in the amount you need to have for this purchase, and put it in a safe place. As you write

the check, visualize the amount you just wrote as if it were already in your bank account. Close your eyes and see yourself having the money to make your purchase. Repeat this visualization each day for forty-five seconds. Now plan your daily *Mini Feats* necessary to reach your goal. Then watch your dream unfold.

★ **Is there something you've been yearning to do, or to have?** Write a detailed short story (a page or two) with you as the main character involved in your activity, achieving your goal, or receiving your desire. Write about the experience as if it were happening now. Be very specific about how it looks, feels, how it turns out, what was said, and what you received from it. Read it out loud each day as you visualize and feel yourself performing your activity or receiving your desire.

It may take a week, a month or even a bit longer to shift the energy from survival to abundance. Patience and persistence are required. You may have moments of feeling frustrated and doubtful of the pending positive changes. Acknowledge those feelings and then bring your thoughts and actions back on track. The reward for all of this intention and action will be well worth the wait. ✪

Is Your Money Ruled by Your Emotions?

Do you spend and save based on the mood you're in? For instance, do you lose five pounds and decide to go on a shopping spree? Or do you gain five pounds and decide to go on a shopping spree?

I'm guilty and this is my confession. I used to sway between splurging on home decor and spending lavishly on shoes until my daughter started asking me to buy her designer purses at age twelve! That was the final straw, and even if I had the money, I felt that my emotional spending was not setting a great example for her money karma. Not that decorating your house is a bad thing, or that adorning your feet with the latest blingy styles isn't fun. I just needed to get clear about the motivation behind my purchases. Was my drive to buy born out of pure need or desire, or was there an inner frustration, longing or angst that could be propelling me to spend? Was I trying to fill an inner sadness, boredom or void with the swipe of my credit card? My honest answer was the latter.

Have you ever experienced feeling very strong, confident and worthy in your work in one moment? Then your boss throws a fit in your office regarding something you've done and you suddenly feel so beaten down and frustrated? As a result, you start thinking, "I feel so tired of struggling month-to-month for praise and money." This is despite the fact that yesterday, when your boss was happy, you were thinking, "I love my job." Do these feelings perpetuate a spending spree on unnecessary stuff to satisfy an emotional craving? Like the time you felt so excited about purchasing that blue velvet couch? Then you felt nauseous all the way home, and when the couch arrived, you wondered what the hell were you thinking!

> "The roots of all goodness lie in the soil of appreciation for goodness."
>
> ~The Dalai Lama,
> The spiritual leader
> and head of state for
> the Tibetan people

When spending is a result of emotional mania, you will not be a happy camper about your purchases later. To prevent emotional money purchases that only build debt and clog your wealth pipes, it's smart to create a backup action plan.

Here's one such plan. The next time the urge comes to spend frenetically rather than logically, *set a determined amount of time that you are committed to wait before acting.* When the pendulum of impulsive energy swings intensely in one direction, if you just wait a bit, maybe an hour or a day, it will surely swing back the other way. What goes up must come down. So you'll feel differently about your spending urge if you just cool your jets for a short while.

Emotional spending is an unhealthy compulsion that can be damaging to your life. Pre-plan alternate activities until the urge to splurge calms and passes, such as:

★ Going to a movie

★ Exercising

★ Writing about the feelings that you're experiencing in your journal to get to the core of what's creating your craving

★ Whatever else you can think of that would work for you

Just like when you're able to avoid a late-night pizza binge, once the cravings subside for spending, you'll feel so much better since you didn't react by frittering away your money. Do I still enjoy shopping? Of course I do. But now my purchases come from true choice, rather than a mood-reactive impulse. And that feels so much better in the moment... and the day after.

The Power of Appreciation

Similar to the Boomerang Principle 1 discussed in the Chapter Five (the Relationship chapter), the energy you create around money will come right back to you. Think about how you feel when you're paying your bills or leaving a tip at a restaurant. If you're focusing on how much money you do *not* have when you're paying your mortgage, you will be projecting to the Universe a feeling and frequency of "lack." The more energy of lack you transmit outwardly, the more lack you will receive. To make a positive shift in your financial situation, the energy you need to be projecting is appreciation—whether you're spending one penny or a million dollars.

The more you manifest appreciation around the money you spend, the more money will flow back to you. And I know you'll appreciate that! Follow the steps below to create *appreciative energy* around money:

- ⋆ Think about something you appreciate very much, such as your partner, your children or your animals.

- ⋆ When you think about them, feel the appreciative feelings emanate from your heart to the rest of your body.

- ⋆ Focus on and feel those appreciative feelings as you spend money or pay your bills.

- ⋆ Even if you don't feel appreciative now, fake it until you feel it!

- ⋆ Think thoughts such as: *"I am so thankful to have this home that I am thrilled to be paying my mortgage bill (or rent). This home gives me such a sense of security and warmth."*

- ⋆ When you're at a restaurant, think something like: *"It feels wonderful to tip this waitress. She did a great job for us tonight, and it gives me great pleasure to give back. I know she'll appreciate that too."*

★ And when you're making your car payment and paying for your auto insurance, think thoughts like: *"I'm so happy to pay this auto payment because my car takes me where I need to go, when I need to get there. My car insurance makes sure that I will be taken care of financially if I were to have an accident. I'm so thankful for that because there is no need to worry or even think about it."*

Appreciative energy is big and free flowing. Just the kind of energy you want flowing in your world.

Blast Off! PRACTICE 5: Thank You, Bills, Thank You

If you're still obsessing about your bills twenty-four hours after you pay them, you are creating nothing but money-sucking energy around you. A positive shift needs to happen to keep your money from running down the drain.

To activate your cash flow, write down each monthly bill that you are paying in a separate notebook. Think and feel appreciative thoughts in relation to these bills. Hold onto these uplifting feelings for at least one minute at a time.

For example:

Bill	New Appreciative Thoughts
Water Bill	I so appreciate having clean, fresh water.
Babysitter	I am going to tip her because she takes great care of our kids.

> "Money was never a big motivation for me, except as a way to keep score. The real excitement is playing the game."
>
> ~Donald Trump, Business entrepreneur, real estate developer, host of the TV show, The Apprentice

By simply shifting the energy from feelings of loss or focusing on what you don't have, to thinking and feeling appreciation, abundance and the great things your money is contributing to, you will attract more of the same feelings of appreciation and abundance you can bank on. ✪

When It Comes to Money, Think Big

Over the years, I've asked many clients how much money they would need in order to make their lives easier on a daily basis. Most of them answered pretty conservatively. They often felt that they were not allowed to ask for what they really want. Remember, we are completely responsible for placing limits on our life and income; therefore, we can also ask for and create the income we desire.

Why ask for $100, when you could ask for $1,000? If you're going to reach for $100,000, why not add another zero and reach for $1,000,000? Just as we need to dream big and take action toward our dreams, you can set a powerful intention for the amount of money you want to create. There is no cap on your capital unless you shut the lid.

As discussed in Chapter Four, I have written my Silver and Gold Platter Numbers each quarter over the past several years. This is how I set my intentions for my financial goals. Then my actions make the goals a reality. It's an approach that has always worked for me and I've seen it make a difference in my clients' lives as well. It can work for you, too.

Money Makes the World Go Round... So Give, Baby, Give

One of the most prosperous things you can do for yourself and others is give of your heart and your wallet. The energy you are creating when you share your wealth is powerful beyond measure. This frequency is similar to that of the ocean tide that rolls out with an energetic force, and then it flows back with a similar energetic force. Create a high tide of money by giving, and the heartfelt rewards you'll receive will be sure to rise above plain material wealth. To start your philanthropic flow of energy, try the following:

> "Let us not be satisfied with just giving money... Spread your love everywhere you go."
>
> ~*Mother Teresa,*
> *Famed missionary, Roman*
> *Catholic nun, and an*
> *advocate for the poor*
> *(1910-1997)*

* When you pay your bills each month, add another payment to your check register toward a charity you feel personally connected with. Make a commitment to increase that amount each year.

* As you send the payment, take a moment and focus on the appreciation you feel to have money to send. Feel the love toward the group you are donating to, and visualize how they will be using the funds.

* If you're not sure what charity or cause to donate to, there are organizations such as www.charitynavigator.org and www.charitywatch.org that research, list and rank thousands of charities for your review.

Have you noticed that most philanthropists are wealthy? A great secret of receiving is giving.

Create Wealth around You

Creating wealth doesn't need to be a solitary endeavor. While meditating on your financial goals, set another intention for your friends and loved ones. Close your eyes, think of those in need, and project abundant energy toward them. Imagine a gold light of abundance surrounding them.

Create a *Blast Off! Manifesting Wealth Group* that meets once a month to set and share financial goals and intentions. Gather up to six people together to motivate each other on your financial and professional goals on a monthly basis. At the end of each session, participate in a group meditation as you all visualize, feel and set the intention for money and financial opportunities to pour in for everyone. The power of group energy is magnanimous. This shared intention-setting can even be done over the phone in a group conferencing meeting if it's more convenient for everyone. Energy travels, so the same locale is not necessary to bring home the bacon. To become a *Certified Blast Off! Group Facilitator*, contact info@MyBlastOff.com.

The Seven Steps to Fiscal Wealth and Prosperity

Incorporate the following seven steps into your life and your money tree will begin to thrive.

1. Flip-switch your beliefs from negative to positive and know that money is abundantly available to you as you need it.

2. Set your mental intention by creating your financial *Big Picture Vision* and meditate on your financial goals.

3. Project your *money knowingness* outward through visually *feeling* your *Big Picture Vision* and financial goals. Do this at least 60 seconds each day.

4. Feel appreciation every time you give or receive money.

5. Take action steps every day, using your *Mini Feats* and *Mile Steps,* to move toward your positive intentions and your *Big Picture Vision.*

6. Think BIGGER than you ever thought possible and watch your wealth grow exponentially!

7. Expect to receive abundant wealth.

Keep this list visible throughout your day. Post it on your bathroom mirror, on your computer screen, on your refrigerator, or wherever you frequently focus your attention. Read it morning and night. Utilizing the Seven Steps of Fiscal Wealth and Prosperity can help you to *Blast Off!* financially in a big way.

The Value of Money versus Time

You may be earning a great income, but are you taking the time to truly enjoy your life? When I was earning a large income from running my advertising agency, my true wealth was in a deficit state. Why? Because I had no time to enjoy anything! I was a monomaniac for work. There was no time for the people and activities that brought me the most joy.

No time for my husband, child, friends, hobbies. I was fiscally wealthy and socially starving. I remember driving by the beach and watching people having fun. I couldn't understand how they had the time to do that. I barely had time to eat and sleep, much less lounge in the sun. I was choosing to run ragged, spending all my time doing something that drained my spirit instead of filling my soul.

> "Abundance is not something we acquire. It is something that we tune into."
>
> ~Wayne Dyer,
> Self-help author and lecturer

In your personal drive for wealth, it's all about balance. In fact, many Fortune 500 entrepreneurs who take more vacations actually make *more* money because they aren't just on a race to fill their bank account. They take time off to refuel their spirit. And a full spirit manifests even more creativity, more joy, and ultimately more wealth.

In the next chapter, you'll learn how to make time for fun, adventure and more spirit in your daily life. Remember, each realm of your life affects every other realm. When you're out of balance and lacking fun, adventure and spirit, your body and mind will talk to you. The key is to listen and act on your behalf. There's no one who can take better care of you than you.

True Wealth

True wealth is a balanced combination of financial, emotional, mental, physical and spiritual prosperity. The key to *blasting off* to success is to create abundance in all areas through the power of acting on your passions and intentions, and the love of your heart and soul. Money is energy, so it flows in and out. When it is attached to something that's meaningful to you, it will endure. Create enduring wealth through the manifestations of a passionate life.

Today is the perfect day to begin!

BLAST OFF! Daily Launch Tools

1. Each morning, write your *Sun-Up Script* and *Rocket Words*.

2. Read your *Rocket Words* to yourself and out loud as often as possible during your day.

3. Create and perform a minimum of *Mini Feats* each day. (These are the smaller steps for moving toward your larger *Mile Step* goals and your *Big Picture Vision*.) For example, today's *Mini Feats* might be:

- *Set up automatic payments from my bank account to pay my outstanding debts so that I don't have to focus any negative or worrisome energy as I pay them down.*

- *Pull out my Gold and Silver Platters, and think about the actions that I'm taking to head in the direction of reaching these goals. (Try taking one action every day this week, e.g., make ten sales calls, raise your fees if applicable, etc.)*

- *Look into developing a small business on the side. (Check out www.mysmallbiz.com for ideas.)*

4. Choose one to two *Blast Off! Practices* from this chapter to do each day over the next week.

5. Fill out your *Weekly Flight Assessment Log* to review your week's progress toward realizing your *Supersonic Life*.

Summary of the Chapter Concepts

➤ When the desire for a more abundant life finally overpowers your fear, you can step out into the world and capture your personal prosperity. Everyone who has achieved greatness in their life has faced fear at one time or another. The difference is that they keep moving forward, regardless.

➤ Survival consciousness is a way of being that creates thoughts like, *"Life is hard and you must struggle,"* and, *"You have to fight for what you have because you could wake up tomorrow and have lost it all."* Thoughts are energy and they create our reality. Therefore, survival consciousness creates survival reality.

➤ By flip-switching your thoughts from negative to positive, you immediately uplift the frequency of the energy in your body, even if the thoughts are forced. This shift in energy will improve your mood and motivation, and as a result, your positive thoughts will come more naturally.

➤ Money is energy. When you spend money, you are creating an outward flow of energy. When you receive money, the energy is flowing right back to you.

➤ Make room for money by surrounding yourself with people who are wise with their money and, at the same time, willing to take risks. Negative people and debt are two money-energy drainers.

➤ Take a close look at your finances regularly. Know where your money is going. Get your base monthly survival number and begin moving beyond that.

➤ *Abundance consciousness* says that you have the ability to create your reality, and that all you desire is possible.

➤ *Money knowingness* is the core belief that money will always be available when you need it. By developing this faith in the Universe, you can let go of your fears and survival thinking, and focus on your passion and your *Big Picture Vision*. If you are using intention and action, you will generate wealth.

➤ Money is a medium that provides freedom of choice and an avenue to pursue our passions. Money alone does not bring happiness, but utilizing it as a catalyst to create positive energy does.

➤ Your actions create a reaction. Your choices with money follow this same law, so spend wisely.

➤ Impulsive spending is ruled by your emotions. Have a financial plan in place so that your spending does not result from your high or low moods.

Summary of the Chapter Concepts (continued)

➤ By reminding yourself how blessed you are to have a home with running water and electricity, you can create an appreciative energy around your bills. You are receiving something in return when you pay your debts, such as a college education or cable television. Create positive, thankful energy when paying your bills. This is a sure way to propel the flow of money right back at you.

➤ You are the only one creating limits on the wealth you can receive. When focusing intention toward your goals and finances, think outside of the box—bigger than you ever have.

➤ Sharing the wealth by giving to those in need creates an extremely positive money frequency. Give and you shall receive.

➤ Read *The Seven Steps of Fiscal Wealth and Prosperity* every single day and project your *money knowingness* for 60 seconds.

➤ Time is of similar or greater value than money energy. If all you are doing is creating money with no space in your life to enjoy it, than you are creating a deficit in your emotional and personal well-being.

➤ True wealth is a balanced combination of financial, emotional, mental, physical and spiritual prosperity.

"Gratitude is not only the greatest of virtues, but the parent of all others."

~*Marcus Tullius Cicero,*
Roman statesman, philosopher, author and orator
(106-43 BC)

CHAPTER 8

BLAST Off!
to Adventure
and Amusement

> "I have always wanted an adventurous life. It took me a long time to realize that I was the only one who was going to make an adventurous life happen to me."
>
> ~*Richard Bach,*
> *Author of* Jonathan Livingston Seagull *and* Illusions

The only thing that stands between you and an ordinary existence, or one of soulfulness and adventure, which would you choose? If an ordinary, safe life is your preference, then protection and predictability are the motivators of your time here on earth. If you choose the latter, congratulations! You have decided to move beyond your fear and embrace a life path full of boldness and passion.

Boredom and frustration result when there is a chasm between attaining your highest calling, and existing in a life-limiting situation. Everyone has the potential to manifest an amazing life-adventure full of unforeseen miracles and treasures at every twist and turn. All you have to do is be willing to implement change, embrace life's surprises, and risk gaining everything.

The truth is that it can be hard to appreciate how great life is unless we have gone through some trying times. When you have experienced the contrast between happy times and times of struggle, you have a means of comparison. For instance, once you've had a great relationship, you don't want to enter into a bad one. Once you've had a fulfilling career, you will not desire to work in a stifling one.

I'm not suggesting that you go out and have a miserable phase in your life to appreciate what you have later. I'm only saying that an inspiration, life change or transformation will often follow a less-than-charming life experience or time period. Challenging or painful times are also some of the most growth-oriented phases. When you activate your will to survive a dark period, you inherently become stronger because your coping muscles are being utilized. You find out what you are made of when you're forced to tap into your power within.

A Flight into Fantasy

I was so determined to improve my life once I had hit a dead-end at age thirty. My transformation came from a primal need to heal and be released from my past, and a deep desire to create a nothing-less-than-brilliant life. Once my proverbial light bulb switched on, I was completely energized to capture every ounce of life that this vibrant world had to offer. My heart began to heal, and then it opened wide. My brain cells awoke from what seemed like an endless slumber, and my body was energized and ready to move. It literally all happened simultaneously, once I made the choice to let my soul breathe and not die.

After my divorce, I decided to travel. I felt the need to get away and regroup for the next chapter in my life, but I had no idea where to go. I had journeyed a great deal in my life, across the U.S. and to many foreign countries. Yet I had never traveled alone. My sister suggested that I get away for a week to a Club Med because it would give me the opportunity to explore a new area and meet new people in a safe environment. I agreed, hesitantly, since this type of excursion would be a completely new experience.

When you travel with another person, you know that there will always be someone to hang out with. Traveling alone was a big step for me, and an opportunity to break out of my comfort zone. I arrived at a gorgeous setting in Mexico where the sea was endlessly blue, and the

March weather was perfectly tropical. There were lots of seemingly fun and friendly people, yet early on, my shy side erupted and I found myself feeling completely out of place. I called my sister for solace and said, "This is just not for me. I'm taking the next flight out." She encouraged me to give it two days, and if I still hated it, then to come back to San Diego. I agreed, reluctantly.

> "There's no half-singing in the shower. You're either a rock star or an opera diva."
>
> ~Josh Groban,
> Singer and songwriter

At that moment, I left my room and sat near a court-yard to watch the salsa dance class. All of a sudden, I felt a tap on my shoulder. It was the dance teacher asking me to join his class. The instructor must have detected my resistance to this place because he wouldn't take my oppositional head-shaking seriously. The next thing I knew, I was moving across the dance floor feeling at one with the Caribbean music. And that was just the beginning of my adventure.

The next day, I went to the rehearsal for the Club Med performance and was selected as the lead character, Rose, for a spoof about the Titanic. We had about an hour to rehearse for the entire show, so you can imagine how disastrous we all were. It was the most fun and laughs I'd had in years! I had entered the vacation with my head between my knees, and now I was center stage, lip-synching the theme song of the movie *Titanic* to a guy I had just met, while he was faking his drowning and hanging onto a boogie board. The audience was in stitches, and my inner child had just died and gone to nirvana. And it didn't stop there. I met interesting people from all over the world there, and it felt so enlivening to talk, laugh and hear about their lives back home. I wasn't surprised to find out that many of them had also recently experienced some major life changes.

Flying with Ease and Joy

On the third day, I decided to explore the other side of the club. The Universe must have been guiding me, because I literally walked right into a sport that has become one of the greatest passions of my life—*the flying trapeze!* Yes, folks, just like in the circus. I don't know about you, but when I went to the Barnum & Bailey show at a very young age, I remember being mesmerized by those gymnasts in the sparkly outfits who flew gracefully and bravely through the air with the greatest of ease. So my palms started sweating and my heart was pounding with anticipation when I saw a trapeze setup at the Club Med. I knew I had to be up there.

I joined in the class that was in process and watched intently to assess what the other flyers were doing. I was so excited, but completely clueless and terrified at the same time. I climbed the thirty-foot ladder up the trapeze rig while strapped tightly in safety lines. For some reason, it seemed at least 100 feet high when I was on the pedestal preparing to jump. I was told by the professional flyer (who was holding onto my life by a rope) that once they called "hep," which means "begin" or "get the heck off the board," to bend my knees and jump while gripping the swinging bar with my hands. They called "hep" three times and, for some reason, my feet remained glued to the board. By the fourth call, they got tired of waiting and pushed me off the pedestal and into the air.

At that moment, the shock was replaced by adrenaline, and I was immediately transported to that young girl in my backyard swinging and flipping on her uneven bars. My muscle memory took over and I was able to throw my legs over the trapeze bar with ease, swing from my knees, and then do a backflip into the net. It was the most exhilarating, freeing moment I had experienced in years, and with that one swing, I was completely hooked.

My sister called during the afternoon of that third day to see if I was still planning to come home early, and I told her that I didn't have time to talk because I was on my way to perform in the trapeze show. She cracked up laughing and replied, "Thank God. The old Allie is back." *I was indeed!* I spent the rest of that week rediscovering what it felt like to play and embrace life. My heart was literally bursting with joy.

This is a perfect example of someone stepping outside of their comfort zone. If I had gone home early, or not visited Club Med at all for that matter, I would have never experienced this extraordinary glimpse of a new reality, and an opportunity to recapture my life.

Bringing the Vacation into My Daily Life

I arrived back in California with a bold, brazen perspective on life. My *Secret Spark* for adventure and the trapeze had been lit and I was determined to not let it die out. I immediately researched a trapeze school and found one in Los Angeles that is run by professional flyer and trainer, Richie Gaona, a fourth-generation circus performer and a member of The Flying Gaonas. I spent the next several years driving back and forth to Los Angeles to challenge myself, to improve on my flying stunts, and to have a blast flying high in the sky. It was completely worth the two-and-one-half-hour drive to Los Angeles and back. I made use of that time for some of my most creative brainstorming.

> "Because of our routines, we forget that life is an adventure."
>
> ~Maya Angelou,
> Author, poet and civil
> rights activist

With Richie's guidance, my array of tricks grew from knee hangs to splits, double flips and seat rolls off of the bar. A few years ago, I was blessed to have a trapeze rig built right in San Diego, called Trapeze High, where I have the opportunity to fly as often as possible.

Do I get fearful up there? *Absolutely.* Every single time I climb the ladder, in fact. But I keep climbing because the other option would be to sit on the sidelines of my life and watch it pass me by. The flying trapeze is a power-packed lesson in letting go, combined with a large dose of trust as you throw your body vulnerably to the catcher. When I am up on the trapeze rig, I'm not thinking of my responsibilities at home or work, or my issues of the day or of the world. Not that those aspects of my life aren't important… but in that moment, I can release it all and be completely and utterly in the moment. And that, my friends, is ecstasy.

Capture Your Bliss

What adventure is out there that you have always wanted to experience, but were afraid to try? Or maybe you feel like the time has never been just right. Well, people, the time will never be right unless you choose to make it so. Today, right now, is the absolute perfect time to step out of your comfort zone and reach for your dreams.

This is your life, and you have complete power over your choices. You will know that you have found your bliss when you are wholly absorbed in that action, and in that moment, as if nothing else exists. Yes, it's time to get off the couch, away from the office, turn off the computer and create some fun. What exciting and challenging sport have you stopped playing? When was the last time you went dancing? What about a biking or running group? Golf or tennis lessons, anyone? How about putting yourself out there in an acting class? There is so much fun just waiting for you to join in. Boredom and stuckness exist out of pure choice. Set the intention for more fun and adventure in your life, and then, as always, take action.

If you're at a loss for fun ideas, pick up your local weekly newspaper and see what's happening around town. The Web is another great resource for all kinds of fun stuff. I realize you have lots to do at home or work, but I promise you that it will all be there when you get back.

Fun is one of the most important aspects of a *Supersonic Life*. As we get older, the focus leans toward responsibilities of work and our personal life, which are obviously important. However, when you're having fun, everything else in your life will shine that much brighter. You'll be lighter at work, at home, with your children and, most importantly, with yourself. Having fun is one of the best things you can ever do for yourself. So don't procrastinate any longer. Start now! Break out of your box and create a newfound relationship with fun.

Blast Off! PRACTICE 1: Fun Finder

In your journal, *The Blast Off! Workbook,* or the *Blastation* software, make a list of fun stuff that you'd like to do. Then make a commitment to give some of the activities a try until you find a few that have that *blast* factor. (Try one for fun, see how it feels. If it's not a match, simply move on to the next.)

Enjoy the process. Experiment, experience... *Blast Off!* ✪

Blast Off! PRACTICE 2: What Are Your Top Three Funtastics?

From the list above, choose three favorite activities that are most fulfilling to you. List them wherever you are recording this series of exercises.

If these three favorites are not already in your life on a regular basis, do whatever it takes to make it a reality. For instance, make a point of regularly scheduling them into your calendar. These fun splurges will add leaps and bounds of joy to your daily experiences, your overall moods and your ability to maintain healthy relationships. They will help build self-confidence and relieve stress, while bringing you more into the present moment. ✪

Love Yourself First

I realize that I have touched on this in a few other chapters, but it's important to mention it again with regard to personal fulfillment. The love and acceptance of yourself and others will change your life. It's difficult to enjoy the special moments or be in the present when you're criticizing yourself or others. If you want to step into a *Supersonic Life* of adventure and fulfillment, it's time to let the negativity go. Shame, hatred, anger, self-deprecation, apathy and fear will only attract more of the same.

> "If you are personally fulfilled in your heart and soul, body and mind, this is the greatest gift of all."
> ~Allison Maslan

Once you begin to let go of these negative emotions, you are literally making room for love and acceptance. Love is powerful and infectious. Spread it far and wide, and it will return right back to you. A great example of this is in the movie, *Pay It Forward,* when a young boy, Trevor, gets inspired by a class assignment about coming up with a concept that will change the world. His idea? To not pay favors back to the originator, but to do nice things for three *other* people. Trevor's idea succeeds after initially appearing a failure, positively affecting people he doesn't even know (as well as those he does), and it helps him cope with his troubled home life.

Blast Off! PRACTICE 3: The Smile Magnet

Nothing is more engaging than a smile or a laugh. What do you do when you walk by a stranger at the shopping mall or the bank? Do you barely say hello, then put your head down and keep walking? Or do you just look the other way pretending not to notice them?

We have become such a fearful, shut-off group of human beings that we miss out on so much magical interaction. One of the easiest ways to quickly connect with others and to manifest happiness is to look directly at a passerby and say, "Hi!" with a smile. Believe it or not, this alone can make someone's day. And the more happiness you create, the more uplifting energy you'll be surrounding yourself with. I challenge you to smile at as many strangers as you can for one week. See the amazing difference in your daily experience. You may just want to make this a permanent way of living! ✪

I Love to Love Those That I Love

Spending time with my loved ones—both family and friends—brings me insurmountable feelings of peace and happiness. Just hanging out with my husband, enjoying great talks with my daughter, going out to dinner with my girlfriends, and laughing with family. These moments are priceless. While I'm experiencing them, I make a point to create an inner snapshot with my eyes, head and heart so these moments will always stay close to me.

I commend you for taking this journey to find and experience your passion in life. Along this path, remember those you love. Their connection, acceptance, and unconditional love will be the motor that pulls you through the bumps in the road. Make time to get together with friends, give extra love to your partner. If you have children, tell them how important they are, and don't forget to call your mother. Spread the joy. These are simple secrets of an abundant love-filled life.

Love from Our Furry Friends

As I am writing this book, I am surrounded by my fan club: Wilbur, our nine-year-old Golden Retriever; Daisy, our nine-month-old Bulldog, and Miko, our fifteen-year-old, full-of-wisdom cat. Writing can be a solitary activity and these furry buddies have kept me company from page one.

Animals are love-actualized. Honestly, I was never a big animal person. We didn't have pets at home when I was younger, so I never developed that natural connection. Now that I'm older, I have had the luxury and blessing of being surrounded by animals, and they have added so much love, peace and entertainment to my life. They just want to "be" with you to give and receive love. It's as simple and beautiful as that.

If you don't already have an animal at home, I encourage you to adopt one. It's a surefire way to open your heart and add tremendous fulfillment to your life.

Travel: The Perspective Shifter

I've traveled to many places over the years, and every single time I take a break away from my daily life, a perspective shift emerges. When you're too close to a problem or situation in your life, it's often hard to see the big picture or find optimum solutions. When you're experiencing angst, frustration, fear, stress or any taxing emotion, sometimes the best thing to do is to take a break from it all.

There are obviously many options for traveling, depending on your budget and time frame. Journeys to foreign countries where you can experience other cultures can be life-altering. To experience the people and their ways of being, foods, language, art and music will completely open a narrowly focused life perspective.

Traveling can be empowering in that you are taking charge of your direction and opening your visual windows to completely new horizons. To travel is to explore. Visit the Great Wall of China, climb Masada in Israel, take the journey to Machu Picchu in Peru, ski the Swiss Alps, sail in the Greek Isles, parasail in the Caribbean, experience the volcanoes of Kauai, wonder at the glaciers of Alaska, and scuba dive at the Great

Barrier Reef in Australia. Stepping into another world will shift you out of your busy mind, and into a soul-filled voyage.

Traveling can be an extremely spiritual quest because getting away from your daily routine will bring you back to yourself. Away from the hustle and bustle of life, you can stop, breathe and ponder over your existence and purpose. When you get some distance, travel will give you the opportunity to take stock of your present life, and give you enough space to strategize your next steps.

> "I think that travel comes from some deep urge to see the world, like the urge that brings up a worm in an Irish bog to see the moon when it is full."
>
> ~Lord Dunsany,
> *Author and playwright, leading figure in the development of modern fantasy literature (1878-1957)*

Traveling with a loved one can rekindle your connection, traveling with friends can be a blast, and traveling alone is empowering and freeing. Traveling with someone you don't enjoy can be miserable, so choose your travel partners wisely.

You don't have to wait for a big block of time to open up so you can take a grand trip. Traveling a short distance can be healing, too. My husband and I take lots of short weekend trips, and we come home feeling completely inspired and refreshed. Short escapes are also a wonderful way to reconnect with your inspiration and creativity. Sometimes your genius-inspired ideas cannot find room in your already crowded brain at home. My senses are awakened whenever I travel, and this stimulates my creative mind. In fact, some of my best ideas were born while traveling. I believe it's time to start packing now. (See the Resource section at the end of the book for sources of travel info.)

Blast Off! PRACTICE 4: Destination Unknown

In your journal, *The Blast Off! Workbook*, or the *Blastation* software, list your favorite travel destinations and new places that you'd love to visit. Be bold, be daring, and explore the world! ✪

Move from Body to Mind and Mind to Body

You may be both physically and mentally centered. However, in most people, there will be a little more energy in one direction or the other—the mental or the physical plane. How about you? Which area do you favor?

For instance, are you a logical, left-brained, analytical type person? Do you spend a lot of your time in the thinking mode? Does your career or passion involve more mental energy rather than physical? Do you live your life from the neck up? If you operate mostly from your brain, I challenge you to involve yourself in activities that are more body-centered. By doing this, your energy and blood will begin to flow from your head down through your torso and limbs, awakening the physical energy of your body. This will actually bring even more oxygen to your brain.

There is absolutely nothing wrong with being a very mentally focused person. You can achieve great things! However, if you stay primarily in your head, one day you will wake up and find yourself cut off from the rest of your body. So get up from your desk and shake that body.

Or, alternately, are you more of a physically centered person? Do you tend to get bored with mind-crunching activities? Are you much happier in motion? Do you enjoy challenging your physical agility or strength? If so, your energy is that of a body-centered person.

One of my athletic clients, Joseph, shared this experience: "I have realized that after long runs while training for my upcoming marathon, I become so brain dead. It's as if my body has taken all of the focus and my mind becomes a bit spacey." All of Joseph's energy is being channeled to support his body during his training; therefore he becomes unfocused mentally after a tough workout.

If you are more body-centered, I challenge you to incorporate more mental stimulation into your life to awaken that part of your being. Having a physically centered life is fantastic, but to fully utilize the amazing equipment you were born with, you need to energize your brain cells. They may be dormant but, trust me, they are anxiously waiting to be ignited. Try going to a museum, taking a class at a local college, reading a non-fiction book or playing backgammon.

Balance is the key, and to achieve this, try accessing and stimulating your *whole* body. For instance, once you experience being in your body after a period of being inactive, you may feel parts of yourself that you didn't know existed. Interestingly, moving the energy from your brain to your body will actually stimulate your creativity and mental capacity.

And by the same token, stimulating your mind after it has been in neutral for some time will feel exhilarating and enlivening.

> "Laugh as much as you breathe and love as long as you live."
>
> *~Unknown*

Be a Kid

Think about the times, as an adult, that you've really let loose and had fun. You laughed with abandon, danced freely without a care, were silly and spontaneous, and it all felt so damn good! What do all of these experiences have in common? It's that childlike energy surging forth from the deepest part of you. The kid in you that, at this moment in time, is releasing any requirements or expectations. You're just being in the moment and fully taking hold of it.

How do children look at life? They see it through eyes that are filled with wonder and amazement. Imagine what it would feel like to have that same wonder and amazement in *your* daily life. You would be so excited to get out of bed in the morning. You would have fun at work connecting with your friends, want to embrace each day, and look forward to experiencing new things. You would find humor in the smallest things, and you wouldn't care what others thought of you. You would express your feelings and then move on, instead of harboring them for days, or even years. You would feel full of energy, ready to go play, rather than sitting and waiting for life to happen. You would have dreams of being a great this, or a famous that, and believe in your heart that one day it would come true. Yes, that is you, just a few decades later.

What if you could bring that excitement and enthusiasm into your present day? You can if you choose to draw out the best of your inner kid-self.

> **Blast Off!** | PRACTICE 5: **It's Kid's Week**

It's time to tap into that kid inside of you and embrace life with fun and curiosity. Pretend that you're looking through your eyes at age seven. Go through your week and experience as much as you can in your ordinary day from a childlike perspective. See how different every moment can feel with a shift in your approach and outlook. Write about this experience in your *Sun-Up Script*. And remember, it's never too late to awaken those innocent childhood dreams. ✪

What's Your Secret Muse?

The word "muse" originates from Greek mythology, where the goddesses or spirits inspired creativity through music, dance, writing and stage performances. Your personal muse could be that special something that inspires you to play, to sing, and to express yourself in artistic ways. It can be anything that inspires you to be creative in your life.

A muse may come from nature, the arts, history, spirituality, society, a relationship or any aspect of your everyday life. For instance, a new romance often inspires lyricists to write beautiful poetry or love songs. A painting or drawing may represent the muse that inspires you to pick up a paint brush too, or a song on the radio could be a muse for starting your day on a high note by singing in the shower.

> "Originality is an unexplored territory. You get there by carrying a canoe—you can't take a taxi."
>
> ~*Alan Alda, Actor, star of the* Mash *TV series*

Learn to recognize and utilize your favorite muses as a way to stimulate your creativity. Practice tapping into your muses when creating new ideas for business or fun, to express and release emotions, and to bring peace to your heart and soul. And, as you will do in the next practice, think of a muse especially when you need inspiration for a creative endeavor.

Blast Off! PRACTICE 6: Put Your Muses to Work

It's time to put your muses to work to inspire re-involvement in one of your past creative passions, or to motivate yourself to come up with a completely new one. How long has it been since you:

* ★ Played a musical instrument?
* ★ Wrote poetry?
* ★ Painted with finger paints or watercolors?
* ★ Tried ballroom dancing?
* ★ Took singing lessons?
* ★ Cooked for fun?
* ★ Worked in your garden?

In either your journal or *The Blast Off! Workbook*, make a list now of all the creative endeavors you want to explore. Try a new one each week, and if you find ones that really click, make them part of your regular schedule.

Creative expressions can be practiced at any age. Try not to take them too seriously. Be in the moment and have fun. That is what matters most. You may be surprised to find how your spirit lifts, your energy improves, and your overall motivation increases. In fact, *your life may never be the same.* ✪

A Catnap Is Our Friend

If you're a productive sort of person, you may have the idea that napping is for the lazy or unmotivated. In reality, napping is one of the healthiest, most rejuvenating practices you can do for yourself. Research shows that you can make yourself more alert, reduce stress, and improve cognitive functioning with a short nap. Even a brief five minutes of shut-eye can make a difference, but fifteen to twenty minutes is preferred. Too long of a nap may cause you to feel more groggy rather than re-energized.

If you're feeling bothered by a certain issue, you'll most likely feel better after a nap. In fact, the term "sleep on it" means taking an idea or situation and digesting it in your sleep. After just a short nap, you're likely to have more clarity, become more relaxed, and be better able to access your creativity. As a result of all this, you'll feel more upbeat.

Some of the most powerful people in our past used short naps to recharge their brains, including Benjamin Franklin, Winston Churchill, Margaret Thatcher and Brahms, the lullaby guy.

> "Dreams are illustrations... from the book your soul is writing about you."
>
> ~Marsha Norman, Playwright, screenwriter, novelist

Your Dream Life

Dreams are the window to your soul. When we shut off our body and mind, dreams are free to roam through the caverns of our unconscious. They can inspire creative ideas, guide you through conflict in your present and past, help you to get to know yourself on a deeper level, and allow you to discover hidden thoughts and meanings related to yourself.

Your dreams might seem silly or strange and may not make any sense at all. It's important to not take dreams literally, but rather to look at the feelings behind your dreams. Two people may have the same dream, but the meaning of the dream can be very different to each person. For instance, if you were chased by someone in your dreams, you may feel terrified and unable to scream, whereas someone else may think the chase experience is exciting and wild. Those differences can tell you a lot about your inner self, and what you are feeling in your waking life.

In general, what happens to the characters in our dreams isn't usually about those people, but rather some aspect of us or our lives. If you dream about having a child, it may be about your desire to be reborn or a craving for major change in your life. If you dream about looking for your childhood home, it may be more about finding that child inside of you, or the security you had (or didn't have) as a child.

Dreams are something we typically don't control. It's a time when we allow our ideas, pains, desires and fears to run amuck, rather than trying to plan the outcome. By taking a closer look at your dreams, you can utilize this special tool, which is completely unique to you, to gain insight, heal from past issues, and to tap into what drives your *Secret Spark*. Let's try this in the next exercise.

Blast Off! PRACTICE 7: Dream-Scaping

Here are some helpful tips for accessing, analyzing, and gaining insight from your dream life.

1. **Write down your dream as soon as you wake up**. If you wait, there's a good chance that the images will have already vanished. I believe our conscious mind is trying to protect us, so it forces these stories out of our head when we open up our eyes.

   It's helpful to keep a dream journal right by your bed. Write down as much detail as you can remember about your dream. Who was in it? What was said and done? What were you wearing? And most important, how were you feeling during the dream?

2. **Right after you have written down your dream, follow this up with writing about what you think the dream means to you.** Jot down any ideas, memories, hunches or thoughts. There is no right or wrong thought that arises or format in which to do this.

3. **Read back through the dream and see if you can come up with any additional detail**. What the people said in the dream, how the rooms were decorated, what the energy felt like in the dream. For instance, if you were watching an approaching tidal wave, what did it look like? Were you facing it alone? Was anyone there to support you? How were you feeling? What was the outcome? If you were alone, it could mean that you're feeling like you have to face overwhelming challenges all alone and you want some support. If you were rescuing someone, it could mean that the responsibilities in your life now (or in the past) feel overwhelming.

4. **Write down any other details and feelings you may have missed concerning the people or characters in your dreams.** See if these people or characters might relate to a particular aspect of your personality or life. Could they represent a hidden part of you, a deeply held desire, or a

betrayal or a guilt that you're carrying around? What would you ask these people if you had the chance?

5. **What do you feel is the overall message or theme of your dream?** Is there anything you can learn from this dream? Is there a fear you would like to overcome? If it was peaceful, is this calming image something you can use in your meditation or as a creative muse? Is there an action that you need to take which your unconscious is trying to push you towards? Is there a gut-knowingness about something in your life that you're not facing? Is your dream calling you to have more fun, to find your purpose or passion, to spread your wings and fly?

6. **Draw, paint or collage your dream, if you are inspired to do so**. Often more insight and memory will be jogged through artistic expression. This is a way to make sense of the dream, release any negative emotions, and help yourself look at it objectively on paper for even deeper understanding.

7. **Utilize stream-of-consciousness writing to release negative feelings in your dreams.** Several years ago, I kept having a recurring dream of an argument with someone I was very angry with, but had no way to express it to them in real life. Night after night, I would rehash this same argument. It was so frustrating and exhausting. One night after having this dream, I awoke and started writing my strong feelings wildly across the paper. I really let it all out. From that point on, I never had that dream again. The reason the dream kept coming up was because I needed to work through it and let it go. Let the paper know how you feel. No holds barred.

> "Where there is love, there is life."
>
> *~Mahatma Gandhi, Spiritual and political leader of India (1869-1948)*

By learning to access, question and analyze your dream life, you open yourself up to a whole other part of your world—the one that exists from dusk until dawn. If you're having disturbing dreams that you cannot seem to shake, I recommend seeking out the counsel of a Jungian, art or sandplay therapist (see Resources) to help unlock and hopefully shift them to more pleasant experiences.

Your *Blast Off!* to adventure continues! ✪

Cherish Your Friendships

My father used to tell me that if you have one great friend for your lifetime, you are a very lucky soul. Having frequent contact with friends is a very healing and fulfilling aspect of life. As you get older, it's easy to lose track of friends. You have gotten busier, maybe you have a family now, and before you know it, months or years go by and you haven't spoken to your friends. Not because anything bad happened, you just didn't take the time or make the necessary effort to stay connected. You may forget how uplifting and fun it is to hang out with friends until you do it again.

As we age, it can take more effort to make and keep friends because we tend to meet people on a deeper level during our growing times in life, or when we shared an experience or bond through a life phase or event. Friends can lend us support, insight, laughter and love. My close girlfriends have added gobs of substance to my life. Knowing they are just a phone call away is extremely comforting.

It's sometimes harder for men to reach out to other male friends because they were often taught at a young age to be tough and work it out for themselves. That is why it is even more important for men to make an effort to keep their friendships alive. My husband gets together with several of his college buddies a few times a year for skiing and mountain biking trips. He has a blast with them, and then he is ready to come home. It's a great balancer for him. When men have an outlet for their emotions, they feel freer, more understood, and they learn to be more open. We girls come out of the womb talking, so there's usually no issue there.

Great friendships can endure for a lifetime. They are part of our history and an important part of a *Blast Off!* life. Pick up the phone and call an old or new friend. You both will be so glad you did.

Nurture Yourself in Nature

When you step back from the ringing phones, cars, pollution, and white noise, then enter the vastness, beauty and serenity of nature, your entire energy will flip-switch to the positive. Have you ever experienced the difference in your breathing when you are in nature? Whether you are camping in the mountains, hiking in the desert, or sailing on the ocean, your body will feel soothed, and your lungs are free to expand rather than constrict.

Being surrounded by nature is one of the most fulfilling, energizing, and profound experiences you can have, whether witnessing the glory of giant redwoods, watching a deer and her fawn walking together, or taking in the calming sounds of a running brook. Nature can also breed wonderful inspiration. It can help clear your mind of clutter so you can actually think, it can bring you back to your childhood dreams, and it is one of the most spiritual environments you will ever be a part of. When you look at the mountains or the trees, they seem to look back and say, "Don't take life so seriously. It's not so important in the big scheme of things, and it will all still be here tomorrow."

Incorporate some time in nature every week, whether it's a morning jog in a park, a hike in the woods with your dog, or a stroll along the ocean or by a lake. Afterwards, it's likely that the issue you were all wigged out about before will have already floated off into the horizon.

People Helping People

One of the best things you can do for your health is to step outside of yourself and help others in need. Giving of your time and energy is one of the most personally fulfilling actions you'll ever do. A smile and a handshake will go a very long way for those who have been hurt, became ill or were neglected. Find a charity or cause that you can connect with in some way. You will put much more into the volunteer work if it is a cause that you can truly get behind.

> "Life is either a daring adventure, or it is nothing."
>
> ~Helen Keller,
> Deaf-blind author,
> lecturer, activist
> (1905-1968)

When I have gone through some of the more painful times in my life, helping others was a monumental aspect of my own healing. It forced me to get out of my own pain and focus on others' needs. Before I knew it, my pain was a memory. Nothing puts your struggles into perspective more than experiencing someone else's woes.

Blast Off! PRACTICE 8: Your Giving List

In your journal or *The Blast Off! Workbook,* make a list of different charities or causes that you would like to give some of your time and energy towards. What causes or organizations have been calling to you? ✪

Blast Off! PRACTICE 9: Your Bucket List

In the 2007 movie called *The Bucket List,* Jack Nicholson and Morgan Freeman serendipitously share the experience of learning that their days on earth are numbered because of their terminal illnesses. Morgan Freeman begins to write his bucket list, the things he wants to experience before he dies. Jack Nicholson encourages him to make the dreams come true and they proceed to leap from airplanes, eat caviar, explore the Great Wall of China by motorcycle, and express love to those who need to hear it.

Don't wait until your time in this world is limited. Live life today like there is no tomorrow!

In this exercise, make a list of all the things you want to do in this lifetime. Jot your ideas in your journal or workbook, or input them into the *Blastation* software at www.InteractiveLifeCoach.com.

Next, do whatever it takes to experience each desire on your list. Mark it as accomplished when completed. ✪

> "All good things are wild and free."
>
> ~Henry David Thoreau, American author, Transcendentalist, naturalist and philosopher (1817-1862)

Blast Off Now!

A *Blast Off!* life is one of passion, personal achievement, peace and fulfillment. If you leave this chapter learning only one thing, I hope you have come to believe that you absolutely deserve a spectacular life experience that includes plenty of fun, love and adventure.

No one is going to do it for you. And most likely, you will not be told to claim it by those around you. It is your responsibility to claim what is meant to be your *Blast Off!* life. Grab it, capture it, and take ownership of your own personal wonder. Start today!

BLAST OFF! Daily Launch Tools

1. Each morning, write your *Sun-Up Script* and *Rocket Words*.

2. Read your *Rocket Words* to yourself and out loud as often as possible during your day.

3. Create and perform a minimum of *Mini Feats* each day. (These are the smaller steps for moving toward your larger *Mile Step* goals and your *Big Picture Vision*.) For example, today's *Mini Feats* might be:

- *Do research online for some travel destinations that I would like to explore.*
- *Call the local running club about joining.*
- *E-mail my friend Kris, who I haven't connected with for a while, and suggest we make a plan for lunch.*

4. Choose one to two *Blast Off! Practices* from this chapter to do each day over the next week.

5. Fill out your *Weekly Flight Assessment Log* to review your week's progress toward realizing your *Supersonic Life*.

Summary of the Chapter Concepts

➤ Taking steps to experience new and exciting activities in your life can feel like you're moving into uncharted territory. In reality, once you do it, this won't be uncharted territory anymore. It will be your new known territory.

➤ Where is your bliss? What fun, adventurous or fulfilling activities can you explore that will bring you happiness and joy?

➤ Are there some fun activities—such as acting, biking, swimming or canoeing—that you have either not done in a long time, or always wanted to try? Now is the time!

➤ Joy starts from the inside. The external things will bring temporary fulfillment until you begin to love and accept yourself. Self-criticism and judgment of others will only keep you in a negative space and hold you back from creating your life potential. But once you feel great about yourself, just the way you are, you can then begin to fully enjoy the external aspects of your life.

➤ Spending time with those you love will provide the mental snapshots that will stay with you for the rest of this lifetime. Finding your passion is incredibly fulfilling, yet being aware of and enjoying the passion and love around you is priceless.

➤ Animals can offer you unconditional love and acceptance. Their unique personalities and devotion can bring you peace, healing and happiness.

➤ Travel is a way to take a break from your everyday life and obtain a big picture perspective on any conflicts or stressors. Travel can be life-changing, spiritually centering, adventurous and exciting, whether you jaunt across the globe or take short breaks to a nearby town.

➤ If you are a mind-centered person, moving your energy down into your physical body will feel energizing and freeing. It's a way to release any mental overload. If you are a body-centered person, awakening your napping brain cells and senses with educational or thought-provoking material or experiences can help to stimulate your whole person, rather than your half person.

➤ When was the last time you were silly, wild with abandon and spontaneous? What would your life be like now if you could let go of the controls and infuse more of the fun, curious kid in you?

➤ What's your muse? What inspires your creativity? What makes you want to sing, dance, paint or write poetry? A muse is inspirational and it creates new life out of nothing.

➤ Catnaps are the secret tool of many great people—including scientists, musicians, inventors and politicians. Just a short snooze each day can restore your body and mind, and get you recharged so you can embrace the rest of your day.

Summary of the Chapter Concepts (continued)

➤ Dreams may seem elusive, but they can hold the key to solutions for conflicts or struggles in your life. They can offer insight, wisdom and help guide you along your path.

➤ Friendships can spark incredible warmth, support and joy. However, when you have more responsibilities, it may take more effort to cultivate and maintain friendships within your busy life. That is all the more reason to keep the connections going. When you make the time to bond, you will be so glad you did.

➤ Nature is one of the most powerfully healing and spiritually fulfilling elements of our planet. Enveloping yourself in nature through hiking, adventure and exploration is like wrapping yourself with the wonders of the Universe.

➤ Giving is a tremendous healer for both the giver and receiver. There's something so precious and exalting when, from your generous heart, you help to create a smile on the face of someone in pain or in need.

➤ Have you written a bucket list? List all the things you want to experience during this lifetime before you kick the bucket. Then start checking them off today, one by one.

➤ What are your top three favorite, most fulfilling activities that you love to do, or have always thought of doing, but have not tried yet? Think about how much happier and personally fulfilling your life will be once you incorporate your 1-2-3!

"Man cannot discover new oceans unless he has the courage to lose sight of the shore."

~Andre Gide,
Nobel Prize-winning French writer
(1869-1951)

CHAPTER 9

Your
BLAST Off!
Plan for Life

"We all have the
extraordinary coded
within us, waiting to
be released."

~Jean Houston,
Scholar, philosopher,
researcher, one of the
founders of the Human
Potential Movement

Congratulations! To have reached the final chapter of this book, you have obviously also reached a new chapter in your life. Chapters in life, as in books, give us the wisdom to succeed with the subsequent life stages. The key, of course, is to draw on the lessons of our past experiences so that we make new and improved choices as our story evolves.

There's nothing that I'm sharing with you in this book that I haven't done myself. As your mentor, I am not just feeding you information; I have walked and continue to walk the talk. I feel confident in saying that if you fully apply the concepts of this book to your own life, you will succeed.

My greatest hope is that my book has empowered you with the passion and wisdom needed to create your new direction, and the fortitude to support your flight toward the dreams of your lifetime. If you experience fear rising from the pit of your stomach, know that this is just part of the process. The fear will begin to subside when you accept that it is there, and take action regardless of its existence.

Do I have all the answers? No, of course not. My journey has had its own chapters of soaring to new heights, and others riddled with comical crashes and burns. (They are comical now that they are in the past.) My grace has been that once I have pronounced a new dream or my *Big Picture Vision*, I've headed in that direction and didn't take "no" for an answer. Snafus and roadblocks are inevitable when you embark upon a new path. Sadly, the challenging times are when many people get paralyzed, overwhelmed and give up. The ironic thing is that they were probably just inches from achieving their goals.

> "Success means having the courage, the determination, and the will to become the person you believe you were meant to be."
>
> ~George Sheehan,
> *Author, track star, cardiologist*
> *(1918-1993)*

Anything worth having will bring about challenges. But if you really want to reach your destination, the challenges make the victory that much sweeter. I was blessed with the knowledge (or you might say the stubborn perspective) that there is always a way—even if the situation seems bleak. If you are told something cannot be done, denied a request, receive disappointing news, or hit the proverbial wall, always, always, always look around the corner or explore the hidden crawl spaces for a solution. If you look hard enough, the open door will appear.

As you begin to apply this book to your life, I invite you to do the following:

1. **Go back and reread the book.** There's a lot of information here to soak up in one reading. On the second time through, review the practices that you benefited from the most and complete the ones that you passed over. Give special attention to the chapters that apply to the areas of your life which are screaming for attention, and those that desire a new way of living. Remember, even if you don't need help in a certain life area, such as a new career or a new relationship, many of the lessons from every chapter can be successfully applied to any area of your life. And let's face it, there is always room for improvement.

If you worked the book alone initially, you can create a *Blast Off! Group* for this seond go-through. The power of a group is priceless to help keep you on task with the program, to assist you in offering insight in how to reach your goals, and most importantly, to throw some fun into the mix. For information on becoming a *Certified Blast Off! Group Facilitator*, contact us at, info@MyBlastOff.com.

2. **Apply the *Blast Off! Launch Tools* as new habits for your everyday life.** Habits are routines and actions that become repetitive. Just as we all, at times, adopt some bad habits, we can just as easily take on good ones. Note that most desires do not appear as a reality in our life without the combination of purposeful intention and action—which result from good habits. (Unless, of course, love comes knocking at your door and you marry your mail carrier. This did happen to one of my clients!)

3. ***Blast Off!* every day.** Do your daily *Sun-Up Scripts*, and stay focused with intention on your *Big Picture Vision*. Then take your *Big Picture Vision* and work backwards from there. Start accomplishing your *Mile Steps* through the action of your daily *Mini Feats*. This fail-proof flight plan will catapult you to the stars.

I tell all my coaching clients that this program is everything but rigid. Instead, it's flexible and can fit within your lifestyle. If you find that your *Sun-Up Scripts* are better done before bed, then make them *Sun-Down Scripts* and go for it. If it's hard to schedule a specific time for each *Mini Feat*, just get them done at some point in your day. This book is designed to make your life more fulfilling, not more complicated. I know that if the tools were inflexible, you might not stay with them. All I ask is that you do them. *Why?* Because, my friend, they work.

4. **Surround yourself with inspiring and motivating people.** You may find that your usual crew begins to thin out as you take on a new life direction. As I've mentioned earlier in the book, making choices to realize your dreams may offend some friends, family or coworkers, and bring up fear in others. This is to be expected and it's just part of their own life process. By surrounding yourself with like-minded individuals, you're less likely to cave into criticism and contagious doubt. If you receive any negative

words of advice, just smile, say, "Thank you for your opinion," and let the person know that they don't need to offer any more suggestions regarding your life changes unless you ask for them. In this manner, you are setting boundaries from an empowered yet respectful space.

5. **Start Your Own *Blast Off! Launching Group*.** There is strength, power and incredible energy that can be generated within a group. Not to mention motivation, inspiration and accountability. You are more likely to stick with your goals knowing that you will be checking in with your team every week or two. Get your friends together, post a flyer at work, a listing on www.Craigslist.com, or www.Meetup.com. See page 265 for specific details on setting up your own *Blast Off! Launching Group*. Create your own *Blast Off!* movement while sharing the motivation, excitement and fun of a team.

6. **Hire a life coach with a successful track record** to help you navigate toward your dreams. A life or career coach will help clarify your dreams and visions and then keep you motivated and on track to attain them. The secret of many prosperous go-getters is that they have at least one personal or life coach. I recommend finding a coach who has experience and is living the wisdom he or she is teaching. The support of a coach or mentor is priceless and your investment will return to you in numerous ways. Check out my coaching website for further opportunities for support and guidance, www.MyBlastOff.com.

7. **Be easy on yourself.** Change and transformation can bring up all sorts of good, bad and ugly stuff. When you feel yourself struggling, take a break. If you make a mistake, big deal! If you're headed in a direction that you're not feeling good about, it may be time to re-assess. You have the freedom to change your mind. This doesn't mean you've failed, it just means that path was not a good fit. You learned something from it, right? Then it has been a benefit to your next endeavor. Give yourself kudos for all your hard work and let's move on to another *Big Picture Vision*.

8. **Start now.** You don't want to look back in ten years and realize that you're still at the same place in your life then as now. Even if you love your life now, growth is a necessary part of your evolvement on this planet. Every single day of your life is precious. Embrace it, and those you love, to the fullest.

9. **Stay in touch.** Send me an e-mail at Allison@MyBlastOff.com and let me know how this book has changed your life. Hearing of the insights, achievements or dreams you've realized through utilizing this process is my greatest reward.

Before you finish the book, here are some key words of advice. Out of everything I've shared with you, the most important point to remember is that *you deserve to be happy*. Whatever the circumstance, there's a way to make positive changes. Never settle for anything less than joy and your highest potential.

May all your dreams come true.

Here's to your *Blast Off!*

> "When you live your life with a knowingness of abundance, and you take steps toward receiving this abundance, you'd better be prepared to receive all that magic that is coming your way."
>
> ~*Allison Maslan*

A Final Note

My husband and I went to the beach today with our three dogs to celebrate the completion of my book. As we walked along the Del Mar shore, I was inhaling the ocean air as I felt a sense of exhilaration in my step. I said to my husband, "I did it!" At that moment, as the dogs were bouncing through the waves, I was overcome with gratitude for all the love and beauty in my life. Mike put his arm around me and said, "This is a sand dollar day. I can feel it." I replied, "Really?" in my curious manner. He said with certainty, "Yes, I feel it. Can't explain it. I just feel it."

Now I've lived in San Diego for the past twenty years and I've never seen a complete sand dollar on the beach. Occasionally, I might find a nickel-size broken piece of one, but never a whole sand dollar. Yet, all of a sudden, we both spotted what looked like a flattened round sand-colored shell with a flower petal imprinted in its center. Oh, my God! How synchronistic is that? I reached down and scooped it up. It was so lovely, complete and whole. I honestly thought it was a mirage. After admiring it for a few minutes, I made a wish and threw it back into

the water where it belonged. As I was still high on elation for receiving this gift, my husband spotted another large one with the graceful petal imprint. I was astounded. They are so rare, and to find two!

We continued on our walk in the glow of our magical find, and right as I looked down at my feet, there was another gorgeous sand dollar. And, I kid you not, another and another! On this extraordinary day, we ended up finding a total of five perfect sand dollars.

> "Dream as if you'll live forever... Live as if you'll die today."
>
> ~James Dean,
> *Movie icon and star of the film* Rebel Without a Cause
> *(1931-1955)*

I'm not sure if that is a world record, but having never laid eyes on a whole one before, it was definitely a personal record for me. At that moment, I was experiencing the acknowledgment of everything I live my life by and everything I had just finished writing about.

How To Create Your Own
Blast Off! Launching Group

Choose people to work with that are at your level or a level above you in reaching your life goals. Each member of the group can act as a catalyst for inspiration and support. If you are surrounding yourself with people that are not willing to do the work and make the necessary changes in their lives, there is a great possibility that you may become stuck or feel held back.

> "You lift me, and I lift you, and we ascend together."
> ~*Anonymous*

Don't be afraid to reach out of your comfort zone and ask people to join your group that are out of your daily life realm. If someone has already achieved a great deal in their lives, it may be time for them to take everything to the next level. This group is the perfect launching pad for this.

I call the groups *Blast Off! Launching Groups* because working through the book while involved in a cohesive group will literally propel each of you to create the dreams and goals you are ready to manifest and achieve.

I recommend anywhere from four to eight people in each group. If there are too many members, each person's share time becomes limited and the meetings will go on too long.

Each *Blast Off! Launching Group* should meet every other week at the same time and place to keep a consistency and flow of action, and to prevent confusion on such details.

Choose the focus of the group. For instance, if you want to focus the group on career and finances, you may not want to work through Chapter Five on relationships, Chapter Six on health and Chapter Eight on adventure and amusement.

If you want to focus only on finding your soulmate, you may not work through Chapter Four on career, or Chapter Seven on financial prosperity. The rest of the chapters can work together to benefit your relationships.

I believe that a truly abundant life is creating fullness in all the areas discussed in *Blast Off!*, so working through each chapter together can only benefit you in your highest calling for success and fulfillment.

Requirements for Group Participants:

1. All members need to take a personal pledge to take responsibility for the choices, actions and scenarios in their lives. For change to happen, you must first take a hard look at yourself and be completely honest about your own contribution to every life situation. This does not mean you need to be critical or hard on yourself. It means you should say, "This is what I have done in the past. It is obviously not working for me, so what am I going to do differently now so that I can feel empowered and reach my goals?" Coming to the group and spouting off blame or victimization only weakens your ability to take control of your life and makes you completely dependent on the past. It also brings everyone else down. Your present and future joy and success depends on this shift in personal ownership thinking. No more excuses!

2. All feedback from group members needs to be honest, yet in a positive and supportive manner. The *Blast Off! Launching Group* needs to be an inspiring and uplifting experience for all members. Insight and suggestions from each member are pertinent for the group's success. However, make sure that your suggestions are expressed in a positive manner, rather than judgmental or critical. You want group members to feel comfortable to express themselves.

3. The *Blast Off! Launching Group* is not a therapy group. Although there will be emotional issues and roadblocks that will arise in your success process, this group is not about continuous venting of your emotional baggage. The intent of your *Blast Off! Launching Group* is a supportive, inspirational and

strategic gathering of like-minded individuals that are setting an intention and taking action to reach their dreams and goals. Fear and emotions will undoubtedly come up. However, the commitment of the group is to use the principles of the *Blast Off!* book to move everyone forward past their roadblocks to make positive changes and results.

The Blast Off! Launching Group Process:

1. Set an intention for the meeting.

Begin the group meeting by setting a positive intention for the groups process such as, "We are all here to share abundance, creativity and fulfillment in one another's lives and to inspire and ignite one another's greatness."

2. Set a time limit for each person to share.

If you want to keep the sharing time to an hour and you have six people, keep the sharing time to ten minutes each. Assign one member to be aware of the time. Allow a few minutes between each member for ideas, observations, and insight from other group members. Make sure your time keeper is cognizant of the clock during this process as well.

3. State your *Big Picture Visions* and Goals.

As each person shares with the group, state your *Big Picture Visions* in the areas of life that you are working on. In each session, state your progress in forward movement toward these goals since the last meeting. Then state what you plan to complete by the next meeting. Make a commitment, to yourself and the group that reflects your intention to take action. If you are feeling stuck or need support or advice from the group, state this out loud and allow the other members to offer positive insight or suggestions.

4. Discuss the reading and exercises assigned the previous week.

At the end of each share, take a minute or two to discuss the exercises you have worked on and what you have realized through their completion.

5. Complete your meeting.

a) Assign exercises for next meeting.

Decide as a group what reading and exercises everyone needs to complete by the next meeting. I suggest two exercises per week. The reading and exercises are pertinent for continued growth and success for the members and group as a whole. Utilize them as a guide to launch you past your barriers and to open up a whole new realm of possibilities.

b) Positive conclusion.

End each *Blast Off! Launching Group* meeting with an inspirational quote from the book. Or have everyone make one positive statement (not a discussion) of something they are grateful for in their lives.

Many Ways to Launch Your Dream Life

There are many more ways to launch your *Blast Off!* experience.

Visit www.MyBlastOff.com for information on:

* Complimentary *Blast Off!* Newsletters full of valuable advice and tips.

* *The Blast Off! Surefire Success Plan Workbook* that is the companion book for working with the practices from the main book, *Blast Off!*

* Free download of the *Big Picture Vision Board* form, the *Mile Steps Spreadsheet*™, the *Mini Feats Calendar*™, and the *Weekly Flight Assessment Log*™.

* Audio Version of *Blast Off! The Surefire Success Plan to Launch Your Dreams into Reality*™.

* E-Book of *Blast Off! The Surefire Success Plan to Launch Your Dreams into Reality*™.

* *Blastation*™, the Interactive Life Coaching and Planning Software Program.

To receive one-on-one support, contact Allison Maslan at Allison@MyBlastOff.com. Or visit www.MyBlastOff.com for background on her *Blast Off! Life Coaching Program*.

To book Allison Maslan for a dynamic speaking engagement or for bulk sale pricing on any of the *Blast Off!* products, please e-mail our sales office at info@MyBlastOff.com, or call us at 888-844-3550.

And for information on the *Blast Off! Group Facilitation Certification*, contact info@MyBlastOff.com.

Here is a selection of recommended resources to complement your *Blast Off!* expedition.

Chapter 1: Blast Off! to a Life of Passion and Meaning

Books

The Architecture of All Abundance by Lenedra J. Carroll

Built to Last: Successful Habits of Visionary Companies by Jim Collins and Jerry I. Porras

Dare to Dream! 25 Extraordinary Lives by Sandra McLeod Humphrey

Happy for No Reason by Marci Shimoff

The Purpose Driven® Life by Rick Warren

Chapter 2: Blast Off! to Soulful Living

Books

Invocations: Calling Forth the Light that Heals by Jacob Glass

The Power of Now: A Guide to Spiritual Enlightenment by Eckhart Tolle

The Science of Success by James Arthur Ray

Siddhartha by Hermann Hesse

Stillness Speaks by Eckhart Tolle

Audio

Your Inner Awakening: The Work of Byron Katie: Four Questions That Will Transform Your Life by Byron Katie

Websites

www.MyBlastOff.com—For guided meditation tapes to help you slow down and enjoy the journey of life.

www.youtube.com/jacobglass—For lectures on YouTube by inspirational teacher Jacob Glass.

www.ashtangayogacenter.com—For worldwide workshops with leading ashtanga yoga teacher, Tim Miller.

Chapter 3: Blast Off! to Limitless Living

Books

Feel the Fear... and Do It Anyway by Susan Jeffers

Feel the Fear... and Beyond by Susan Jeffers

You'll See It When You Believe It by Wayne W. Dyer

Websites

www.MyBlastOff.com—For guided meditation tapes to break through fear that is related to your dream career, to calm your mind, and to overcome daily stresses.

Chapter 4: Blast Off! to the Career of Your Dreams

Books

Discover Your Passion: An Intuitive Search to Find Your Purpose in Life by Gail A. Cassidy

Go With Your Gut by Mary Goulet

Little Red Book of Selling: 12.5 Principles of Sales Greatness by Jeffrey Gitomer

The Mozart Effect: Tapping the Power of Music to Heal the Body, Strengthen the Mind, and Unlock the Creative Spirit by Don Campbell

Small Business Success by Mark Leblanc

The Western Guide to Feng Shui: Creating Balance, Harmony, and Prosperity in Your Environment by Terah Kathryn Collins

Whiff: The Revolution of Scent Communication in the Information Age by C. Russell Brumfield

Websites

www.braingym.com—A website featuring an effective process for using movement to open and activate right and left brain functions for better focus and processing capabilities.

www.businessownersideacafe.com—A gathering place for budding entrepreneurs with information on financing, networking, and marketing; it also offers inspiration from others who are following their dreams.

www.careerplanner.com—Lists over 12,000 careers, including educational requirements, job outlook, salary ranges, work environment, etc. This is a very comprehensive tool.

www.InteractiveLifeCoach.com—*Blastation* software that helps you to create a vision for your dream career through *Big Picture Vision Boards* and *Dream Career* exercises, and then supports the necessary actions steps with electronic versions of the *Mini Feat Calendar* and the *Mile Steps Spreadsheet*.

www.jobstar.org—A website offering free templates for effective resumes.

www.monster.com—A website where you can post your resume and receive career advice. Offers an extensive career database.

www.mysmallbiz.com—A resource site for small business ideas.

www.score.org—An organization that provides volunteer mentors for new business owners and entrepreneurs.

www.toastmasters.org—A non-profit organization founded in 1924 that helps individuals develop public speaking and leadership skills through practice and feedback in local clubs.

www.vocationvacations.com—Test drive your dream career by taking a dream job holiday as you work with an expert mentor in the ultimate career of your choice.

Chapter 5: Blast Off! to the "Love-of-Your-Life" Relationship

Books

Getting the Love You Want: A Guide for Couples, 20th Anniversary Edition by Harville Hendrix

In the Meantime: Finding Yourself and the Love You Want by Iyanla Vanzant

Love Is a Choice: The Definitive Book on Letting Go of Unhealthy Relationships by Robert Hemfelt, Frank Minirth, and Paul Meier

DVD/CDs

The Soulmate Kit by Arielle Ford

Websites

www.chemistry.com—Online dating service.

www.InteractiveLifeCoach.com—Go here for help with creating your *Soulmate Shopping List* and *Soulmate Statement*, and begin attracting the partner of your dreams into your life or take the relationship you are in now to the next level.

www.match.com—An online dating service.

www.perfectmatch.com—An online dating service.

Chapter 6: Blast Off! to New Heights for a Healthy Body and Mind

Books

Accepting Your Power to Heal: The Personal Practice of Therapeutic Touch by Dolores Krieger, Ph.D., RN

Family Guide to Homeopathy: Symptoms and Natural Solutions by Andrew Lockie

Healing Visualizations: Creating Health Through Imagery by Gerald Epstein

The Homeopathic Guide to Stress by Miranda Castro

The Homeopathic Revolution: Why Famous People and Cultural Heroes Choose Homeopathy by Dana Ullman, MPH

Impossible Cure: The Promise of Homeopathy by Amy L. Lansky

Pilates by Rael Isacowitz

Sam the Cooking Guy: Just a Bunch of Recipes by Sam Zien

Staying Healthy With Nutrition, 21st Century Edition: The Complete Guide to Diet & Nutritional Medicine by Elson M. Haas and Buck Levin

Ultimate Core Ball Workout: Strengthening and Sculpting Exercises with Over 200 Step-by-Step Photos by Jeanine Detz

Yoga as Medicine: The Yogic Prescription for Health and Healing by *Yoga Journal* and Timothy McCall, M.D.

Websites

www.healingtouch.net—This Healing Touch Program website provides referrals for practitioners, as well as publications and information.

www.homeopathic-academy.com—Three-year Homeopathic Certification Program in Southern California founded by Allison Maslan, CCH.

www.homeopathicdirectory.com—The Council for Homeopathic Certification website provides a directory of certified classical homeopaths.

www.homeopathy.org—The North American Society of Homeopaths (NASH) website offers a resource directory of professional homeopaths who are registered with the Society in the United States.

www.jinshinjyutsu.com—The official site for Jin Shin Jyutsu (Oriental medicine style of healing touch), which contains a practitioner locator.

www.nationalcenterforhomeopathy.org—Non-profit organization that educates and provides information on homeopathy.

www.olivija.com/meditate2/—A website with information on prana-yama breathing for calmness and clearing unhealthy emotions.

www.youcanhealyourlifemovie.com—an inspirational and healing movie about the life and work of Louise Hay, author of the best-seller *You Can Heal Your Life*. The film is also about compassionate self-healing.

Chapter 7: Blast Off! to Financial Freedom and Prosperity

Books

The Abundance Book by John Randolph Price

Harmonic Wealth by James Arthur Ray

Secrets of the Millionaire Mind by T. Harv Eker

Soul Currency by Ernest D. Chu

The Success Principles by Jack Canfield

Websites

www.InteractiveLifeCoach.com—*Blastation* Software that gives financial exercises and budgeting capabilities to help you move from your *Blue Plate Special* Number to *Silver Platter* and your ultimate *Gold Platter*.

www.thisismoney.co.uk/calculators—Interactive calculators to compute potential savings, money-saver budgets, loan repayments, mortgage, taxes, insurance and pensions.

Chapter 8: Blast Off! to Adventure and Amusement

Books

Dreams, Symbols, and Homeopathy: Archetypal Dimensions of Healing by Jane Cicchetti, RSHom

Just a Bunch of Recipes, by Sam Zien

Websites

www.connectthedogs.com—A service that helps you find the perfect dog for your lifestyle.

www.dreammoods.com—Dream Moods is a free online source that assists you in interpreting your dreams.

www.flytrapeze.com—Fourth-generation circus performer Richie Gaona's trapeze school in Woodland Hills, California.

www.learningtogive.org—A resource site for The League, an organization that teaches giving and volunteerism.

www.nationalgeographicexpeditions.com—Originated in 1999, this travel program of the National Geographic Society operates more than 200 trips a year.

www.virtuoso.com—A leading provider of adventure, nature and luxury travel.

www.sandplay.org—Site for the Sandplay Therapists of America (STA), which offers information on this approach to personal exploration and development.

www.trapezehigh.com—A flying trapeze training facility in Escondido, California.

Note: All the resource website addresses were current at the time of publication. *Blast Off!* is not responsible for domain or content changes related to any of the recommended Internet sites.

How to Use the Forms

Here's a recap on how to use the *Blast Off!* forms provided in the upcoming pages:

First, you can use a copy of the *Big Picture Vision Board* form to write each *Big Picture Vision*. Create *Big Picture Visions* for each area in which you want to create change or wish to move to higher levels of success and prosperity. Every *Big Picture Vision* should be the ultimate, most beautiful and satisfying end-result you could ever imagine. Write about your *Big Picture Vision* as if it is actually happening right now as you wish in the present moment.

Now turn to the *Mile Steps Spreadsheet*. Using the spreadsheet, you'll break down each into the crucial *Mile Steps*—these are BIG steps needed to make your vision a reality. List the *Miles Steps* horizontally across the top of the spreadsheet. Then it's time to break down the *Miles Steps* into small daily *Mini Feats*—the valued activities or tasks that move you forward to the accomplishment of a *Mile Step*. *Mini Feats* only take a minimum of five minutes each to complete, but you may be so motivated that you will do the feat for a longer time. On the spreadsheet, list the necessary *Mini Feats*, vertically under the *Mile Step* it pertains to.

The third form is the *Mini Feat Calendar*. Use this calendar to chart out the timing (day and actual time of day) of your *Mini Feats* each week. Plan three *Mini Feats* for each day. Sunday is a good day to plan this out. This way you'll start your week on an upswing with a clear roadmap toward your goals. *(Note: Subscribers could do all of the work above in the* Blastation *software.)*

And last but not least, the fourth form is the *Weekly Flight Assessment Log*. This log will help you evaluate and track your progress each week. You'll see what you're doing well, and what you need to work on more. To help yourself keep the commitment to fill out the log weekly, you may want to make it a habit to fax it to a supportive friend or *Blast Off! Group* member.

Note: There are filled out samples ahead of all the forms for your information and inspiration.

Big Picture Vision Board™

Describe your personal or professional vision in the first person
as if it is happening right this very moment.

Epic goal: _____

_____

_____

_____

_____

_____

_____

_____

_____

_____

_____

_____

_____

_____

_____

_____

_____

_____

_____

_____

_____

Sample: Big Picture Vision Board™

Author's note: This would be the *Big Picture Vision* for someone like Sherry in Chapter One.

Describe your personal or professional vision in the first person
as if it is happening right this very moment.

Epic goal: _Own my own clothing store in three years._

I am on the way to work at my clothing store called The Finer Things.
I actually love going to work now because it doesn't feel like a job.

I enjoy taking care of my clients and seeing them so happy when they find
an outfit they love. Merchandising my window displays is fun and
challenging. It's an artistic outlet for me and I always do my best to draw in
clients. My business has been open a year now and last weekend we had our
biggest sales record to date! I am getting many return clients and they
are referring The Finer Things to their friends. I also really love going to
the marts and buying merchandise. It's always exciting to see the next
season's styles from the designers. I've made some great friends in the
industry, too. I am so thrilled and proud of myself that I took a risk and
went after my dream. My business is already turning a profit and will
double in sales in the next few years. After five years, I plan to open my
next location.

Mile Steps Spreadsheet™

Write your Mile Steps℠ (the large steps that need to happen to reach your *Big Picture Vision*℠) on the top row of this spreadsheet. Vertically, under each Mile Step, write out all the Mini Feats℠ that need to happen to make this Mile Step actualize. Then select the Mini Feats to input into your Mini Feat Calendar™. *Copyright © 2009 Allison Maslan. All Rights Reserved.*

Sample: Mile Steps Spreadsheet™

Write a Business Plan	Find Location	Get Financing	Take a Business Class	Learn Buying/ Merchandising	Register Business	Set-up Accounting
Research business plans	Call area realtors	Call SBA for information	Research local colleges	Research area fashion colleges	File fictitious name	Research bookkeepers
Contact Score.org	Meet with realtors	Apply for credit line	Register for classes	Research online classes	Apply for resale license	Research tax accountants
Write business plan	Go visit locations	Research investors		Register for class	Open business bank account	Buy accounting software
	Research Craigslist	Ask Uncle Joey for $$				

Write your Mile Steps℠ (the large steps that need to happen to reach your *Big Picture Vision*℠) on the top row of this spreadsheet. Vertically, under each Mile Step, write out all the Mini Feats℠ that need to happen to make this Mile Step actualize. Then select the Mini Feats to input into your Mini Feat Calendar™. *Copyright © 2009 Allison Maslan. All Rights Reserved.*

Mini Feat Calendar™

Week from _____ **to** _____

	MiniFeat	Hour	MiniFeat	Hour	MiniFeat	Hour
Monday						
Tuesday						
Wednesday						
Thursday						
Friday						
Saturday						
Sunday						

Week from _____ **to** _____

	MiniFeat	Hour	MiniFeat	Hour	MiniFeat	Hour
Monday						
Tuesday						
Wednesday						
Thursday						
Friday						
Saturday						
Sunday						

Enter three valued activities each day in your Mini Feat Calendar™ that will move you toward your *Big Picture Vision*℠. Write the time of day you will be performing your Mini Feat activity so that you will be more committed to following through. Each Mini Feat needs to be a minimum of five minutes in length. You might plan the Mini Feats for the coming week on the weekend.

Sample: Mini Feat Calendar™

Week from	January 5, 2009		to	January 11, 2009		
	MiniFeat	**Hour**	**MiniFeat**	**Hour**	**MiniFeat**	**Hour**
Monday	Research business classes	7:30 AM	Study business plan writing	12:30 PM	Research clothing stores	7:00 PM
Tuesday	Research business books	7:30 AM	Research financing	12:30 PM	Pick 5 stores to apply	8:00 PM
Wednesday	Research business class	7:30 AM	Research financing	12:30 PM	Fill out finance applications	4:30 PM
Thursday	Organize my office	11:00 AM	Study business plan writing	12:30 PM	Turn in finance applications	4:30 PM
Friday	Organize my office	11:00 AM	Research business coaches	7:00 PM	Study fashion magazines	8:00 PM
Saturday	Go hiking	8:00 AM	Meet Susan for lunch	noon	Finish office organizing	2:30 PM
Sunday	Read business books	9:30 AM	Start writing business plan	1:30 PM	Call Kathy to discuss my plan	4:00 PM

Enter three valued activities each day in your Mini Feat Calendar™ that will move you toward your *Big Picture Vision*™. Write the time of day you will be performing your Mini Feat activity so that you will be more committed to following through. Each Mini Feat needs to be a minimum of five minutes in length. You might plan the Mini Feats for the coming week on the weekend.

Copyright © 2009 Allison Maslan. All Rights Reserved.

Weekly Flight Assessment Log™

Date: _____

This evaluation is to assess the gains and roadblocks scattered along your new path. At the end of each week, fill out this assessment to evaluate your journey and your progress. Choose the keywords from below that resonate with you in each particular sector. Mark the applicable ranking in the space provided. Then briefly describe any gains or roadblocks for this past week. (Gains are any personal, emotional or tangible movement forward. Roadblocks are personal, mental or tangible challenges or detours.)

Gains & Roadblocks Keywords:

1. Stuck, trapped

2. Drained

3. Frustrated

4. Indecisive

5. Unmotivated

6. Bored

7. Exploring new options

8. Confused about what option to take

9. At a plateau, enjoyable but ready for more

10. So far so good, but time for the next level

11. Successful

12. Fulfilling

13. Inspiring and exciting

14. Supersonic Wow!

Career

Ranking _____

Gains _____

_____

Roadblocks _____

_____

Relationship

Ranking _____

Gains _____

_____

Roadblocks _____

_____

Health

Ranking _____

Gains _____

_____

Roadblocks _____

_____

Financial

Ranking _____

Gains _____

_____

Roadblocks _____

_____

Personal Fulfillment

Ranking _____

Gains _____

_____

Roadblocks _____

_____

Spiritual

Ranking _____

Gains _____

_____

Roadblocks _____

_____

Sample: Weekly Flight Assessment Log™

Date: _____ January 8, 2009 _____

This evaluation is to assess the gains and roadblocks scattered along your new path. At the end of each week, fill out this assessment to evaluate your journey and your progress. Choose the keywords from below that resonate with you in each particular sector. Mark the applicable ranking in the space provided. Then briefly describe any gains or roadblocks for this past week. (Gains are any personal, emotional or tangible movement forward. Roadblocks are personal, mental or tangible challenges or detours.)

Gains & Roadblocks Keywords:

1. Stuck, trapped

2. Drained

3. Frustrated

4. Indecisive

5. Unmotivated

6. Bored

7. Exploring new options

8. Confused about what option to take

9. At a plateau, enjoyable but ready for more

10. So far so good, but time for the next level

11. Successful

12. Fulfilling

13. Inspiring and exciting

14. Supersonic Wow!

Career

Ranking _____ 9 _____

Gains _I have reached the top level of management in my career._
I learned so much and feel good about my accomplishment.

Roadblocks _I am missing the feeling of challenge and stimulation at work._
I am feeling bored and ready to create a new path for myself.

Relationship

Ranking _____10_____

Gains _I am putting more time and energy into my relationship. We've been_ _having much more fun together and this has lightened my feelings of stress_ _in other parts of my life._

Roadblocks _I would like to create a lifestyle that allows us to take more_ _time away together. I am feeling stuck on how to do this._

Health

Ranking _____9_____

Gains _I made it to the gym four times this week. I felt tired but I was able_ _to motivate my body to get there anyway. I now have so much more energy!_

Roadblocks _I want to figure out a way to exercise during my lunch hour so_ _that I have more time to do fun things after work._

Financial

Ranking _____8_____

Gains _It looks like I will be receiving a nice bonus this year for all of my efforts!_

Roadblocks _I want to create a side business to supplement my income and to_ _express more creativity and passion in my life. I need to find a coach to help_ _me do this._

Personal Fulfillment

Ranking _____6_____

Gains _I am having more fun in my relationship._

Roadblocks _I am realizing that I have not tried any new activities in a long_ _time. I am in need of some adventure._

Spiritual

Ranking _____3_____

Gains _None_

Roadblocks _I planned to try some meditation or yoga and I have not been_ _motivated enough to make it happen. I am going to create Mini Feats to make_ _both of these happen. I feel that they help me clear my head and feel more_ _connected to myself and others in all aspects of my life._

Acknowledgments

This book is a culmination of my personal and professional journey. I have been blessed with much love and support along the way. I would like to extend my heartfelt gratitude to...

My soulmate, Michael Rees. You are the love of my life, and have encouraged my dream since Day One. It took a while to find you, but you were worth the wait. Thank you for your unending love and patience during this past year of late-night and weekend writing marathons. Now you have your wife back. Tahiti, here we come! And my beautiful daughter, Gabriella. You fill my heart daily with your bright light. Never stop believing in yourself and your dreams. I love you.

Thanks to my mom, Phyllis Marcum. You always told me I could achieve anything I set out to do. See, I did listen. And to my dad, Herbert Maslan, for passing your entrepreneurial spirit down to me, and the belief that all is possible.

My sister, Wendy. Thanks for being my cheerleader. You have always believed in me and made me laugh until my stomach hurt. My big brother, Jeff, who I have always looked to for sound advice. Your marketing savvy has been instrumental in the growth of *Blast Off Life Coaching*. Bobbie Ruff for being my second mom and teaching me about love.

My path has been adorned with gifted mentors and coaches who have been catalysts to my personal and professional growth. My heartfelt gratitude to Sid Wolf, Ph.D., for rescuing me from the hamster wheel, seeing and revealing the healer in me, and directing me down my personal Yellow Brick Road. I am forever grateful for all the knowledge and wisdom you bestowed onto me. You have helped me to help so many.

My deepest gratitude to Mark LeBlanc. When I came to you for direction on the next turn on my path, you said, "You already have it. You just need to tell the world." Without your guidance and encouragement, this book would not have been born. You rock!

To Markus Heon, my trainer and friend. You have pushed me beyond my limits three grueling and gratifying days a week for over a decade. Thank you for revealing my strength and reminding me to never settle for anything less than the best. Richard Pitt for his unending support and guidance as a homeopath, school director and friend. Louis Klein, my teacher, for opening my eyes to the possibilities. Thank you Jayesh Shah for sharing your gift, wisdom and kindness. My clients have been blessed from all that I have learned from you. Corrine McMullen, for holding my hand that very first year as a homeopath. Thank you, Rita Dove, my college creative writing professor and Pulitzer-Prize-winning poet, for teaching me to translate and shape my words so that the audience would really hear and understand me. And Ms. Chappell, my high school English teacher, for encouraging me to keep writing. The influence from these two women made a powerful impact on my life.

Some of my biggest gifts are the rare friendships that I have been bestowed in this lifetime. My friends are like family. Susan Sandler, my soul sister, for sharing twenty-five years of tears of joy, laughter and love on this merry-go-round we call life. Even though you are three thousand miles away, it feels like you're right here. I so respect your ability to speak and live your truth. You are truly congruent and your friendship continues to make my life so much richer. Kelly Zien, for your strength, love and forthright communication. Your honesty and directness has helped me at crucial turning points to open my eyes when I was not seeing straight. You have been my rock. Mary Goulet for your unending friendship. We have lived many lifetimes together over the last fifteen years. My gratitude for your divine loyalty and love. You forged this path as an author before me. Thank you for lighting the way and holding my hand in this process. My love to Lori Stephenson-Strickland for your beautiful spirit and depth that nourishes me so. Dahlia Shemtob and Bara Waters, fast friends since the first day of homeopathic school. We share a language and a road that is foreign to many. Cindy Sanders for keeping me laughing during those ludicrous moments in life. You have been a huge support ever since you walked into my office those many years ago. Thank you Malcolm Smith for your entertaining and loving support as we cruise down similar *Blast Off!* paths. And to Sam. My heartfelt gratitude to you. You raised the bar in my eyes on how a stand-up guy should be. You are the man.

My appreciation to my assistant, Samantha Conboy, for all the attention you give my private practice. Thank you for taking such great care of me and my clients.

Many thanks to Stephanie Gunning, my publishing consultant, for your perceptive ear and helping me to blast off into the publishing world. It was destiny that we met. Your finesse and guidance have been instrumental to the book's success. My gratitude to Robin Quinn for her editing skills and valuable input in my writing process, and to Sarah Sleeper for your editing magic. Your keen eye saved this book! Thank you, Sarah. My graciousness goes to William Gladstone, my literary agent, for believing in my message and my spirit. I am thrilled to have you as my guiding light on this new pathway. *Blast Off!* has found a perfect home with Morgan James Publishing. Thank you for inviting me to be part of your enthusiastic and talented team.

And lastly, I am awestruck at how I am continually blessed with wonderful clients who have nourished me over the years. Thanks to all of you for inviting me to support your process. How lucky I am to have a dream career where I can witness your lives being transformed.

About the Author

Allison Maslan has been an entrepreneur for the past 25 years, and she has a vibrant and powerful array of successful businesses to her credit. Allison is an author, an international speaker, the originator and President of the *Blast Off! Life Coaching Program*, and the President of The Homeopathic Wellness Center where she practices as a Nationally Certified Homeopath and Licensed Holistic Health Practitioner. She is also the Founder of the Homeopathic Academy of Southern California, the largest and most comprehensive homeopathic certification academy in the United States.

In her twenties, Allison was co-founder and co-director of the Barali Group, a full-service advertising and public relations firm. Her client list included Supercuts, Allstate Insurance, Merrill Lynch, Charlotte Russe and MCI. She also co-developed, co-owned and sold a scuba diving certification program, Dive Pro San Diego, and a hair salon. And as a successful real estate investor, Allison manages several properties and coaches others to do the same. She is the author of many well-received articles in local, national and international publications. *Blast Off!* is her first book and others are being developed.

Allison Maslan has a doctorate in homeopathy from The British Institute of Homeopathy. She received her holistic health degree from Body Mind College in San Diego. Allison is certified as a homeopath through the Council for Homeopathic Certification, and she is registered with the North American Society of Homeopaths (NASH). She also served as the marketing director for NASH, which promotes homeopathy nationwide.

Through her years of working with clients on a one-on-one basis, Allison has come to understand how and why human beings create their own personal limits in different aspects of their lives, including in their relationships, personal joy, career, health, prosperity and spirituality. She developed the *Blast Off! Program* to help people learn to identify and release self-imposed roadblocks and create solution-oriented road maps to living abundant, richer and freer lives.

As a Master Life Coach and President of the *Blast Off! Life Coaching Program*, Allison utilizes her years of experience in building thriving businesses as well as healing, counseling and motivating thousands of individuals. Allison conducts one-on-one coaching consultations for personal and professional prosperity, and she can be reached at Allison@MyBlastOff.com and www.MyBlastOff.com.

The *Blast Off!* adventure continues. In addition to her *Blast Off! Life Coaching Program*, Allison has launched an online interactive coaching program called *Blastation,* available at www.InteractiveLifeCoach.com.

Allison Maslan lives in San Diego with her husband, Mike, three dogs, Daisy, Madison and Samson, and her cat, Miko. Her daughter Gabriella, who she raised largely as a single mom after her own life changes, is currently in college.